Presented to
Master Henry M. Le Count
by
his Teacher
Mr. Moulton Smith
for
Proficiency in
Spelling

TURKISH EVENING ENTERTAINMENTS.

THE

WONDERS OF REMARKABLE INCIDENTS

AND THE

RARITIES OF ANECDOTES,

BY

AHMED IBN HEMDEM THE KETKHODA,

CALLED "SOHAILEE."

TRANSLATED FROM THE TURKISH

BY JOHN P. BROWN,

DRAGOMAN OF THE U. S. LEGATION AT CONSTANTINOPLE

NEW YORK:

GEORGE P. PUTNAM, 155 BROADWAY.

LONDON:

PUTNAM'S AMERICAN AGENCY,

49 BOW LANE, CHEAPSIDE.

MDCCCL.

Printed by D. Fanshaw,
35 Ann-street, corner of Nassau.

INTRODUCTORY NOTE.

The manuscript of the following translation was sent to me by Mr. Brown, with the request that I would offer it to some publisher, in his name. It may, therefore, be proper for me to introduce it to the reader with a brief statement of the circumstances under which it was prepared, and is now presented to the public.

The translator has resided for several years in Constantinople, as Dragoman of the United States Legation at the Ottoman Porte; and this work of Suheily having been published in that city in 1840, Mr. Brown, at an early period of his residence there, formed the design of translating it, in which he was encouraged by the approbation of the celebrated orientalist Baron Von Hammer, who characterized the work as "by far the most interesting book that has been published at Constantinople for a long time." It is but justice to Mr. Brown, however, to add, that he does not claim to have made a translation which, in all respects, meets the demands of the scholar. On the contrary, in clothing this popular oriental work in an English dress, he thought only to amuse the general reader with a pleasant representation of oriental sentiments and manners, and not to challenge the criticism of the orientalist by a scrupulous accuracy of rendering, although he aimed, indeed, "to preserve it as much like the original as possible." Conscious of the imperfections of his translation, yet hoping it may entertain and instruct the unlearned, he sends it forth "as a promise of something better in future."

The proof-sheets have been revised by a gentleman of New York, who first kindly gave some touches to the translator's manuscript, with the help of a copy of the original, presented by Mr. Brown to the American Oriental Society, which an acquaintance with the Turkish enabled him to make use of. But I am restricted to the simple acknowledgment, in behalf of Mr. Brown, of this kind service, without having the liberty to mention the name of the able scholar by whom it has been rendered.

The plan of the work, and the sources of its materials, are sufficiently indicated in the author's truly oriental preface. The personage to whom it is dedicated was the fourth Ottoman sovereign of the name Murad, who reigned between 1623 and 1640.

To the credit of the publisher under whose favorable auspices this work appears, the first ever introduced to readers in the United States directly from the East, it should be distinctly understood that he has liberally assumed the whole expense of the publication.

EDWARD E. SALISBURY.

Yale College, November, 1849.

PREFACE.

In the name of Allah, the merciful, the clement.

O Lord, immerse me in the light of the true path; bind me with the thread of resignation and contentment; preserve the true mirror of my heart from the rust of affliction; and show me thy countenance, O Thou who art my most ardent desire!

If any one attempts to dispose the order of the jewels of thy praises and adulations, or to arrange the strung pearls of thanksgiving and satisfaction, to Thee who sittest enthroned on high, the God of might and grandeur, (the Merciful on the firmament above*), the vast plain of whose kingdom is heaven,—the faculty of speech and the zone of eloquence excuses itself from the task, under the plea of weakness and inability, and acknowledges its want of power, saying:

"O Sultan of the climes of eternity,
Who can express sufficient thanks for all thy benefits!
That He, himself, is above all mundane necessities, is an additional benefit."

In expressing his great glory, the eloquent tongue is a sterile mute; and in the exposition of his mightiness, the mind of the learned is tongueless and diseased. The most knowing of the erudite are amazed at the commencement of the beams of His beauty; and the most eminent of the doctors of science and knowledge, are astonished at the sound of the hymns of His grandeur.

The strung pearls of the laws of prayer and devotion, the pure necklace of the gems of praise and exultation; the praise of the pure grave (of Mohammed); the offering of the illuminated garden (the cemetery wherein the Prophet is interred); the summary of the degrees of created things; the royal verse of the poem of beings; the essence of all creatures, and the quintessence of all possible things in the niches of brilliancy,—Mohammed,—"Allah is the light of heaven;" he who is seated in the tent

* These exclamations, thrown in the Preface by the Author, are from the Koran. —A. T.

of *Thum dena;* the sultan of the canopy known by the name of "It was approached at the distance of two bow-shots or less;" he who is addressed in thy noble discourse, saying, "We will relate to you the best of narratives;" he who was thus honored (of Allah), with the sagest of language, and the wisest of words; Allah adding, "He will tell you concerning the prophets, and strengthen your heart with it,"—thus again was he distinguished; may Allah have peace and satisfaction with him!

The meaning of the Koran; the sallies of the Psalms of David; the reflected mirror of the light of God; the source of the two streams of entity and nonentity; the union of the two seas of the past and the future; the crown of prophets; the sovereign of apostles; the moon of pure path; the beloved of Allah; the great Prophet;—peace and the best of benedictions be on his excellent person, and on the pure individuals, the blessed bodies and glorious souls of his family, friends, sons, forefathers, and posterity! because they are the sovereigns of the thrones of the cities of religion, and because they are the commanders of the battle-fields of true knowledge. May the satisfaction of God be upon them all!

On the praise of the sovereign whose armies are as numerous as the hosts of heaven,—may God eternalize his empire, and prolong it!

Allah be praised! He whose world-adorning beauty ennobles the throne of majesty; whose imperial accession to the throne of the caliphat, has given thereunto honor and magnificence.

VERSE.

"The fortunate prince, who is the heroic Darius of the globe,
The world-conquerer, the sultan, the lord of his creatures."

The resplendent sun of the extremity of greatness; the star of majesty and of splendor; the sultan of the sultans of the age, Sultan Murad, son of Sultan Ahmed Khan, son of Sultan Mohammed Khan; may Allah glorify the throne of state with his person, and bless the two worlds with acts of his justice and generosity; may the sound of the report of the equity of the hero resound in the dome of the universe, and the voice of his justice reach the place and inhabitants of the most distant part of the world! Sivar, he whose royal diploma of majesty (*berat* or patent of sovereignty) and monogram of good fortune has been honored with his illustrious name and high title, the honorable divan (or council) of the universe has never beheld so glorious a padishah—so intelligent, so fortunate, so illustrious, so felicitous, and auspicious a sovereign. O Allah, protect him within the fold of safety and security, for the sake of him whom thou appointedst a prophet out of the children of Adam. It is our prayer and request of the glorious throne of God's omnipotence, that his person may ever repose on the breast of felicity; and that prosperity and empire, success and victory, be, day and night, attached to his noble and fortunate stirrup; that he be yet far nobler than his forefathers; that wherever he may extend his armies both east and west, he may find success. Amen, in the name of the faithful Prophet!

Lastly, It is evident as the sun in the midst of the heavens, to those who seek for knowledge and information, that history polishes man's nature, and rubs away the rust of his afflictions; and that the talent of evening narrators is one which enlivens the circle of society, and is the true source of joy and pleasure. And thus the intelligent know that narrators who are gifted with affability of disposition, quickness of perception, and judgment, are possessed of sciences like strong pearls. "Say, are the ignorant and the knowing equal?"* Persons of experience and trial have acquired their knowledge from history and biography, and collected whatever was strange and remarkable. But surely this kind of compilation cannot be easy to every one; and its attainment cannot be perfected without deep study in voluminous books. Therefore, I, the parasite of the the table of the love of my affectionate brethren—that is to say—the humble Ahmed bin Hemdem the Ketkhoda, known by the name of "*Sohailee*," (may Allah spread his benefits over him, and pardon him and his parents!) have collected the following pearls from the seas of authentic works, and these sparkling jewels from the mines of celebrated authors, in which are folded and contained the histories of the ancients, with the accounts of the best of the learned and the philosophers. I have selected its contents from the most remarkable events and the strangest occurrences, and have spent the capital of my life in acquiring the valuable and choice extracts found in it. I translated them from the Arabic and Persian tongues, wrought them into a new form, and gave them new light and expression in the Turkish idiom; giving to my book the the title of "Remarkable Events and Strange Occurrences." In this work I have particularly attached myself to collecting such tales and narratives as are authentic and instructive, and, at the same time, more or less curious; so that their moral application will be seen by every one.

* From the Koran.

"The following are some of the works from which the extraordinary events and remarkable occurrences have been extracted:

Tareekhi Mohammed bin Ahmed bin Mustevfee.—History by Mohammed bin Ahmed bin Mustevfee.
Murudj uz Zehb lil Mesoodee.—The Golden Meadows, by Mesoodee.
Jami ut Tevareekh li Khodja Resheed Vazeer.—Collection of Histories by Khodja Resheed Vazeer.
Mirat uz Zemani li Subt ibin el Jevzee.—Mirror of the Age, by Subt ibin el Jevzee.
Tareekhi Kivam ul Mulk ber Kohee—History of Kivam ul Mulk ber Kohee.
Tareekhi Tabaree.—History of Tabaree.
Jamei ul Hikayat.—Collection of Stories.
Tareekhi Billaderee.—History by Billaderee, Hamee, and others.
Muntazam ul Jewzee.—Collection of the Poetry of Jewzee.
Tareekhi ul Futuh Tasneefi Ibin Athem Coofee.—History of Conquests, by Ibin Athem Coofee.
Keshf ul Gammet Taleefi Alee bin Isa Ardibeelee.—Relief of Sorrows, by Alee bin Isa Ardibeelee.
Tareekhi Guzziday.—Choice History.
Nuzhet ul Kuloobi Harad Illah Mustevfee.—Joys of the Heart, by Harad Illah Mustevfee.
Vassayai Khodja Nizam ul Milk Vazeer.—Testaments of Khodja ul Mulk Vazeer.
Tareekhi Kivam ul Mulk Tabbaket Nasiree, by Min Hadj bin Seradj Jurjan.
Tareekhi Vassaf Abdallah bin Fazel Sheerazee.
Tareekhi Fakhi Eddin Daood Benakee.
Medjeinah un Nevadir Nizam Aruzi Samarkandi.
Zafer Namehi Sharef ud Deen Tabreezee.
Tareekhi Jehan Kushai Khodja Ata Melik Jaweenee.
Matta uz Saadain Abd ur Rizzak Samarkandee.—Rising of the Fortunate Stars,* by Abd ur Rizzak of Samarkand.
Ravzat us Saffai, by Mohammed bin Rashavend Shah el Balkh, known by the name of Mirkhond Shah.
Habeeb us Sier Gias ud Deen Khondimeer.—The Friend of Biographers, by Sier Gias ud Deen Khondimeer.
Tezkereti Devlet Shah. Memoirs by Devlet Shah.
Medjales un Neffaisi Meer Alee Sheer.—Meetings of the Select, by Meer Alee Sheer.

From these works I compiled my book, and changed their Arabic and Deri (Persian) dress to robes of Turkish. So that when my brethren of faithful narratives, and the friends of pleasant literature derive delight by reading the contents, may they remember their humble servant for good, and recite a Fatha for the repose of his soul!

VERSE.

"If brethren, from good feeling and friendship,
Bestow on it one atom of regard,
From being a coarse, rough stone, it will
Become a ruby of Bedakshan;
And from a simple atom, it will be a sun of glory."

* In the East, Jupiter and Venus are fortunate, and Mars and Saturn are unfortunate.—A. T.

CONTENTS.

CHAPTER FIRST.

Illustrative of Intelligence and Piety.

CHAPTER SECOND.

Illustrative of Generosity and Benevolence.

CHAPTER THIRD.

Illustrative of Promise and Performance.

CHAPTER FOURTH.

CHAPTER FIFTH.

CHAPTER SIXTH.

CHAPTER SEVENTH.

CHAPTER EIGHTH.

CHAPTER NINTH.

On Justice and fostering Care.

CHAPTER TENTH.

CHAPTER ELEVENTH.

CHAPTER TWELFTH.

CHAPTER THIRTEENTH.

CHAPTER FOURTEENTH.

CHAPTER FIFTEENTH.

CHAPTER SIXTEENTH.

CHAPTER SEVENTEENTH.

Anecdotes about the Abbaside Caliphs.

CHAPTER EIGHTEENTH.

On the Government of Ali Booyeh.

CHAPTER NINETEENTH.

On the Censure of Folly and Evil Qualities.

CHAPTER TWENTIETH.

On Civility and Gentleness.

CHAPTER TWENTY-FIRST.

On the Subject of Elevated Qualities in Man.

CHAPTER TWENTY-SECOND.

On the Wonders of Creation.

CHAPTER TWENTY-THIRD.

Anecdotes about Astrologers and Soothsayers.

CHAPTER TWENTY-FOURTH.

CHAPTER TWENTY-FIFTH.

On Perfidy.

CHAPTER TWENTY-SIXTH.

Anecdotes about Gluttons.

CHAPTER TWENTY-SEVENTH.

On Avarice.

CHAPTER TWENTY-EIGHTH.

Anecdotes of Lovers and Mistresses.

CHAPTER TWENTY-NINTH.

Amusing Anecdotes.

CHAPTER THIRTIETH.

On the Subject of Confidence in Allah.

CHAPTER THIRTY-FIRST.

On the Subject of Benevolent Qualities.

CHAPTER THIRTY-SECOND.

On Beneficence and Bounty.

CHAPTER THIRTY-THIRD.

CHAPTER THIRTY-FOURTH.

CHAPTER THIRTY-FIFTH.

Of Enchantment and Sorcery.

CHAPTER THIRTY-SIXTH.

CHAPTER THIRTY-SEVENTH.

Of Extraordinary Occurrences and Miracles.

TURKISH

EVENING ENTERTAINMENTS.

CHAPTER FIRST,

Relative to those individuals who were gifted with judgment, ingenuity and penetration, and possessed of agreeable and pleasant qualities.

In the books of Commentators and Historians, it is a fact frequently mentioned, and true without doubt, that on a certain day, two men entered the presence of David the Prophet to make a complaint.

They were adversaries; and one of them said, "This man's sheep entered my garden by night; and destroyed all the twigs growing on my vines, so that they, and the branches of the vines, are all destroyed." The Prophet judged the case, and sentenced the owner of the sheep to compensate the owner of the vines, for the loss which he had sustained, by giving him his sheep.

The parties left his presence, and when proceeding on their way met Solomon, the Prophet's son, then only in his twelfth year. Solomon asked them from whence they came, and they forthwith told him what had occured, and how his father David had judged the sheep to the owner of the vines.

Solomon answered that there was a more just and proper sentence. "Come," said he, "into my father's presence, and you will hear what he will order." So they returned with him, and when they were before his father they repeated their complaint. The Prophet then asked his son, "What more just and proper sentence could be pronounced on this case?" Solomon answered, "This man's sheep entered that man's garden, and so far as they could reach them, cropped off the twigs and sprouts from his vines, but did not injure their roots. These latter being still in the earth, will again in a short time produce. Let, therefore, the milk of this man's sheep be given as a remuneration to the owner of the injured vines, until such time as the sprigs and sprouts, having grown, can benefit the owner; after which, restore the sheep to their original owner."

The Prophet David praying, "May God be satisfied with thee and thy father, and be bounteous to them both," observed to his son, "you have judged justly and uprightly." The two complainants were satisfied with the judgment; and conformably to its injunctions, when the vines had again sprouted, the original owner received his sheep. This circumstance, God makes mention of in his book, the Koran, in the following manner. "When David and Solomon sat in judgment on the plants, and then inquired on the subject of the sheep and the tribe, we (dual) were witnesses to their sentence, and we made them to understand Solomon, and he them."

May God verify their deeds. They (the disputants) departed, praising the knowledge and talent of Solomon, and lauded their (his) divine greatness and goodness.

It is related in the books of historians, and well known to men of letters, that Nezar ben Maad ben Adnaan, one highly gifted, had four sons, to whom he gave the names of Ayaz, Mirzir, Anmaz, and Rebiah, all of whom were men of celebrity. When their much respected father was about to depart this life, he divided all his wealth and possessions between them ; all red domed things, he gave to Mirzir; the black herbs and other similar things to Rebiah ; the long haired maiden slaves to Ayaz, and the sofas and all white things to Anmaz, and in this manner willed his property. "If," added he, " when I am gone, any difficulty or dispute should arise between you, go to the celebrated judge of the age, the Ameer Hatti Bahran, make the same known to him, and leave him to judge justly between you.

Now some time after this, these four brothers disputed, and forthwith set out for the residence of the learned judge mentioned in the will of their deceased parent. On their way they passed through a meadow, where a camel had been grazing, though then gone, and no longer in sight.

Mirzir on observing the marks, remarked, that they were those of an one eyed camel; Rebiah said it was also greedy; Ayaz, that it was laden with oil and honey, and ridden by a woman; Anmaz, that it was a stray camel. The Arabs call a one eyed camel Aâver, one that has a crooked breast Azvre, and one with no tail Ebter, and a stray, or wandering one, Sherood. Whilst these four brothers were yet talking on the subject of the camel, they met the person to whom it belonged; who, when he asked them if they had seen his lost camel, Mirzir answered by asking, was it one eyed ? " Yes," said the camel driver. " Was it crooked breasted ?" asked Rebiah. " Yes," answered the man. Ayaz asked, " Had it oil on one side, and honey on the other; and had it not a woman on its back?" " Yes," was again the answer. " Was it not astray ?" demanded Anmaz. " Yes, indeed," was the eager reply, " pray give me back my camel." The brothers now said that none of them had even seen his camel. On this they had a long altercation with the driver, and he finally accompanied them to the presence of the celebrated judge, whom the camel driver informed, that these men knew of his camel, for they could describe it. The brothers, however, answered, that they had not seen it; the owner of the beast insisted that they had, and demanded his camel.

Now the judge spoke to the brothers and asked how they could know the description of a camel which they had never seen. They answered, that on their way they had passed through a meadow of which they observed the grass on one side was cropped, whilst on the other, it remained untouched, from which, said Mirzir, I understood that the camel was blind of one eye. Rebiah said, that having observed the print of its fore feet, he remarked that one was deep, whilst the other was scarcely perceptible, and he knew the animal was crooked breasted; and Anmar said, that from observing how the camel in grazing had not passed on the other side, he deemed it must be one eyed. When they had finished, the judge exclaimed in astonishment, "Blessed God! what sagacity and discernment! but pray from what did you know that the camel was loaded with honey and oil, and that a woman rode on it?" Ayaz answered, I came to that conclusion from the number of flies about our path, which seek for honey, and a quantity of ants on the way-side, which search for oil; and the rider having had need to dismount from the camel, I remarked the prints of her feet, where she had stepped, making impressions upon the ground handsome as the painted ones of roses.

The judge on hearing this praised their discernment, and sent away the camel driver, saying; "These are not the men you thought them to be, go and search for your camel." Then complimenting the four brothers, he invited them to dine with him, inquiring at the same time the object of their visit. They informed the Ameer of the will of their father, and how he had desired them, in case of any disagreement on the subject of their inheritance, to apply to him for its adjustment. The learned judge replied that it was not proper for any one to interfere between such wise and ingenious persons as they, "But," added he, "I welcome you, and am happy to see you. A sumptuous repast closed their visit, and the judge and the young men departed with mutual admiration: the former struck with amazement at the sagacity of the brethren, and they, in their turn, admiring the adroitness with which the judge had avoided passing upon their father's will.

Ayas ben Monavich bin Kara was a person possessed of great talent and perspicuity, was well versed in the abstruse sciences, and works of history, and narrative, and of quick and correct discernment. Among the examples of his judgment, it is related, that one day a guest came to visit him, and offer a complaint, saying, "I deposited with such a monk a purse of gold, and departed on a pilgrimage to Mecca. Latterly I returned, and when I asked my money of him he denied having ever received it, what shall I do?" The cadi answered, "Have you spoken of this to any one but myself?" The guest answered in the negative. "Then go," said the cadi, "and some two or three days hence come to me and receive an answer." The cadi then sent to the monk, and invited him to his presence, which invitation he accepted, and received from the cadi marked attentions and regard. Afterwards, turning to the monk, he said, "I am compelled by business to leave this country, and have a few purses of money which I desire to deposit with you. As there can be no person more honorable than yourself, God alone shall be a witness between us. To-morrow I will send them to you, and it is your duty to take good care and guard over them. After this the monk departed, and on the morrow the guest again appeared for his answer. "Go," said the cadi, "demand your deposit, and if he refuses it, tell him that you will complain to the cadi, and let us see what will be the result."

The guest, as directed, went to the monk and demanded his deposit. The monk smiling replied, "My intention the other day was only to test your temper, and not to deny the pledge, see, here it is," and handed him his purse of gold. The guest returned to the cadi, and after overwhelming him with thanks and expressions of gratitude, went to his business.

Some days after this the monk re-visited the cadi, and was received with the grossest reproaches and abuse, the cadi exclaiming, "So, hypocrite, your villainous conduct has let the world know your character for duplicity." The cadi's method for obtaining the guest's purse of money was applauded by every one. May God have mercy on them all.

The Ameer of the faithful, Mutasim Billah, one of the caliphs of the Abassides, was a most just and equitable sovereign, as well as a man of much courage and lion-heartedness. He carried on a continued war against infidels, and for amiability of disposition, followed in the footsteps of his upright predecessors. On the decease of this caliph the avaricious unbelievers, thinking it a good moment to make an attack upon the faithful, collected all their forces and took council upon their future operations. "Great divisions," said they, "exist among the Islamites, and as they are each engaged in their own pleasures and amusements, now is a good occasion to attack them."

With this idea they resolved upon hostilities. Now one of the chiefs of the unbelievers was an aged man of great intelligence and experience, who, from being their elder, directed them in their undertaking. His co-religionests arose and proceeded to the dwelling of this individual, whom, when they asked council, answered them. "Your enterprise is neither just nor worthy, and would be rejected by sensible people; for it has been seen in numerous works that, notwithstanding the people of Islam are apparently divided, when opposed they unite and act together. Therefore you had better attend to your own affairs, and give over this wild undertaking." They followed the old man's good advice, and were governed by his councils.

One of the caliphs of the Abassides, named Mutaasid Billah Yansur bi nour Ullah, was a sovereign of great good judgment and careful justice. He, one day, in company with his attendants, visited a palace situated on the banks of the Tigris, where he observed an expert fisherman throw his net into the river, and, after hauling it out, found only three or four fish in it. The caliph remarking this, commanded the fisherman to throw it into the water again, for his sake, "and let us see," said he, "what my luck will be." The man did as he was ordered and soon after hauling his net out, felt something weighty among its meshes. In consequence of the increased weight, the attendants of the caliph had to aid him, and when the net was on shore, they found in it a leather bag, tightly bound round the mouth. In this bag they at first perceived a number of tile, and finally at its bottom the hand of a tender and young female, bent and shrivelled. The caliph, on seeing the hand, exclaimed, "Poor creature, what work is this, that the servants of God (Mussulmans) should be thus cut to pieces and thrown into the river without our knowledge; we must find the committer of this wicked act." Now, with the caliph was one of his cadies, (judges,) who spoke and said, "Oh! Ameer of the faithful, give your precious self no trouble about this matter, for by your favor, we will investigate, and with proper care and circumspection bring it to light."

The caliph at the same time called the governor of the city of Bagdad, and giving the bag into his hands, said, "Go to the Bazaar, show it to the sack-sewers, and inquire whose work it is; they know each other's work; and if you find the individual who sewed it, bring him to me."

The cadi had the sack shown to the sewers, and an old, grave looking man, on seeing it, exclaimed that it was his own work. "Lately, I sold it," added he, "and two others, to one Yahiya Ilha, a native of Damascus, of the family of the Mahides." The cadi on hearing this, said, "Come with me to the caliph, fear nothing, he has only a few questions to ask you." So the old man accompanied him into the presence of the caliph, who demanded of him to whom he had sold it. The old man answered as before, adding, 'Oh! prince of the faithful, he is a man of high rank, but very wicked and tyrannical, and continually does injury and vexation to true believers. Every one fears him, and none dare complain against him to the caliph. Lately, a lady, named Inaan Magennee, purchased a female slave for one thousand dinars, who was very fair and beautiful, and moreover, a poetess. This man supposed her mistress would sell her to him, but receiving the lady's reply, that she had already given her her freedom, he sent her word that there was to be a wedding in the house, and requested that the female should be loaned him for the occasion. The lady, therefore, sent her as a loan for three days, and, after four or five had elapsed, sending to demand her, received for answer, that she had already left his house two or three days ago, and notwithstanding the lady's tears and complaints, she could not obtain her slave, nor even hear any news of her.

The lady, from fear of this man's violence, held her peace, and left the quarter wherein she had resided, for it is said he had already put several of his neighbors to death.

When the old man was done speaking, the caliph seemed greatly rejoiced, and commanded that Yahiya Ilha should forthwith be brought before him. He came, and when he was shown the hand found in the bag, his color changed, and he falsely endeavored to exculpate himself. The lady was likewise brought, and so soon as she saw the hand, she commenced weeping, and exclaimed, "Yes, indeed, it is the hand of my poor murdered slave." "Speak," said the caliph to the Mahides, "for by my head, I swear to know the truth of this affair." So the man acknowledged that he had killed the slave; and the caliph, in consideration of his being of the family of Hasheem,* sentenced him to pay to the owner of the slave one thousand pieces of gold for the loss which

* Beni Hasheem, one of the most ancient Arabian tribes, from which the Prophet desended.—A. T.

she had sustained, and one hundred thousand more for the law of taolion; after which he allowed him three days, in which to settle his affairs in the city, and then leave it for ever.

On learning this sentence, the public loudly praised the caliph's judgment, and commended his justice and equity.

It is mentioned in the celebrated Arabic work, entitled the "Mirror of the Age," that one of the caliphs of the house of Abbass, Mutâsid Billah, besides being a very brave and courageous person, was also possessed of keen observation, and the faculty of knowing men by their physiognomy. One day as he was inspecting the erection of a palace on the banks of the Tigris, which he was wont to do once a week, and encourage the builders with presents and other acts of favor, he observed that each of the men employed carrying stones to the edifice, bore but one at a time, and that with great gravity and slowness. Among them, however, he perceived one, with black hands and dark complexion, who invariably lifted two at a time, put them on his back, and with evident joy and elasticity carried them from the wharf to the masons. On seeing this, the caliph pointed him out to Hussian, one of his attendants, and asked the cause of this man's unnatural gayety. The attendant answered, that the caliph was more competent to form an opinion of the case than himself. The caliph then added, that the man was probably possessed of a large sum of money, and was therefore happy from the consciousness of his wealth; or, that he was a thief, who had only sought employment among the workmen for the purpose of concealment. I do not like his appearance, continued the prince of the faithful, have him brought into my presence.

So, when the man was come, the caliph asked him what his occupation was, and he answered, that he was a common laborer. "Have you any money laid by?" demanded the caliph, "None," replied the man. Tell me the truth, again asked the caliph, repeating the question, and again the man answered in the negative.

Then the caliph ordered an officer to strike the man, which being done, he immediately cried out for pity and pardon. Speak the truth, said the officer, or the caliph will punish you as long as you live: So the man avowed that his trade was that of a tile-maker; and one day, added he, when I had prepared my kiln, and lit the fire, a man approached me, mounted on an ass, who dismounting before my kiln, let the ass go, and beginning to undress himself, took from around his waist a girdle, which he placed by his side and began fleeing himself. I, seeing that the man was quite alone, caught him, and throwing him into the furnace of my kiln, closed it down. I then took his girdle, and after killing the ass threw it also into the fire; "see, here is the girdle." The caliph took it, and on examining it, found it contained some thousands of gold pieces, and, moreover, had its owner's name written upon it. On this discovery the caliph sent criers out, to ask in the streets whether any family had lost a member, or a friend, and if so, to come before him. Soon an aged woman approached, and exclaimed, "My son left me with some thousands of pieces of gold, with which to purchase merchandise, and is lost." They showed her the girdle, which she immediately recognised as her son's, and said that it had his name upon it.

The caliph now gave the girdle into the old woman's hands, saying, "See before you the murderer of your son." She demanded the right of talion, and the man was forthwith hung upon the door of him whom he had murdered.

All the world admired the caliph's sagacity and commended his justice.

CHAPTER SECOND,

On the subject of the qualities of generosity and liberality, and the sentiments of mildness and moderation, with which some individuals are gifted.

One of the Abbasside caliphs, Memoon, was celebrated for his superior knowledge of the sciences, the excellence of his moral qualities, his eloquence, and for his profound sense of justice and equity. He was accustomed to travel about his provinces, and by inquiry learn the condition and state of his people.

In the 204th of Hegirah he took his seat upon the throne of the caliphat. It is written in the work of that very correct historian, Iben el Juzee, that Yahiza ben Ektem relates as follows. "I was once with the caliph Memoon, in Damascus; it was near the time of paying the troops their monthly stipend; and he, the caliph, desired to make war; but, upon examining his treasury, he, finding that it did not contain sufficient money for that purpose, was greatly distressed. One day he was seated near a reservoir of water with his brother Mutasim Billah, and several of the most notable gentlemen of Damascus, engaged in conversation, when two money cases arrived, and were brought into his presence.—The caliph turning to Yahiya ben Ektem and the others, said, 'Come, let us have a look at the cases, and make merry the hearts of those who have brought them.' With these words he arose, and, followed by his companions, proceeded to a high seat where he usually reposed. Many other individuals also followed the caliph, to see the money cases, which were opened before him with much taste and ceremony.

"The caliph turned to Mohamed ben Daoud, and said, 'Since our treasure has arrived, and so many persons are assembled to see it, it would be a pity were we to take it and enjoy ourselves in secret; particularly since it having been the object of their attention and cupidity, they would return dissatisfied.' So he commanded that every individual, each one according to his condition and grade, should be presented with from one hundred thousand pieces of gold down to five hundred, and two thousand, as a royal gift. Now, when all those around him, had each received this amount, and their number was noted, it was found that they had received in all one hundred and fifty-eight thousand pieces of gold. With the remainder the caliph ordered the soldiers to be paid, after which, saluting the people assembled, he returned to his royal abode."

Now from this incident, judge of the power and majesty, and the grandeur of the house of Abbass.

One of the Abbassides, Mustaeen Billah, was considered as one of the most noble and generous among men, and one of the most just and valiant of that house. One of the great men of the state, named Ahmed ben Hemdoon, relates, that Mustaeen Billah erected a most beautiful palace on the banks of the Tigris, at Bagdad, and, that his respected mother had a carpet woven for it, on the silk of which she had worked in gold and silver thread, the figures of all kinds of animals and birds. The figures were all of the purest metals, their eyes rubies and turquois, and other precious stones; indeed so rich was the carpet, that she had spent the sum of one hundred and thirty thousand dinars upon it; and the instruments and other articles, necessary for its construction, were registered, the whole costing twenty thousand dinars.

When the palace was finished, his mother made it known to him, saying, "I have a request to make you; come some day with your suite, and inspect the palace, amuse yourself, and afterwards do as you like best." Mustaeen Billah neglected to go that day.

Ahmed ben Hemdoon narrates, that one of the caliph's suite named, Atargee Hashemee told him, that the palace was actually strewed with jewelry, and that they ought to go to see it. So, adds he, Atargee and myself went, and the door-keeper let us in. We had never seen any palace so ornamented before. Among other remarkable things, was a gazelle of gold; its eyes were red rubies. This, I took and put into my sleeve, and thus left the palace. We went before the caliph, and commencing to praise the palace, and its incomparable carpet, and the other strange things that we had seen, begged him, before giving any part of it away, to pay it a visit. Whilst yet praising it, Atargee remarked, that I had captured a gazelle; so I took it out from my sleeve and showed it to all present.

The caliph addressing the courtiers around him, said, "Those of you who love me are at liberty to go and take from the palace whatever you please."

So we all arose, and proceeded to the palace, where we filled our pockets and breasts with the most costly things it contained, after which we returned to the caliph, who was in excellent spirits, and evinced his gayety. The other persons present now said, "What is our crime, oh! Emir of the faithful?" on which he answered them, "Go you are all at liberty to do the same," at which they all arose and plundered the palace; the delighted caliph at the same time observing them from a window. The courtiers, and other persons present, became sick, and the caliph noticing that one of them, named Ibin Mihleb bore away a package of odoriferous musk, and another of amber, exclaimed—"Where are you going?" to which being answered, "To the bath," he was greatly pleased, and ordered all his servants to go also, and dividing the carpet among themselves, be merry.

In this interval his mother arrived, and said "Could I only have seen you once on that carpet, my labor and pains would have been amply requited." The caliph, touched with her tenderness, ordered the whole expense to be paid her out of his treasury, and that another carpet, just like the former, should be made, for which he allotted one hundred and thirty thousand dinars. A richer one than the first was therefore made for the new palace, with other furniture correspondingly valuable. After this the caliph, attended by all his courtiers, spent some time at the palace in merry enjoyment and there gave permission to them to take that carpet likewise, adding, "Our portion is health, without which wealth and riches are worthless; let our friends and followers partake of whatever is ours." So great and generous a prince was Mustaeen Billah.

It is related, in the history called the "Mirror of the Age," that there was, in the government of the Abbassides, a man among the ranks of the princes of Arabia who was famous for his hospitality, generosity and liberality; and one whose door was ever open to the needy. This person's name was Mâân bin Ziad; his jurisdiction extended, and his courage was renowned from the region of Damascus to Bagdad. This ameer was once amusing himself with a few friends, in a most incomparably beautiful garden, when a poet of much celebrity and talent came in search of an opportunity to make known to the ameer an injustice which he had suffered.

None offered, or even when any was found who could present him to the ameer, a pretext was wanting to excuse his visit. Finally, as there was a reservoir in the garden, the source of which was beyond the walls, the poet, taking a smooth piece of board, wrote on it the following lines, explicative of his feeling, and putting the board into the stream, let it be born down to the reservoir. It so happened that the ameer was seated near the reservoir, and when the board reached him, seizing with his hand, he read,—

"Oh! generosity of Mâân, make my necessities be heard, for I have no other intermediate than thee between me and Mâân."

The worthy Mâân exclaimed, "Hasten, go and see who is beyond the enclosure, and bring him before me." Immediately some of those near him sprang to their feet, and finding the poet, brought him before the ameer, who treated him kindly and civilly. The ameer inquired after his health, &c. and, after quieting his mind, asked how many days since he had come to the city. "It is three days," answered the poet, "that I have been endeavoring to speak with you." "Please pardon our negligence," continued the ameer, at the same time endeavoring to conciliate his good will, he ordered the sum of three hundred thousand aktchas* to be presented him, as an indemnity for the delay. That day the ameer spent in merriment, and at night returned to his residence. On the following day he caused his guest the poet, to be inquired after, and invited him to accompany him to his garden, where he feasted him, and after evincing his respect for him, presented him with the sum of one hundred thousand aktchas more. Finally, for three days the poet received the same treatment, each day being presented with a like sum, greatly to his astonishment; at length he wrote Mâân a letter, full of thanks and good wishes, and on the following day set out for his own country; so that when Mâân sent again to invite him to his presence he had disappeared, leaving only the said letter, from which it was evident his modesty had constrained him to depart. At this Mâân was grieved, and made an oath, swearing that if the poet had not departed he would daily have given him one hundred thousand aktchas, until not a coin remained in his treasury. Strange, added he, that he should go away before informing us of it.

* Aktcha: it is probable that the Turkish translation here means pieces of silver, as the word signifies white money. It is equivalent to the 120th part of a piaster, of which there are now (1848) some twenty-three and a half to a dollar.

In a work entitled the "Annals of the Generous," it is written, and is a fact therein well narrated by that correct historian of past times, Abdullah bin Jaafeer Radavee, that one day he and Abon Dahich Ansaree and Hassan were journeying from Mecca, the venerated, to Medina, the enlightened, when they were overtaken by a heavy fall of rain. Whilst in search of a place of shelter, they perceived, in a plain near to Damascus, an Arab's tent, to which they bent their steps, hoping therein to find an asylum. An Arab coming out, he invited them in, and they spent the night there. The Arab killed a goat, his wife prepared it for her husband's guests, and spread before them a good meal. That night they ate and drank with pleasure, and slept comfortably; and on the morrow, desiring to depart, Abdullah said to the Arab, "You have been good and kind to us, we, therefore, request that some day, when you come to Medina, you will be our guest, and allow us to do as much for you. This request he strengthened by entreaty, and the Arab, answering, "On my head and eyes be it;" they departed.

Now, some years after this incident the Arab became reduced to poverty, and the world was subtle to him. So his wife one day said to him, "If we go to Medina, perhaps the persons to whom we ever offered hospitality may succor us." "But we are ignorant of their names," answered the husband. "Inquire for Ibin ed Deyar," continued she; "I saw signs of generosity in their faces, and hope your visit will not be fruitless."

The Arab therefore mounted his female camel and proceeded to Medina, where he inquired for Ibin de Deyar. It so happened that Imaam Hassan was just then passing, and when the Arab inquired of him for his old guests, he answered, that "he was his uncle's son," and inquired, "How do you happen to know him?" The Arab answered by saying, that once he had been his guest. The Imaam on hearing this exclaimed, "Welcome, oh! Arab, brother, he has often spoken in praise of you," and calling a slave, ordered him to conduct the Arab to his own dwelling, where he showed him every attention, and presented him with a hundred camels. Soon afterwards the Imaam Hassan arrived, followed by a train of servants, and he added one hundred camels more to the gift; Abdullah bin Jaafeer Radavee next came in, who gave him his hands (in salutation,) and presented him with one hundred thousand dirhems, sending fifty thousand more to his wife. Immediately after this Abee Dehieh Ausaree entered, who excused himself from doing what his friends had done, but, ordering the camels given him to be brought before them, he loaded them all with dates of Medina.

Finally, the Arab left Medina rich and happy, and returned to his tribe with great state and magnificence, and was never more troubled with the inconvenience of adversity.

It is related in those celebrated works, which record good qualities and whatever is remarkable among the noble and generous, that Abdullah bin Abbas, that most liberal of men, was one day visited by a man of eloquent tongue, who, addressing him, said, "Oh! son of the uncle of the prophet, on whom be peace, this night a son was born to me, and, in compliment and friendly regard for you, I have named it after your own noble self; but its mother died in giving birth to it, and all that remains for me is to wish for *you* long life and prosperity."

Ibin Abbas consolingly answered him, "Oh! brother of the assistant of the Prophet, may God bless thee with good qualities, and recompense thee for this affliction," at the same moment ordered his steward to give the man a female slave, who could take care of the child, and thus free the father from the cares of a nurse He also gave him two hundred thousand pieces of silver, with which to purchase whatever necessaries he might need. Likewise he directed the man to come to him in a few days, for, said he,

"You have come at a moment when my treasury is poor, so pray excuse me, and do not fail to come."

"God bless and prosper you, oh! son of Abbas," answered the man, "had you come into the world a little earlier, men would never have mentioned in Arabia, as they now do, the name of Khatem.*

It is related of that most generous and brave hearted of men, Yezid bin Mehleb, that Hadgadguz Zalem having appointed him to the office of governor of Vasith, Akeel bin Abee relates that, as he, Yezid bin Mehleb, was on his way to it, I went to take leave of him: he was very attentive to me, and made me promise to pay him a visit in his new office, and spend some days with him. He insisted so much, that I finally promised, and some time afterwards, he having by a letter reminded me of my promise, I sat out for his residence. When I approached it, he came forth to meet me, and conducted me to a suitable apartment, in which I found every object I could possibly need.

At night one of his people came to invite me to his presence. I went, and found him engaged in conversation with a number of friends, by whom he was surrounded, and the discourse turning on the subject of female slaves, he asked me, saying, "Oh! Akeel, pray tell me your thoughts on this matter." I answered in the following verse, which I extemporized at the moment. "Those who have known them may speak, but those who are strangers to them, how can they offer any praises?"

When I had said this, he came to me and asked, "Are you not also a stranger?" He spent yet two hours, after which I arose,

* Khatem Tay. The tale of this generous Arab has been translated into English.

and taking leave, returned to my lodgings. There I found a slave as beautiful as the resplendent moon, a young horse, and ten thousand dirhems for my expenses, which the generous ameer had sent me. In fine, I remained yet ten days, every evening of which he sent me the same sum of money, so that at length I began to be ashamed, and begged his permission to depart, saying, "Oh! ameer, you have plentifully enriched me, pray now let me go and share your favors among my friends and relations." To this he answered, "What I gave you, you are justly entitled to, go in peace;" and presenting me with ten thousand dirhems more, he was pleased to make me promise to visit him again, and not to forget him in my prayers.

It is related about that man of unique generosity and courage, that most noble, worthy and gentle being, Ibin Mehleb, that there was a deficiency in the revenue of the charge to which Hedjadj ez Zalim* had appointed him; and to obtain it, this cruel tyrant threw him in prison, saying, "If by the next day you do not produce one hundred thousand aktchas, and deliver them over to me, I will have you severely punished with stripes. In consequence of this treatment Ibin Mehleb's people collected the requisite sum and brought it to him.

The ancient poet Farazdack having received great benefits and acts of kindness from him, now paid him a visit of consolation, and asked his people if he could have access to him. Ibin Mehleb from inside his prison, hearing Farazdack's voice, said, "He is my good friend, let him enter," which being done, the poet wept at the sight of his benefactor, and expressed his feelings in the following lines.

* Hedjadj ez Zalim, or the cruel. This governor is famed in eastern tales for his cruelty and severity.

"Oh! Mehleb, your goodness has filled Khorassan; its recipients ask, where now is Yazid? after you, not a drop of rain (goodness) can fall in the east, nor any tree flourish in the land of Mardin; no joy ever be felt when your glory is gone, nor any one ever be generous beyond thee."

Yazid Ibin Mehleb on hearing these sweet verses, said to his porter, "Where are the one hundred thousand dirhems which my friends collected for me? give them to Farazdack, and let them thus be spent honorably, rather than as Hedjadj desired; after which, let the tyrant do with me as he may wish." Farazdack took the money and departed; and as some of Hedjadj's people were present when the scene occurred, they went and informed their master of Yazid's generosity in his misfortune.

Hedjadj was greatly astonished, and exclaiming that Yazid possessed a mountain of generosity, ordered him to be forthwith released from prison, conciliated his good will, dressed him in a robe of honor, and treated him with every possible mark of attention.

Behold what effect an act of generosity had upon the mind of one so merciless as Hedjadj; and how it changed his fierce character into one of friendship and love.

The Emir Esaw, one of the famous princes of the victorious age of Mutamid Billah, of the Abbasside caliphs, was the very quintessence of liberality. He was governor of Diarbikir and Mardin, and for generosity, was without one equal.

It is related by that most correct of historians, Molana Asulee, that one day this prince was enjoying himself in the company of his friends, when a stranger presented himself before him, and after offering his respects, extemporized the following lines.

"I saw, in my dream, that you clothed me in a robe of honor of a violet color, and presented me with money to the full amount of my debts; my parents I devote to thee; only pray fulfil the dream which my eyes have seen."

The noble minded ameer turning to his treasurer, asked him what stuffs were then in the treasury of a violet color, and was answered that there were seventy rolls of violet silk, besides satins and Damascus silks. "Go," continued the generous prince, "give them all to this person, and present him also with ten thousand dirhems with which to purchase other necessaries." At the same time, he said to the poet in a jocular tone, "be careful not to have any more dreams, lest you do not find so favorable an interpreter as myself."

He then treated the stranger with benevolence and kindness, and sent him away rejoicing. May Allah have mercy on them all.

Hamid ben Abbass, Vizir of Muktadir Billah, one of the caliphs of the house of Abbass, was a most generous, and one of the best of men. One day as he was making a visit to his gardens, attended by a numerous escort, he met an aged man of a respectable exterior, weeping, and evidently in great grief. The poor man's house, and all he possessed, having been destroyed by fire, he, with his wife and children, remained exposed and destitute on the public road. The sight of the old man lamenting his misfortune, and the grief of the family all in tears, touched the sensible heart of the vizir, and feeling nodesire to visit his rose-buds, he called one of his attendants and ordered him, as the man's distress had effected so sensibly his breast, to perform a service for him.

"As I return," said he, "from my garden to-day, let me find his dwelling rebuilt as before, himself and family in it, free from sorrow, and happy. If I find this, your work will be praised, and whatever you ask, I will grant. Let this be your charge."

"Get a list of all his clothes and effects, his animals, &c. in fine, of all which he lately possessed, even more, and place them in the new house which you will erect, so that the service which I ask of you be completed, and you gain honor thereby." After again recommending the charge to his attendant, he continued on to the gardens.

The attendant forthwith collected innumerable building materials and workmen, paid the latter bountifully, and commenced erecting the building. The public assembled in great numbers to witness the care which was taken of the sufferer, and loudly commended the benevolence of the vizir of Abin Abbass. The attendant, by great labor and attention, had a dwelling re-built between morning and sun set, in several respects more elegant than before; its door-way and walls lit up with torches, and all the neighborhood brightly illuminated: and, according to the list, procured every article which had been destroyed. He also dressed the wife and children of the poor man in richly embroidered robes, each according to their stature, thus turning their grief into great joy.

After supper, Mohamed ben Abbass, in returning from his garden, saw that the grief and despair which he had witnessed in the morning, was changed to mirth and enjoyment; the people praised the vizir for his generosity to the poor man; and, in fine, his heart being satisfied with what his attendant had done, he expressed his satisfaction, and dressed him in several robes of honor, one over the other.

When the owner of the house, and his wife and children, kissed his hands and implored blessings on him for his benevolence and generosity, he asked them if they were contented and was answered, that every thing they formerly possessed, was restored to them two-fold. "May God, the bestower of all gifts," added they, "prolong your life in prosperity and bless all you undertake." The register of the expenses was now brought, and when the items were added up it was seen that the house and effects purchased cost just twelve thousand dinars. The vizir returned to his house in great good spirits and mirth, and when, on the following day, the man visited him again to repeat his thanks, he treated him with great attention and distinction, and presented him with one hundred thousand dirhems more, saying, "Let it be a capital with which to commence business."

What noble generosity and benevolence; may God be merciful to them all!

It is related, in historical works, that Abdallah bin Abi Bekir was a man of choice generosity, and noble feelings; courageous, and of pure conduct, and character, and a respected and revered master.

One day having left his house, with the desire of enjoying the chase, he, whilst on the road, became very thirsty, and approaching a house which he saw near by, asked for water: a female made her appearance with a cup, which she handed him, her person remaining concealed behind the door. Abdallah, having drank the water, received new life from it, and said, "Where is the servant? let her take the cup." The woman answered; "Long life to you; our servant is dead, pray therefore excuse me, I am alone; be pleased to put the cup on the sill of the door." Abdallah directed one of his followers to give the excellent woman twenty thousand aktchas. The woman from behind the door exclaimed; "I ask God to give you and yours health." "Give her twenty thousand more, continued Abdallah," and the attendant, after doing so, retired; they all then proceeded to the chase.

Now Abdallah was a good and benevolent man, and it is related of him, that every holy day or festival, he freed one hundred slaves, and supplied provision for the forty neighboring families on the right and left of his dwelling. He gave also many gifts to the passers by and he was altogether a charitable and good person.

It is related that when Moaviah (on whom be peace and the divine satisfaction) died, and his son Yazid succeeded him to the caliphat, Abdallah Radavee came to Damascus and visited him. He both complimented and consoled him, and prayed for the soul of Moaviah. Yazid showed him great respect and attention, and asked him, "What was my father in the habit of giving you every year?" Abdallah answered "Three hundred thousand dirhems." Yazid replied, "Welcome, my good friend, I will also give you three hundred thousand as your own rightful revenue, and three hundred thousand more for the prayer you offered for my deceased father's soul, and three hundred thousand additional on my own part," so he had this amount counted out and sent to Abdallah's dwelling.

Now after the latter named person had departed, one of Yazid's companions said to him; "Why did you give so much money to one person, would it not have been better to distribute it among the needy?" "No," replied Yazid, "it is not all to one man;—perhaps it is a great deed done to the people of Medina. It is evident that you do not know whose master he is; but appoint a person to follow him to Medinah, and if he sees him distribute this money, let him come and let us know."

Abdallah continued on to Medina, and the day after his arrival there, distributed the whole of the sum to the inhabitants of that city; and as it was insufficient, borrowed forty thousand aktchas more, and divided them among the widows and the orphans; so that no one was left portionless. On seeing this the person departed, returned to Damascus, and related what he had seen to Yazid, who exclaimed, "Do you now see?" So they all sincerely praised the benevolence and generosity of Abdallah.

The emir of the faithful, Mutasid Billah, that magnificent sovereign of the house of Abbass, was unique for generosity, the protection which he showed to his people, and the manner in which he conciliated their regard.

In the work entitled Mirati Zaman, "Mirror of the Age," it is related that this caliph once made an attack upon the Greeks; that he set out with an innumerable number of troops, and one day encamped near a village. His royal pavilion was pitched near to a vineyard, where he alighted. Soon after his arrival the gardener cried out with a voice of complaint; hearing which the caliph exclaimed, "Go quickly, and see what is the cause of this man's cries." The attendants departed, and soon returning, brought word that the gardener had planted a few melons in his ground, and that some of the soldiers had entered it, and robbed him of his property. So the caliph appointed men to go, and wherever they found melon-rinds before a tent, to bring its occupants before him. The men found traces of the melons before two or three tents, the occupants of which, being conducted to the caliph, denied all knowledge of the melons, saying that their servants must have put them there. So the caliph next asked for the servants; and they likewise being brought into his presence, he had them put in prison, and at the same time gave the gardener a handful of gold, to conciliate his good will.

On the following day, early in the morning, when the army was about to set out on its march, the caliph had it proclaimed to the troops that an execution was about to take place; and, after having had the heads of the prisoners struck off before him, he mounted his horse and set out.

One of the caliph's suite was named Cadi Hussain. This person having approached the caliph, the latter, as they rode on together, asked him if he was satisfied, or not, with the sentence. "Speak out," added he, "fear nothing, but whatever you feel, tell it truly." Cadi Hussain answered, "You are a true Muslim in every thing, but although of a magnanimous disposition, you are too regardless of life; if you had delayed the shedding of blood, and showed a little more respect for the holy law of our Prophet, it would have been more becoming." Mutasid Billah exclaimed, "God is great! I swear by the souls of my ancestors, that since my accession to the caliphat, I have never issued a judgment disrespectful of the holy law, nor have I shed wrongfully any one's blood." Cadi Hussain answered, "Good; was it then according to the law, that you yesterday shed the blood of those persons who stole the melons?" The caliph answered, "There were three persons worthy of death, confined in prison; and, to frighten the people by an execution, I had their heads struck off." Cadi Hussain adds, that in truth, soon after this conversation, he saw the prisoners who had been confined for the theft of the melons, and complimented the caliph. The cadi also said to the caliph, "The day that we met a dark colored man in the midst of the way, you had him executed without question or answer; why was this?" The caliph answered, "That faithless Caramata* once came and professed obedience to my father; he was a most merciless and tyrannical man, and he subsequently not only turned against my father, but caused also all his comrades, who were very numerous, to do the same, under pretence of excessive regard for their foolish creed. This accursed man is from the village of Kahay, beyond the Oxus, and, during the caliphat of my father, endeavored to do violence to a pure and innocent youth: on his crying out for succor, the Mussulmans ran to his rescue, but too late; for this evil-minded man, drawing his khandjar, martyrized the young man before their eyes. Those present witnessed the act, and catching the monster, brought him before my father, and represented the crime to him. My father, on whom God has had mercy, did not have the right of talion inflicted; and I, happening to be near him on business at the time, made the determination, which at length you saw me execute, that if the All-just should ever give me the caliphat, I would expiate the blood of the innocent youth. Up to that moment it was not in my power; and not before the day when

* Caramata, name of a heretical sect which originated A. H. 278. (A. D. 891.)

I unexpectedly met him, could I fulfil the divine laws, by practising retaliation."

Cadi Hussain, and all those present, praised the religious sentiments of the Commander of the faithful. May Allah have mercy upon him!

CHAPTER THIRD,

Explaining that fulfilment of promises is a trait of character among the well-born. On this subject it is written in the eternal and everlasting book, the Koran, "Those who believe, fulfil their promises."

"The principle of the fulfilment of promises proceeds from a holy personal sensibility and a gracious nature. To act contrary to it, is blamed everywhere; and that it is censured and disapproved of, is borne witness to by all mankind."

"If you say 'Yes,' to any thing, do it; for a promise is obligatory to the good man. But should you say 'No,' both yourself and your companion are relieved and are at ease, and no one can then call you a liar."

THE STORY OF NAAM AND BOS.

One of the most remarkable anecdotes in history is found in the story of Tiey and Sharik. Numan bin el Manzer was one of the noblest of the great and noble; he was considered among the Arabs as a famous prince, gracious and generous, and celebrated in the pages of liberality; and as one who gave great gifts to all goers and comers. To two days in the week he had given names: one he called Naâm, (good fortune,) and the other Bōs, (ill fortune,)

This was a custom handed down to him from his ancestors, to fulfil which he was always very attentive. All those persons who came to see him on the day called Naâm, he considered as being in every respect worthy of his bounty, and always dismissed them well-pleased with their reception; but as for those who were so unlucky as to come during that called Bōs, he rolled their heads in the dust of the earth with the decree of execution, and made their blood to flow like tears from the eyes of the innocent.

By divine providence, once it happened that a man of good birth, named Tiey, by a blast of misfortune, became afflicted and impoverished; and his wife and children being miserable in adversity, he, with a hope of relief, bade them farewell, and sat out for the prosperous sill of Numan's gate. Without knowing anything of Numan's custom, he forthwith entered his presence, and, commencing to offer his respects, recited a few lines explaining his situation. Now it happened that this was the unfortunate day called Bōs, and, as Numan's eye fell upon the luckless Tiey, he remembered the custom of the day, and made known that the life of the devoted and ignorant man would fall a prey to fate. Tiey with the tongue of eloquence commenced a melodious compliment, which at the same time explained his situation. "O emir! this unfortunate being has a number of children, who are without provisions or the means of procuring any; and he is come, hoping by the water of his face (sweat of his brow) to gain them food. They famishing await his return; he left them lamenting and in tears, and on account of having come on this day his head must be the forfeit. Wisdom is with God, but my children are ready to die of hunger; do therefore, I beseech you, delay awhile my execution, and I will fail in nothing; but after bearing the food which you give me to my children, will return before the sun has set. Then do with me whatever you may deem proper."

When the Emir Numan heard these words, he pitied the man from his heart, and the generosity of his disposition would not suffer the children to die for want of food; so he said to Tiey, "I grant your request; but a security for your person is necessary, and if you fail to return I will surely execute him in your stead." Tiey cast his eyes from one side to the other; but no one had the courage to volunteer, except one of Numan's officers, who happened to be nearest to him, named Sharik—a man celebrated for his noble and excellent feelings. Tiey looked in this man's face, and repeated these lines on his generosity:

ARABIC VERSES.

"Oh! Sharik bin Aadee, there is no escape from death.
"Who will befriend helpless children, who know not even the taste of food?
"Children who are in the midst of hunger, expectation of relief, poverty, and disease.
"O thou who art brother of the generous, and a member of the family of the generous!
"O brother of Numan, bestow upon me the liberality of your security, and I will return to you before you make your evening meal."

Sharik arose to his feet and said, "O emir! I will be this man's security. Give him leave to depart." So the emir gave him the desired permission; and Tiey, saying, "Expect me before the sun sets," hastily departed to his children.

Now the afternoon prayer-time (*aser*) came, and Numan said, "Be ready, O Sharik, there is but little expectation of the Arab's ever returning." Sharik replied, "The time on which we agreed was sunset; I am ready." Soon evening came, and Numan said, "Be ready, O Sharik, and, if you have any will to make, make it now." Sharik performed the ablution called *voozoo*, and knelt down before the place of execution.

At that moment, lo! a man was seen running in great haste across the desert towards them, who proved to be none other than the unfortunate Tiey, bathed in perspiration; and when he saw Sharik at the place of execution, he kissed his eyes, raised him up, and putting himself in his place, said, "Our engagement is now fulfilled; whatever is to be, oh! let it be done quickly."

But the Emir Numan inclined his head for a moment upon the knee of admiration, and after a little reflection, again raising it said, "Never, in all my life, have I seen anything, O Tiey, more admirable than what you have just done."

"You have left no room henceforth for any one to excel in exactitude of fulfilment of promise; and you, O Sharik, have placed a seal on the chapter of generosity which evermore leaves no place for the name of 'generous.' I for ever abandon the unworthy custom of our tribe, called Bōs, which has existed so long among us; and may Allah pardon us for the acts of the past. With this innovation, let Naâm truly be Naâm, and those who come into our presence on either day, be bountifully supplied."

Behold in this true greatness and generosity; and surely nothing could be conceived more illustrative of good faith and fulfilment of promise.

There is a tradition extant in the country about Syria and Irak, regarding Samuel bin Adyia, which is as follows: The Emir el Kais, on setting out for his own kingdom of Room, had placed all his most valuable goods, clothes, and arms, in the hands of Samuel. On his way he died, and the king sent one of his own men to demand the property of the deceased. But Samuel answered: "The nature of the pledge is such that I can only give the articles confided to my care to their right owner." On this the king commanded his soldiers to surround the town in which Samuel resided. Samuel had a son, who, coming to his father's assistance, fell into the hands of the soldiers. They bound him and brought him under the castle in which his father resided, and sent word to the father, that if he wanted his son he must send them the pledge, or otherwise they would put him to death.

Now Samuel returning for answer, "It is impossible to be treacherous to a pledge," they at once put his son to death before his eyes. After this, not being able to take the castle, they departed; and soon afterwards the sons of Emir el Kais, coming to Samuel, endeavored to console him for the loss of his son. Samuel received them with many tokens of respect, and delivered to them every thing which their father had confided to his care, thus preferring the death of a beloved child to the commission of a breach of faith. In consequence of this act, the sincerity and fidelity of Samuel became proverbial on the tongues of men.

Among the acts tending to show praiseworthy qualities and noble traits of character in the performance of promises, is one related in history of Hassan bin Akbah, as written by Abool Fatih.*

Kafoor Akshadee, sultan of Egypt and Syria, once held a council in which I happened to be present. All the great men of his court were there, each one seated in his proper place, according to his rank. Kafoor arose and retired for a moment's repose, after which he returned and took his seat. He then demanded if, in such a place, there did not yet live an astrologer, blind of one eye? "Go," continued he, "see and bring me news of him. If he is still living, bring him before me; and if dead, bring whatever children he may have left." The officer went as directed, and learnt that the astrologer was dead, but had left two children, a boy and a girl, both in great poverty. These they brought to the sultan, who inquired after their circumstances, and they answered that it was a long time since their father had died. Kafoor, forthwith had them both dressed in rich clothes, and after buying two houses, gave one to each, accompanied with every thing requi-

* History of Hassan bin Akbah.

site. He also married the daughter to one of his attendants, made a great wedding for her, and told his courtiers that those who loved him should show it by the respect they paid to these two orphans, adding that he would tell them something about himself and them.

When I was the servant, said the sultan, of the clerk of Ibin Abbas, my master one day ordered me to go and bring an astrologer to him. I went, and saw a crowd around his shop, to whom he was acting the part of a necromancer; whilst I informed him that my master wanted him, I took up his stick and made a trial of my own fate and fortune. When I had thrown the stick, the astrologer looking at it said: "I must give you great good news, but indeed the same information is of much import to myself.—Before you there is great prosperity and honor; your star is in great power and strength, your horoscope is high in the constellation of majesty; and you will certainly one day possess all the palaces and fortresses, and reign over all the kings (*krals*) and governors of this land. This is not far distant, and will take place very suddenly."

Now at that time I owned but two dirhems in the whole world; so with many excuses I placed them before him. "Your excuses are excepted," said he; but at the same time he refused to receive the money, adding, "Let it remain with you as a loan at interest: if, at the time of your prosperity, I am alive, then show me whatever favor you please, only do not forget me; and if I am dead, inquire for my children, and fulfil your promise in their behalf."

So this man was the first to give me news of my present good fortune, and since that day my star has been on the increase (or advancement). From the multiplicity of my affairs, the occurrence escaped my memory up to the present time; but just now, after consulting with you, I felt fatigued, and retiring to my chamber for a moment's repose, the astrologer appeared to me in a dream and asked me, "Is this the way to perform a promise?" at the same time adding the following verses:

"Put the hand of fulfilment upon the belt of promise;—endeavor not to be among the faithless.

"Do good to the man that does good to you; and if you are unable to do him good, pray for him."

Hereupon I awoke; and thanks be to the Most High, who caused his servant to fulfil his promise! This is why I asked you if you knew the astrologer.

CHAPTER FOURTH.

On the subject of making proper returns for benefits received. The Prophet has said, "Do good to him who does good to you; and if you are not able to do this, pray for him." *

It is related of Hassin bin Sahil, that one day during the vizirat of Yahiya bin Halid the Barmakide, (I was in his company,) Some necessitous persons coming in, they represented their circumstances, and each one was sent away with gratifications, blessing the vizir. One Ahmed bin Halid il Ahvel arose and went out; and the vizir, pointing out this man, said, "After our divan is closed, do not forget to ask me about him." This the vizir's own son did not fail to do at the proper time, and he thus said:

It was during the caliphat of Muhtadee Billah that I first came to this country. This man's father was at that time director of the caliph's government. I was then in the greatest poverty, and moreover, very ill. One day my wife, with tears in her eyes, said to me, "They do not tell you of our sufferings, lest they should increase your afflictions; but indeed, it is now three days

* This is a Hadis, or saying of the Prophet, handed down by tradition.

since there has been bread or any other provisions in the house." On hearing this I rushed out of my dwelling, overcome with grief, and weeping as I went. I took my shawl from around my waist, sold it for seventeen paras, and gave the money to my wife, telling her to make use of it. After this I again left my house, and went straight to the palace of Halid; but on my arrival I found he had gone, surrounded by his suite, to the palace of the caliph. I followed him, and when I had come near, he perceived and saluted me, asking me what I desired. I answered, "Long life to you, O Ibin Halid, what must be the wants of him who sells his shawl for seventeen paras?" He passed on, and went to the palace of Muhtadee Billah; whilst I returned to my house, and told my wife what had occurred. "Would that you had not told him so," said she; "for you have now divulged your secret, and debased yourself in your own eyes." "But," I replied, "What is done is by God's order; he alone is able to save and to shield his servants."

The following morning I arose early, and went direct to the caliph's palace. On my way there I met a man, who said to me, "The vizir made mention of you in the divan, but I do not know wherefore." At the same moment another man came and informed me that the vizir desired to see me. Passing on I met the vizir, who had left the divan and was returning to his own residence. As soon as he saw me, he looked at me graciously; I approached his horse, and wall the ay to his dwelling he questioned me about my circumstances. Arrived at his gate he said to his attendants, "Bring in the petitioners from such a province;" and when they were come he said to them, "I will give you the produce of your country for the sum of eighteen thousand dinars, on the consideration, however, that this man, Yahiya, be one of your company." This they accepted, and as soon as they had left his presence he called to me and said, "Go and possess the produce of that place in company with these men." Doing as I was commanded, I joined the men, who said to me, "Save yourself much trouble and labor, and leave us in the full enjoyment of this matter, and we will pay you down now your share of the same, namely, two hundred thousand dirhems." This proposition I made known to the vizir, and as soon as he had heard it he recommended me to accept it, and make use of it for my family, adding, "I give you a charge in his majesty's government; go, enjoy it in a seeming manner; what I have done for you is in return for the favors which I received from your deceased father."

At the close of these words the vizir, turning to his son, asked him, saying, "Were any one to do such an act to your father, what should his recompense be?" The son answered, "It would be proper to reward him in a manner worthy of the favor conferred." The vizir added, "I do not know how to repay sufficiently such an act, unless indeed I resign my own office of vizir in his favor. This is my intention; and if God pleases, I will execute it."

So of a truth, after ending his business, he exalted the man most highly to the caliph, resigned his vizirat, and had him appointed in his place. May God be contented with them all! Such should be the regard paid to the right of bread and benefits. Generosity is a quality innate with pure and just men.

Ali ben Abbas, who was the Water Intendant of the city of Bagdad, under the Caliph Mamoon, related as follows:

"One day I was in the presence of the Emir of the faithful, when a man was brought bound before him. It was near night, and the caliph calling for me, said, 'Ali, take this man, keep him in close but genteel confinement, and bring him to me to-morrow.' So I forthwith took the man, and, mounting him on an ass, conveyed him to my house. Seeing that the anger of the caliph was very great against him, and lest he should escape, I took him into a part of my harem, and confined him there. I then for the first time saw that he was covered with severe bruises; so I brought in a surgeon, who applied a salve for their cure. I asked him from what country he had come, and he answered, 'I am from a quarter in Damascus, called *Bab el Jabieh*.' I then told him that I also was from Damascus; on hearing which, he said, 'Is there not cause for you to love that place?' 'Yes,' answered I, 'it gave me birth, and, moreover, an incident occurred to me there.' 'Be pleased to relate it,' said the man.

"So I told him that I once went there with an individual who had received the command of the city from the caliph. The effects of the previous commander were yet being transported from the palace as we took possession of it. The two commanders, in the course of conversation, came to words; and finally, the ex-commander falling upon the new one and his attendants, with a number of men, they chased them before them with swords in their hands. I threw myself out of the window, and, whilst the assailants were surrounding the palace, fled to that quarter of the city called Bab el Jabieh, where, seeing a man standing at his door, I cried out for aid and assistance against the hands of my enemies. The man bade me enter, and secrete myself in a corner of his harem. Soon my pursuers came to the house; and after searching every part of it for me, they at length went so far as to burst into the harem. The man's wife screamed out, and the men desisted. As soon as they were gone, the man and his wife said to me, 'Now calm your apprehensions, and fear nothing.' They then showed me every attention, and the kindness which I received from them was beyond description. Some time afterwards they informed me that the caravan for Bagdad would leave the city on the following day. I, however, had neither horse nor servants, nor even a groat of money, and therefore made up my mind to return on foot. But early in the morning of the next day they came to me, and said, 'If you are determined on going, be quick.' To my surprise, the man had provided a well caparisoned horse for myself, another for my baggage, and a black slave for my service, all well provided; and after handing me a sum of money sufficient for all my expenses, he and his wife and children accompanied me to the caravan, where he recommended me to one of his friends who was about to undertake the same journey, took leave of me, and returned to the city. This is the incident which occurred to me in Damascus, and I have often desired to be permitted, before my death, to repay the kindness which I then received.

"As I ended these words the bound and imprisoned man suddenly exclaimed, 'God bless you, my brother, behold at your feet the man whom you desire to recompense,' at the same time telling me all about the occurrences of that period, and my conduct and conversation with him whilst his guest. Immediately I struck the chains from off his neck, and freed his hands from the irons which confined them. I kissed his eyes and face, saying, 'There is no sorrow for you from this day forth.' Afterwards I questioned him as to what had happened to him; and he told me all his story, which was as follows: 'The same trouble which came upon your head has now visited mine: they accused me of a great crime which I had not committed, and conveyed me in chains before the Commander of the faithful. But the worst of all my affliction is, that my wife and children are ignorant of what has happened to me; and the greatest favor which I can ask at your hands, is, that if I am condemned to death, you will let them know, by a letter, that I have ceased to exist.'

"But I answered, 'O brother, cease to be afflicted! with God's permission you will again return in life and health to your family, and rejoice the hearts of your children.' I immediately got ready a number of the choicest things of Bagdad, gave the man many presents, and prepared others for his wife. Moreover, I bestowed on him one hundred thousand dirhems with which to cover his expenses, and restore him to his family; and said, 'Let the caliph now do with me whatever he pleases.' But the man was dissatisfied, and said, 'It would be ungenerous in me to accept your kindness, you must not incur the anger of the caliph on my account: let us, therefore, now agree, that if he pardons me on your request, good; but if his anger against me is not appeased, I will go to him, and he may do with me whatever he sees proper, so that no misfortune befalls you.'

"On the following morning I went to the presence of the caliph, and saw that he was in anger; for as soon as he saw me he exclaimed, 'Ali, where is the man?' at the same time inquiring for the executioner. I remained silent, and he repeated the question; when I answered, 'O Commander of the faithful! a strange accident has befallen him; pray permit me to relate it to you.' 'Speak, then,' said he; and his anger increasing, he added, 'if you say he has escaped, by my father's soul I swear to cut off your head.' 'Hear me,' answered I; 'behold we are both here, and your orders, whatever they are, shall be obeyed.' So he at length permitted me to speak, and I then narrated all that had occurred to each of us, telling him the generosity and kindness which I had received from the man, and how he in turn had become a prey to misfortune. 'The Commander of the faithful is generous,' said I; 'and can appreciate the nobleness of soul which made him refuse to escape lest he should bring trouble on his benefactor. It now remains for your majesty to order what shall be done.'

"Mamoon was astonished at the generous humanity of the man, and said, '*Afvna an hoo,* we have pardoned him.' Overwhelmed with such condescension, I threw myself at the caliph's feet, and kissed them. He continued, 'He did this noble act to one who was a stranger to him; if we had known it when he was here, we would have bestowed upon him a reward.' I expressed the grateful feelings with which these words inspired me, and begged the caliph to grant him the honor of kissing his feet.

"When I returned for him and gave him the joyful news, he devoutly returned thanks to God for his deliverance, and then went with me to the presence of the caliph, who made many inquiries of him, and finally clothed him in a dress of honor. He also gave him ten horses, ten mules, and ten camels, besides many other valuable things, and ten thousand pieces of silver. He also ordered letters of recommendation to be written to the hakeem (governor) of Syria, that every attention should be paid him, and no other tax be levied on him than the religious tithe, called *asher*. 'Write to us,' added the caliph, as he dismissed him, 'news from Syria.' And whenever his letters came to the caliph, he would call me, and tell me that he had heard from my friend."

See in this anecdote the goodness and generosity of the noble Caliph Mamoon; and learn to do good acts, and bestow favors without their being asked of you.

It is related by Messoody,* that Hedjadj ez Zalim was desirous of injuring Yazid bin Mehlebee, and made a foray into his kingdom, where, seizing upon his person, he offered him every indignity and degradation. During his confinement, Yazid, by means of gifts and kind words, gained the hearts of his keepers, so that they were ready to risk their lives and souls for him. One night they let him escape from prison; and forthwith setting out for Damascus, he fled to the dwelling of Suliman bin Abd el Melek, who was the brother of the then reigning caliph, and claimed his protection. This individual was to be the heir and successor of the caliph. He received Yazid with much civility and courtesy, showing him every attention and respect, and left him at liberty to do as he should think proper regarding the disposal of his time.

Soon after this, Hedjadj ez Zalim heard of Yazid's flight, and wrote a letter to the caliph in which he grossly calumniated Yazid, charging him with several false crimes, and adding that he

* Messoody is one of the most pleasant and sprightly of Arabian authors, and the composer of this work has drawn largely on his Meroodj ez Zeheb.

had escaped from prison and fled to his brother, having with him a great sum belonging to the royal treasury. "It remains for you to decide what shall be done with him," said he. When the caliph read the letter he became very much angered, and gave orders to his men to go and seize Yazid, and, after putting him in chains, to bring him before him. "If my brother," continued the caliph, "refuses to give him up, and makes any difficulty, remember what my orders to you are, this letter will inform him of the same."

When the letter reached Suliman, he read it, and wrote an answer to the caliph, as follows:

"Yazid bin Mehleb has from the most ancient times been on terms of true friendship with our ancestors, and now the faithless Hedjadj, not having received the marks of regard and distinction from him which he expected, is envious, and wishes to shed his blood unjustly. The accusations made against him are false; for he had at first but four hundred thousand aktchas, and yet retains three hundred thousand: therefore this unfortunate man has been compelled to seek refuge with me, and to ask our assistance. If the caliph will permit me, I will pay over that amount from my own treasury, and the public can then say nothing reproachful of us." So he sent a man with this letter to the caliph, who, when he read it, became greatly enraged at the calumnies of Hedjadj, but sent again another to his brother commanding him without fail to deliver Yazid up to him. When the envoy reached Suliman, he read its contents and was greatly grieved. He filled a belt with gold, and attached it to the neck of the "light of his eyes," that is to say, his son Ayub; he also filled another with silver, and put it around the neck of Yazid, and then addressing a letter to his brother wrote, "O Commander of the faithful, my desire was to be the third of these two chained persons, and to preserve the good name of the caliphat. But I will obey whatever you may order, and have sent your brother's son Ayub with Yazid. If Hedjadj the accused injures Yazid bin Mehleb, then let me be the next to die." This letter he sent to the caliph, who, when he saw Yazid bin Mehleb in chains, and read the letter, was greatly ashamed, and said, "If we have injured your father's feelings, O Ayub, we did wrong;" and springing from his seat, he took the chains from off Ayub's neck and kissed his face and eyes. Then dressing Yazid bin Mehleb in a rich cloak of honor, he said to him, "The tyranny of Hedjadj is now known to me." Afterwards he gave Ayub three hundred thousand dirhems, and to Yazid one hundred thousand; he likewise made for them a royal feast, and showed them great favor. He wrote a letter to Hedjadj saying that Yazid had brought to him whatever he had taken in money or effects, and made over to him all his debts and obligations. "Be you caréful," added he, "to see that no harm or wrong is done to any of his people, who may have remained with you." At the same time he addressed a letter to his brother excusing himself and conciliating his friendship, and ordered that whatever government Yazid bin Mehleb desired should, without delay, be given to him; after which, he sent Ayub and Yazid back to his brother at Damascus.

The day they arrived there, Suliman bin Abd el Melek and all his chief officers went out to meet them; and placing Yazid at his side, Suliman treated him like the most distinguished of his subjects.

What protection and generosity in one who, being himself the heir apparent of the caliphat, would condescend to petition the caliph for an act of liberality, and expose his own life, and, what is still dearer, that of his child, for the attainment of the just dues of an unfortunate individual! Such indeed should be the great heart of a sovereign.

CHAPTER FIFTH,

It is known to the pious, all-intelligent, and believing, that the wealth and riches of a sovereign increase in the ratio of his pure intentions and the protection and care accorded by him to his subjects; and that on the other hand, evil intention is the source of degradation and abasement, and the cause of poverty and indigence. It has been handed down by Veheb bin Menich, as a saying of the Prophet, on whom be peace, "That whenever a governor purposes injustice, and acts accordingly, God will send misfortune upon his country by a loss of business in its streets, dearth in its products, and barrenness among its animals; but when his intentions are good and just, and he executes them, God blesses that country with plenty." The relator spoke in sincerity and truth.

It is related that in the country of Morocco, on the west, there was once a king who had heard a certain woman's garden highly praised, as being of a generous soil, and productive of fruit, such as was found in no other Arab country; its sugar-canes, in particular, were the wonder of the age. In fact, so much did they praise it, that the king one day mounted his horse and set out for the garden, with the intention of paying it a visit. On his arrival he found that it had not been praised too much; for when they had cut some of its canes, he found them most delicious. From each one they filled a cup of juice, at the sight of which the king was astonished; and avarice getting the better of him, he said, "I will give the owner of this garden whatever he may ask, so that it be mine." Soon afterwards he ordered one of his attendants to squeeze one or two more of the canes; but although they squeezed an entire armful, they did not get as much out of all of them as they did from the two first: at which the king being astonished, he inquired of the woman if there were any difference among the canes. The woman answered "No," adding that they were all of one kind, and up to that time had produced a glass of juice a piece; "but now," said she, "they seem to differ from their usual custom, and we do not know the reason, unless it be that the intention of the king has been changed from what it was at first."

When the king heard these words he repented of his avaricious desires, and asked pardon (of God). A while after, he requested the woman to squeeze one or two more of the canes, which being done, the cup was filled as formerly; and handing the cup to the king, she returned thanks to God that he had had compassion upon the king's honor and corrected the royal mind. "Evidently," said she, "this remarkable plenty is a proof of the change in his intentions: for the good intentions and protection of kings and princes draw down plenty and prosperity; whilst on the contrary evil dispositions blast all abundance and affection, and prevent what would otherwise be beneficial." The king was greatly pleased at these words, gave the woman numerous presents, and for ever afterwards was upon his guard against envy and avarice.

It is related as follows of one of the caliphs of the house of Abbas, named Mehdi Billah, who was seated on the throne of the caliphat in the one hundred and fifty-eighth year of the Hedjreh.

One day being desirous of amusing himself with the chase, he mounted his horse, and, attended by his domestic officers and other attendants, proceeded to the mountains, where they started a flock of antelopes. The soldiers and attendants of the caliph immediately pursued them, each one following a different antelope; the caliph himself choosing out one and chasing it. In this sport the company soon became separated, and the caliph was lost from his suite. After pursuing the antelope until his strength was exhausted, he succeeded in coming up with and killing it; but on looking round he found no trace or sign of his attendants: he was quite alone, night was near, and he was thirsty. At a distance he perceived a black tent, and proceeding towards it found that it was the residence of an Arab, who had pitched it near the banks of a stream which had once watered the valley, but was now dry. As he came near he perceived an Arab woman, with two children, a boy and a girl; and when she approached him, he saluted her, and claimed her hospitality. "You are welcome, O friend," answered she, holding his stirrup and assisting him to dismount from his horse. She tied the horse and spread a mat for the caliph, on which he seated himself, and from fatigue soon fell asleep. On awaking he found that night had set in, and yet none of his people had made their appearance. He asked the woman if the town was near; she replied that it was a considerable distance off, and added her hopes that he would accept of her humble dwelling for that night. He consented and passed the night in her tent.

In the morning he arose and went to the edge of the plain, and said to the Arab woman, "How strange that the water of such a stream should be dried up! do you reside here alone?" She replied, "Yes, good sir; formerly we were not here alone: but may God grant vigilance to the caliph, so that he may learn what passes in the world; the bed which you see was once that of a great stream of running water, and twenty thousand Arabs and many Turkmen tribes dwelt with us near it; but it was God's providence that our late sovereign should die—he who had been a just person, and moreover was one who paid attention to passing events, and protected the poor against the hand of the oppressor. The caliph who succeeded him is occupied only with his pleasures and pastimes, and as he neglects the affairs of his kingdom, his ministers and other high officers become also of his disposition and character. To such a length have matters gone, that oppression is openly practised, and no one ever asks who are the oppressed, or who the oppressor; for the hand of the poor and tyrannized cannot reach the caliph and make known its grievances. No one pities the fate of those who go to the gates of justice, or to his vizirs, to make known their complaints; no attention is paid to them, and their patience is worn away. For this reason the people of this neighborhood have, one by one, emigrated from their homes; and as honor is gone, they also are departed. Good fortune brought you to us last night; for to-morrow I also am going to leave the country."

When the caliph heard these words, he was grieved from the bottom of his heart, repented of his misconduct, and determined in future to change it. "Hereafter," thought he, "I will attend to the affairs of the faithful. Let it be a covenant between God and me, one that I will surely fulfil, that the interests of the poor shall be henceforth judged according to the holy laws."

The Arab brought before the caliph whatever she had to eat, consisting of a cup of yaoort (curdled milk) and a lamb which she roasted. "I have also a cup of sharab, (wine,)" added she, "is it admissible? The caliph answered in the affirmative; and she placed it before him in two bowls, which he drank, and was greatly exhilarated by it. Then turning to the Arab he said, "I am one of the caliph's favorite attendants, and by God's permission will certainly be of use to you." The woman answered, "Much prosperity to you, you have done us great honor by this visit;" and filling another bowl gave it to the caliph, who also drank it, much to the increase of his good humor. After this he said to the woman, "Do you know me?" She answered, "just now you told me who you were." The caliph said, "I am the caliph's chief vizir, and lieutenant, possessed of full powers." The Arab woman on hearing this arose, and bowing low, filled another bowl of wine, which she handed to the caliph. He drank it and said, "O Arab, do you know who is your guest?" "Yes," answered she. "I will now tell you truly," continued the caliph, "for you have done me a great service; behold in me the caliph of the universe and the sultan of the family of Adam." At this the Arab jumped on her feet and exclaimed, "May God glorify you!" The caliph told her that to-morrow she should see his words verified. The Arab answered, "God be praised; you have deigned to honor us with your noble feet, and all favor is from God." After a little more conversation the caliph asked for another bowl of wine; but was refused by the Arab, who, when asked the reason said, "When I gave you the first bowl, you told me that you were one of the favorite attendants of the caliph; on the second, you called yourself his chief vizir; and on the third, you asserted that you were the caliph himself. Now I fear that if I give you one more you will lay claim even to the character of the most holy Prophet." At this answer, the caliph, much pleased, laughed, and became very merry; and as he felt pleased with the wit of the Arab, he passed there yet another night. In the morning when he awoke he observed the Arab's wife going out to milk two goats which she had, and calling as she did so to her little daughter to bring her a kettle to hold the milk. The child had scarcely obeyed her and returned, when she screamed out to her mother to hasten and escape with the kettle, for the bed of the river was fast filling with water. The woman ran towards the tent; and indeed behold the river, which for such a length of time had been dry, was now filled with water rushing impetuously. The Arab returned thanks and hastened to impart the news to the caliph, saying, "Blessed be God! Your noble footsteps have been the cause of giving back to us this river which was the source of our support. Perhaps your majesty by God's aid has changed your intentions from evil to good, and this is the cause of this compassion and mercy on us. Come forth and behold the effect of this divine favor." The caliph did as he was desired, and returned thanks to the Most High.

The Arab's words made a deep impression upon the mind of the caliph; and while he prayed, he wept. The Arab now aided him to mount his horse; and as he rode away he told her to assemble all her tribe and people, for he designed to make her their chief, and giving her a written paper to this effect, he added, "I also free you from all taxation for ever: sow and reap and enjoy your produce, live in quiet and peace, and no tithe shall ever be required of you. Let me see how you will conduct yourself, and I will aid you accordingly."

When the caliph had reached the city he sent criers into the streets to proclaim a reign of justice for the future; and in fact ever afterwards he paid strict attention to the affairs of his kingdom, and every thing was adjusted agreeably to law and equity, so much so, that his reign became proverbial in the mouth of the world. Ever afterwards, during the whole course of his life, he was attentive to the affairs of his subjects and rayahs, so that even as in Adam's time, the wolf and the sheep walked quietly and in equality together, in the meadows and the plains.

Divine favor led him thus in the true and straight path. May God have mercy on them all!

Ibin Abbas narrates, that there was once a king who, being desirous of seeing his dominions, set out on his travels and one day dismounted at the dwelling of a village peasant. At nightfall the man's cows, as usual, returned from their pasture; and after milking one of them, the peasant brought the milk and sat it before the king. From two cows alone he got thirty batmans of milk. Now when the king had drunk the milk, he was so much pleased with its flavor, that he conceived the idea of paying the man whatever he might ask, and taking away a cow.

On the next day the villager again commencing to milk his cows got from three of them only five batmans of milk (thirteen and a half pounds to the batman); afterwards he milked the others, and found that he had not got as much from them all, as on the other days he got from one.

The king was greatly astonished at this, and exclaimed, "How is this? The pasture is the same; what then is the cause of this diminution?" The villager answered, "God alone knows the reason; it is possible that the king's intentions have undergone a change, and the diminution may be the result of a covetous desire to possess what belongs to his subjects. It is a saying well verified by the experience of time, that if the sovereign of the age looks with the eye of envy upon his subjects and regards their property with a look of covetousness, God will withdraw his blessing from that people."

The king repented on hearing this, asked pardon of God, and changed his intentions. At sunset the cows again came in from their pasture; and when the villager milked them, behold! they gave even more than usual; which the villager seeing, he exclaimed, "God be praised! Our king has changed his evil purposes, and see in this a divine proof of it."

CHAPTER SIXTH.

On the actions of upright sovereigns, and their obedience to the Mohammedan law.

Mutasid Billah, one of the caliphs of the race of Abbas, was a brave, lion-hearted, liberal, and just man. Actuated by feelings of uprightness, he protected the holy law, and ordered punishment whenever it was deemed necessary.

During his caliphat, his cadi asker, or supreme military judge, was one Hussain, the most learned man of that period. The Cadi Aboo Omar, relates as follows: One day I was in the office of the Judge Hussain, when one of the caliph's favorite attendants came to answer to a charge of debt brought against him by a merchant. The judge ordered the parties to stand up side by side and be judged; but the attendant refused, saying, 'Have you no regard for me, that you order me to stand up with a low-born man?" The cadi at this became angered, and said, "Not only you, but your master, would I make to stand up with this opponent." At the same time the cadi ordering some of his people to make the attendant arise, the case was tried, and sentence pronounced against him. Then the cadi ordered the officer in whose charge he was, in case the attendant dared to refuse to pay the debt, to take him into the street, and there sell him to the highest bidder, and pay over the amount to his creditor the merchant. "If it is greater than the debt," added he, "give the overplus to the Commander of the faithful." The officer, however, received the full amount from the attendant; who, after paying it, went away weeping to the caliph, before whom he threw his turban on the ground, and exclaimed, "Is this the protection of the Commander of the faithful, that the Cadi Hussain should abuse me in this manner, and order me to be sold—me, who am a faithful servant of the caliph?"

The caliph took offence at this language, scolded the attendant, and said: "By the souls of my ancestors, had he even sold you, I, for the sake of the holy law, would have confirmed the sale, and received the surplus. If you had felt an interest in my honor and good name, you would, by paying the debt justly due to the merchant, have avoided the necessity of going to law with him."

God be praised, such is the manner in which kings ought to show their obedience to the holy law of the Prophet, to the end that their places be exalted both in this life and in that which is to come.

Mohammed bin Abdallah bin Abd el Melek relates, that during the reign of the Caliph Mutazid Billah it became necessary to send troops against the infidels; but it being the first year of the caliphat, there was not sufficient money in the public treasury to meet the expenses. Indeed, had it not been for Mutazid Billah, the prosperity of the house of Abbas would have come to an end; for enemies were rising up every where, particularly among the tribe called Caramata, which ruled in Syria, Yemin, and Aden, where it trampled faithful Mussulmans under foot, and, finding a foot-hold in Bussorah and Lahta, made an attack upon Bagdad.

During the reign of the Caliph Mutamid Billah, Mutazid Billah was charged with the power of rendering justice, and he sent soldiers in all directions to cut off the enemies of the true faith. One by one he seized upon the chiefs of the Caramatees, and had them executed in the city of Bagdad. When the caliphat descended to him, so general were security and justice, that it surpassed the age of Haroon er Rasheed; and the people gave him the name of the second Seffah,* because he had, as it were, resuscitated the kingdom.

Still it was urgently necessary to send troops against the infidels; but the treasury was in a very low condition.

At that time there was a rich merchant, a magian, in Bagdad, and the caliph was advised to borrow money from him; to which advice he having acceded, he invited the merchant to visit him. When he arrived, Mutazid Billah asked him, "Can you lend us one hundred thousand pieces of silver until our revenues are collected?" The magian replied, "Not only I, but all I possess, is at your disposal. Give me your orders, and whatever you wish shall be immediately brought to you." The caliph was astonished at the confidence the man showed, and asked him how he could place so much faith in him as to offer so large an amount of money; to which the magian answered, "O Emir of the faithful, God having confided this vast country and so many subjects to your care, and you having always governed them with justice and equity, failing in nothing, cannot I, for a few coins, put faith in you?" When the caliph heard these words his eyes filled with tears, and he expressed his thanks to God; after which he said to the magian, "May God bless your store and preserve us from the necessity of

* Seffah was the name of the founder of the caliphat.

making loans. You have not failed in your duty to us: if we need your money, we will accept it; and should you ever hereafter need our assistance, come to us freely and do not fail, for our door will be always open to you."

The magian departed, thanking God for the noble sentiments with which he had inspired the caliph.

Ismail ibin Bulbul was the most favored and worthy attendant of the caliph of his time. He relates that one day when the Emir of the faithful, Mutazid Billah, was amusing himself in the company of his vizir and attendants, one of the latter presented him with a petition, in which it was represented that in a certain place there was a number of men assembled, whose conduct was injurious to the prosperity and good name of the state, and therefore required observation.

Whilst Mutazid Billah read the petition, anger was visible in his countenance; and asking of his grand-vizir, Abdallah, what he thought had better be done with these people, the vizir answered, "Let us send a number of men and disperse the meeting, then act towards each in turn as may seem just, and make them an example to others."

To this the caliph replied, "May your heart's severity and want of mercy never be mine; for it has made my anger disappear, and gained my best feelings in their favor. Do you not know that rayahs and subjects are so many pledges confided to me by the Creator of all things, and that they will be asked of me at the day of judgment? I thought you were more merciful and benevolent than myself, but now I see that you are less pitiful than a cannibal; go now examine well this matter, and see why this people have acted in this unlawful manner. There certainly is a cause for it; they have either experienced injustice and oppression from their governor, been burdened with excessive taxes, or some calamity has befallen their relatives and friends. If they have been dealt with unjustly, do them justice; if they are in poverty, assist them from the public treasury; in fine, do for them whatever their nêcessities may require. Put in prison and punish those who have dared to injure them; and by this means the good laws of the state will secure peace and quiet to every one. Do not confound the innocent with the guilty, and thus turn the edge of the sword of justice from those who merit it; for what would our Creator do in the world to come, and how could we answer for it before the All-just?"

The vizir left the royal presence, and examined attentively the whole affair. He learnt who were the guilty and who the innocent, saw them dealt justly by, and acted towards them agreeably to the views of the caliph. And when the caliph's kindness and consideration for his subjects, and the advice which he gave to his vizir, were made known, every one prayed for his prosperity, and he became celebrated in the whole seven climes of the world for his equity and justice. Truly, kings should be attentive to the affairs of their people, and attend to them in person. If they confide all to their vizir, and neglect their government, they do a vain and imprudent thing, and give cause to the enemies who surround their empire to attack them. When a sovereign devotes himself closely to the affairs of his state, his officers, seeing that he is vigilant, fear him, and make efforts to perform properly their respective charges; and thus good order and system are preserved.

Mohammed Khan, the Ghazi, the conqueror of Constantinople, one of the sultans of the family of Othman the unique and chosen, was a talented and learned as well as a brave and courageous man, and a sovereign who was attentive to the affairs of his kingdom. He was in the habit of always uniting the Ulemas to his company, when he would take delight in engaging them in learned and erudite conversation. It was also his habit to walk the streets and bazaars by night and day in disguise, for the purpose of acquiring information of what was passing among his people. His vizirs and other ministers were all very learned men, and, in all their actions, had at heart the welfare of the state and the faith.

One day Mollah Kevzanee, who was the most excellent of the great men of the age, was in his council hall, when, the conversation turning upon affairs of state, Sultan Mohammed Khan, the conqueror, asked the Mollah, saying, "It is said that the Crimea was once a thickly populated and very wealthy country, famous for its excellent and very learned men, and that it has had no less than twelve thousand muftees, whose decrees are worthy of being recorded. It is related in the history of the Mollah Tashkendee, that it was gifted with great men and immense wealth. Why, therefore, did it, in so short a time, become impoverished and ruined?" Mollah Kevzanee answered, "The cause of the ruin of that country was, that its sovereign had no vizir of talent or capability." When Sultan Mohammed heard this, he said, "Hasten, and call my respected vizir, Mahmood, to me;" and when he had come, addressing him, he said, "I asked of Mollah Kevzanee what was the cause of the ruin of the kingdom of the Crimea, and he answered that it was the want of a talented and capable vizir."

So Mahmood Pasha said, "Yes, my sovereign, they have answered truly; but Mollah Mahmood has respected the rules of civility in the presence of majesty. Now, the truth is this, that the real cause of the ruin of that country was the want of an attentive sovereign; for, if a king is acquainted with and watchful over the condition of the realms under his empire, those who are in his service will be zealous accordingly: therefore, my much respected sovereign, the vizir is not the cause of this ruin, but, rather, the sultan himself, who makes his vizir arbitrator over the affairs of religion and state, of this life and eternity, and places him as an absolute decider over the fates of the subjects of his kingdom, particularly the Ulema or religious doctors of the Holy Law. Assuredly affairs should not be left wholly to a vizir; he is but an humble servant, who, if he fills his office with uprightness, is worthy of his charge, but, should he not do so, ought to be dismissed and degraded, and another found who will perform his duty. When a sovereign employs himself with the affairs of his empire, his lieutenant is zealous and attentive to fulfil whatever is given to his charge; the governors in the different parts of his kingdom, aware that the sultan examines into their administration and knows who of them are good and who bad, perform their respective duties accordingly, and abstain from misconduct; and the enemies who surround his country, knowing the attention of the sovereign to the affairs of his state, learn to fear and respect him."

When Mahmood Pasha had ended these words, the sultan said to him, "You have spoken truly; and may you ever be prosperous and happy. Mahmood, you have awakened me, as from the sleep of negligence." He then dressed him in a robe of honor, and conferred numerous marks of favor upon him. A sovereign should not be grieved on learning the truth, nor close his ear against it; and this is the choicest and best quality of a prince.

CHAPTER SEVENTH.

On the subject of good faith, religious observances, and evil machinations.

In the year of the Hedjreh 501, reigned Sultan Sinjar Malek Shah Ogloo, one of the Seljook sultans, a prince of upright and just sentiments, and true piety. Once upon a time he marched his troops and followers to the city of Talikan, for the purpose of letting them repose there; and when its inhabitants heard the sound of armed men, and the commotion around the sultan, each sought a place from which to witness their passage. It so happened that near the city was a high hill, with a pointed summit or cone, up which a child of one of the families of the city had climbed for the purpose of seeing the passing soldiery, and was there seated alone. The sultan's troops, like a torrent, passed by there; and Sultan Sinjar, casting his eyes around him, espied something on the summit of the hill which resembled a bird. Supposing it to be such, the sultan, who was extremely expert with the bow, as he passed by let fly an arrow at the object, which, by God's providence, attained its mark, struck the body of the child and killed it on the spot where it sat. He called one of his attendants and directed him to go and bring him the bird. The attendant, hastening to do as he was bid, mounted the hill, and found a dead child covered with blood. Putting it on his shield, he brought it down to the presence of the sultan; and the just and merciful prince, perceiving that in place of a bird he had killed a child, uttered an exclamation of painful surprise, dismounted from his horse, threw himself upon the ground, his breast burning with the fire of affliction, and his eyes filled with tears of sorrow. "How strangely and grievously have I sinned," exclaimed he, "and in a manner how unexpectedly am I pained! I will endeavor to do justice for this crime." So he sent criers throughout the city to summon the parents of the child, who were not long in being found. They proved to be poor indigent inhabitants of the place. When the father saw his child in this condition, grief overcame him and he wept bitterly. The sultan, seeing the man's affliction, took him by the hand and led him to his tent, and there, in the presence of his officers, placed before him a pile of gold and a sword; he then swore that the child met his death by accident. "But there," continued he, "is gold, and here is my head: satisfy yourself with the former, and pardon me, or strike off my head with the latter; kill me beside your son, so that at the day of judgment you deliver me not up to torment. The choice is in your hand: either pardon me, or execute the right of talion, and thus free me from this misfortune."

But the poor man answered, "My noble-hearted and justly minded sovereign is absolved from all criminality; for the accident occurred by divine destiny and providence: long may he live to be the soul of the world and the spirit of his empire! The favors and gifts which you offer me are worthy of your greatness of heart; and may your reign be ever prosperous. Let all our heads and lives be devoted to your welfare: you are the shadow of God; be ever faithful to the charge given you by Him. I have absolved you from the blood of my child; may he, at the day of punishment, not ask it at your hands, and let those now around you be witnesses to your innocence."

The poor man's words consoled the sultan, and made a deep impression on him. The father did not wish to accept the money; but the just king added another equal sum, and pressed them upon him against his will. He also conferred upon him the government of the country of Talikan and made him one of his chief officers.

What an upright and merciful sovereign, in whose mind power and poverty are one and equal, and whose noble character and conduct made him one of the best of kings!

May God have mercy on them all!

It is written in books of history, that Suliman bin Abd el Melek of the family of the Ommiades, was a most benevolent, intelligent, and worthy man. He always cultivated the acquaintance and society of persons of mind and talent, and took pleasure in having the histories of preceding sultans, and the virtues of sovereigns of just principles, read to him.

Once in the course of conversation Suliman bin Abd el Melek made this remark: "Praise be to God the benevolent, the most high and holy, whose grace to his servant of this kingdom and empire is, if not greater, certainly not less than that shown to Suliman bin Daood.* He had power over the Deevs, Perees, wild beasts, birds, and winds, which we have not; but for wealth and troops, honor and fame, we have nearly reached our expectations." One of the learned persons present said, "You do not possess that which is more important than all others to your kingdom, and is as the running water of your empire." The sovereign inquired what it was. "You have not a vizir worthy of your glory and reign. You are a king, son of a king, and you should have a vizir excellent, and versed in the affairs of government, one who is possessed of personal purity, famous for his piety and charity, free from haughtiness, pride, and hypocrisy." The sovereign replied, "But none knows where there is to be found a vizir possessed of such excellent qualities and brilliant talents as those you recommend." Then the person said, "There is now in the city of Balk, one named Baramikee, descended from the vizirs of Ardashir Babek, whose office has come down to him by inheritance. When the kingdom of the kings of Adjem departed from them, that country became Islamite. It was then that the Baramikees took up their residence in Balk, and received the true faith. They possessed works on the knowledge necessary to a vizir, and taught their sons the science of belles lettres, as well as other necessary attainments; so that they became superior to their equals, and the most learned of the age." In such terms of praise as the preceding he commended them.

So Suliman bin Abd el Melek sent royal missives to Balk, and had Jaafer brought to Damascus. The principal officers of the court went out to meet him with great honor and distinction, and conducted him before the sovereign. After kissing the hand of

* The reader is here reminded of the Eastern traditions that give to Suliman the powers above spoken of.

the shah, he showed him a place near the throne; but as Jaafer took his seat the countenance of the shah changed its color, and he turned away from him in evident displeasure. "Take him out," exclaimed he: and as no one knew the reason, the officers of the king were astonished. One of the padishah's near attendants inquired, why, after having Jaafer brought from Balk to Damascus with so much honor, he showed such sudden aversion for him? The king replied, "Had it not been for his merit and abilities, I would have had him executed on the spot; for this man has prepared poison about him, and one must beware of him." The attendant said, "If you so command, we will inquire about this matter of himself; and if he denies it, your sovereign aversion will be a just one: but should he avow it, and explain a motive for it, it will remain with our sovereign to accept or not of his excuses."

So Jaafer was called to the presence of the king a second time, when Suliman bin Abd el Melek said, "The reason of our sending you out of our presence was this, that I became aware you had a deadly poison about you." Jaafer saluted the sovereign and said, "Yes, my padishah, in my ring there is a prepared poison; but it is inherited from my forefathers, and is designed for myself alone: up to this day it has injured no true believer, nor is it intended for any other purpose than that of protecting myself. How many accidents occur, and what numerous sorrows and tribulations are endured in the service of kings and sovereigns! mayhap one day they might require of me an important service, which it would be beyond my powers to perform; or it might be that an enemy brought upon us a disgrace beyond our endurance; in which case we would then destroy ourselves, to free us from the shame."

Sultan Suliman bin Abd el Melek was a man of judgment, and replied, "To persons of mind and talent both rashness and haste are at first sight faulty; for a subject which at first appears disagreeable, upon reflection becomes praiseworthy and commendable, particularly to sovereigns and other governors: therefore is deliberation beneficial and useful in the proper administration of their government." Suliman bin Abd el Melek also praised Jaafer's talents and judgment, as well as his prudence and care; and he ordered one of his own riding horses with its rich equipments to be brought forth for his use, on which he mounted him, and, preceded by all the high officers of his court, went to his court of justice, where he counseled with them.

One day when Jaafer was with the king, he asked of him, "From what did his majesty, our sovereign, know that I had poison concealed about me?" Suliman bin Abd el Melek replied, "In the treasury of my predecessors were found two royal rings which I inherited, and their qualities are as follows. When any one has poison about him, or there is poison near, these two seals become agitated, and rub against each other." Then taking off the rings from his finger, he showed them to Jaafer. All the persons present were greatly astonished at the sight. Jaafer exclaimed, "Barik Allah! There are two wonderful things connected with this matter. One is this seal; and the other, that once being in the society of the sovereign of Tabristan, he asked your servant whether he had ever beheld the sea, or been rowed upon it. I replied that I had not; so he remarked, that as I was his guest, I should go upon it with him. He went to the sea, where sailors brought a bark which we entered; a meal also was got ready, of which we were partaking, when I perceived a ring on his finger, made of a red ruby, the like of which I had never seen before. The sovereign, of delicate feelings, perceiving that I observed the ring attentively, took it off and offered it to me. As we sailed along, I kissed the seal and returned it to him. Upon which he remarked, 'Keep it, it is yours,' and gave it back to your servant; adding that a thing which was once taken from the finger and given away, could not be returned to it. Your servant replied, that a thing worthy of a sovereign was not proper for a servant; when, as I begged to return it to him, much to my regret, he threw it into the sea. I said, 'Had I known your intention of throwing it into the sea, I would have accepted it; as it is, I fear I have been impolite in this matter.' The sovereign replied, 'There is now no remedy; you are to blame for not taking it, but there is something else curious connected with the ring.' So he turned and ordered one of his attendants to go, and from a certain place bring him a particular box. The attendant departed, and soon returned with a small box, out of which the king took a little fish made of fine wrought gold and threw it into the sea. It moved about for an instant and descended to the bottom of the sea; then taking the ring into its mouth, it swam back to the surface, and the sailors received and handed it to the king. He then took the ring from the mouth of the fish and once more presented it to your servant. I put it on my finger and kissed his hand; after which he placed the fish in the box and locked it. This is that ring," said Jaafer Baramikee, taking it out of his breast and handing it to Suliman Abd el Melek; who, highly praising it, said, "If ever there was a miracle, it is this." He then returned it to Jaafer and observed, "It is a sovereign's gift, and ought to be guarded with care."*

After this Abd el Melek placed full confidence in Jaafer's intelligence and knowledge, and on all occasions took counsel with him.

The moral of this story is, that sovereigns should on all occasions act without haste, lest its end be repentance, and that they may be free before the just God from punishment and shame; for reflection is the source of happiness in this world and in the other. A vizir who with due gravity attends to matters of religion and faith patiently, and who, confiding in God, properly reflects beforehand, sincerely and justly serves his sovereign and fellow-subjects. If in every circumstance his eyes are steadfastly fixed on the All-just, and he is obedient to the holy law of the most excellent Prophet, his end will be attained with success.

* This tale is mentioned by D'Herbelot as taken from the "Majma'al Tavarikh."

CHAPTER EIGHTH.

On the subject of those generous persons who habitually act with benevolence and goodness.

Some of the most virtuous of the Arabs were once seated around the vestibule of the Caabah, discussing the subject of who were the most generous and benevolent of Arabs; when one of them said, "Of the present time Abdallah Radavee, the son of Jaafer bin abi Talib is among the most generous." Another said that Kais bin Abadeh was the most generous and benevolent of his tribe; and yet another observed, that indeed he was the most excellent and liberal of all, to a remarkable degree. Another asserted that Grabet el Uvsa was superior to all others. So the discussion grew warm among them as they remarked on the character of the different candidates; when one of the hearers, who was the governor, exclaimed, "What need of words? let some one go to each and make a request of him and explain his wants, and we will see the degree of his generosity." All approved of the proposal, and they deputed a person to each of the individuals under discussion.

One, in going to Abdallah Radavee, found that he had gone to the country; so, having prepared a loaded camel, he was just putting his foot into the stirrup of the horse on which he intended to ride, when the man arrived. "O son of the uncle of the Prophet," said the man, "I was travelling, and having become separated from my companions, am reduced to beggary; generosity accompanies your character for honor." Abdallah Radavee dismounted from his horse and said, "You have come at a most inauspicious moment; pray excuse my want of means. Mount on this camel, and take what is on it, namely, four thousand dinars and a lot of clothes; among the latter is a sword which was a souvenir to me from the conquering lion of God, Ali ben Abi Talib, on whom be the divine satisfaction;* it also I give to you, and let you know its value." The asker of alms mounted the camel, thanked Abdallah Radavee, and returned.

When he had come to the place where the subject had been discussed, he dismounted from the camel; and all present, on seeing him take out of the saddle-bags clothes of costly silk, four thousand dinars, and the flashing sabre of the valiant lion, praised and extolled the generosity of the donor.

One of the party went also to Kais bin Abadeh, and on reaching his palace found that he had retired to rest with a maiden at his side. Kais told the maiden to inquire the cause of the visit of the beggar, and to ask what he desired. The beggar replied, "I am a poor man in great poverty, and am come with the hope of benefiting by the known generosity of Kais." "Here are seven hundred pieces of gold in a purse; take them," said the maiden, "and do not disturb Kais." Opposite her stood a black slave. "Take him also," said she. She likewise gave him a token, and added, "Go to such a caravan, and let them give you a camel to ride upon, and pray excuse the humbleness of the gift." The beggar, greatly pleased with this present, departed, taking the camel with him.

He who went to the greatest wonder of all, found him; but he was blind, wholly deprived of the light of seeing. The beggar went to his gate, and found that Grabet el Uvsa had gone out to the chapel, leaning on the shoulders of two slaves. The beggar met him and exclaimed, "O Grabet el Uvsa, I, a poor unfortunate traveller, ill and with the hope of receiving something from your generous hands, have come to see you. I depend upon your liberality." Grabet el Uvsa forthwith raised his hands from off the two slaves, and placing his right hand on his left, said, "Ay! Vah! you have come at a moment of poverty for Grabet el Uvsa; take, however, these two slaves who have been my guides and support—they are thine." The beggar replied, "These two

* Ali bin Abi Talib, the third caliph, a successor of the Prophet Mohammed.

are your wings; should I take them you would be left alone, and what would become of you." But he answered, "I have given them to you: take them and keep them as slaves, or free them; and if you do not, I will give them their liberty." So saying, he felt for the wall, and continued on to the chapel. The beggar taking the two slaves returned to the place of the discussion, where the generosity of each was narrated. One of them they proclaimed the chief, and that was Grabet el Uvsa, on account of his being the greatest in generosity.

But if one justly discriminates, the preference was due to him who presented the four thousand dinars and the souvenir of the lion of God.

CHAPTER NINTH.

On the subject of those noble sultans who have excelled in justice and protection to their subjects, and whose magnificence has been surpassingly great.

In the time of Mustansir Billah, in the four hundred and eighty-sixth year of the Hedjreh, Mohammed bin Melek Shah, the Seljookide, was sultan of Transoxania. His sons after him became very powerful, conquered the neighboring sultans, took possession of their countries, and held them in subjection. Even so great a king as Mohammed Sebektageen, a powerful sovereign, and owner of numberless troops, was conquered by them; but after Sultan Mahmood's death, the son of the latter, Sultan Mesood, conquered them, and took the throne of Mahmood the Seljookide, the father of Alb Arslan.

He became very powerful: and passing over to the opposite

side of the Euphrates on a bridge, which none of his tribe had done before, with two hundred thousand men, conquered Aleppo and Damascus, and kept possession of them.

He became a martyr in the affair of Yusup Khavarezmy; and his son and successor, Melek Shah, was a just sovereign, courageous, lion-hearted, and benevolent to his subjects. In his time the wolf and the sheep, the lion and the gazelle, lived in quiet companionship together. It is related that he left home one day with the desire of going to the chase, and on his way out observed a man on foot, weeping, and approaching the city. He had the man called to him, and inquired the cause of his tears; to which he replied, "I possessed a small capital of money, with which I bought a load of water-melons, desiring to take them to the city, and sell them, so as to provide food for my wife and children. But two soldiers took them from me, and thus I lost all my capital." When Melek Shah heard this, he bade the man not to be grieved, "Weep not," said he, "your property shall be given you again." So calling one of his attendants, he told him that he wished a water-melon; "go to the camp and seek, perhaps you may find one." The servant departed, and going round the camp, came to a tent where he found a melon, and brought it to Melek Shah. The padishah said to him, "Go, bring the owner of it to me." Departing, he did as he was directed, and on his return the padishah asked the man where he got the melon. He replied, that his servant brought it to him. "Go then," replied the padishah, "and bring your servant to me." The man went, but sent away his servant and returned, saying that he could not find him. The padishah became very angry; and forthwith putting a cord around the man's throat, he called to the owner of the melons, saying, "This man is one of my purchased slaves, and I now present him to you; go and use him as your own, and be careful not to let him escape." They both left the Shah's presence and departed for the city. On the way the man threw himself at the feet of the owner of the melons, and begged that he might be allowed to purchase himself for five hundred dinars. The poor man returned to the padishah and informed him that he could sell the man, if his majesty would give his noble consent, for five hundred dinars. The just Melek Shah replied, "How, my poor fellow, could you sell him for so small a sum? I gave him to you with all he possessed." The poor man thanked the Shah and with a gladdened heart returned to his wife.

That is justice and good judgment which inflicts a punishment that serves as an example to others against oppression, while it is a source of felicity to those who practise it, both in this world and in the world to come. Those are the principles entertained by the sultans who protected religion and showed mercy towards the faithful. May Allah have mercy on them all!

CHAPTER TENTH.

On the subject of the justice and religious principles of Mahmood Khan.

Ferdusee dedicated the work entitled the "Shah Nameh" to Sultan Mahmood, one of the Sebektageen sultans. He was a perfectly just and munificent, as well as a most religious and virtuous sovereign and hero.

Once a Turkish soldier, when drunk, entered the dwelling of an humble dervish, and raised his hand to the latter's wife with evil intentions. The poor dervish presented a petition against the man to Sultan Mahmood, complaining of the injury and oppression done towards him.

Shah Mahmood had the dervish brought to him privately; he bestowed presents upon him, and said, "Should that faithless man ever go near you again, come and inform me of it without fail." He directed his door-keeper, at whatever time this man came, to conduct him immediately to him, even should he be in his harem. The dervish of humble attire offered up a prayer for the shah and departed.

Three days afterwards, after nightfall, the same drunken Turk came again to the dervish's house after his wife; and the dervish said to the latter, "Leave your bed and engage him for a short time in conversation, whilst I go and give notice of the affair to Shah Mahmood and return." He reached the sultan's palace, and seeking the gate-keeper, gave the shah news of his arrival. He immediately arose, and taking a sharp sword in his hand set out with the dervish for his house. The dervich entered the house first, and seeing that the fellow had got into his bed, he returned and informed the shah; whereupon the shah, also entering, ordered the dervish to extinguish the light. He then slowly approached the bed, and with one keen blow cut the man in two pieces; after which he called for a light, and on looking at the Turk's face, returned thanks to God. The dervish asked him why he did so. The padishah replied, "The reason why I asked you to put out the light was, that I feared the person who had dared to commit this act was my own son; and had the light remained, I might, on seeing his face, have had compassion on him. But when the light was brought, and I saw that it was not my son, I thanked God. If," continued he, to the dervish, "you have any thing to eat, bring it." The man brought out a little honey and a piece of bread, which the padishah ate, and offered thanks to God. He also said to the dervish, "Know, that since the day you presented me the petition, not a morsel has entered my mouth; I was excessively hungry, and asked you for something which would appease my hunger. Thanks be to God that you have been able to take vengeance on that oppressor!" added the shah, as he bade the dervish farewell.

Mustazid Billah, one of the Abbaside caliphs, had a vizir named Abd Allah. The latter relates that, one night, as the caliph was taking his pleasure, one of the pages of the treasury, becoming drowsy, struck the caliph on the head, so as to knock off his turban. The caliph took it up, and putting it on again, said to the page, "Go and repose yourself, and call another page to me." The vizir says: God knows that my senses had left my head, and I came near falling to the ground; but when I heard this I turned to him, and exclaimed, "How admirable is such mildness!" To which he replied, "How could I do otherwise, seeing it was only an accident occasioned by drowsiness?" It is not proper that the poor fellow should die of fear, but rather become wiser by reflection upon his negligence." So he ordered that the number of pages in waiting should be increased by one or two more, to render their duties lighter.

Such good qualities are hereditary; for it is related that the ornament of the vizirat of religion, Zeen el Abideen, had a child which was standing at his side when the table of favors was served. A boy brought in a dish of food with the intention of putting it on the table, but let it fall. The contents were very hot, and, lighting on the Imam's child, scalded it severely. The servant, in great alarm, exclaimed, "Those who retain their anger, and pardon the faults of men."* The generous Imam, without the least change of manner, replied, "Slave, in God's name I pronounce thee free;" and thus at once pardoned the servant and gave him his freedom. In another narative it is added, that the Imam's child immediately expired.

One of the Baramikides, who have filled the world with the report of their generosity, and adorned it with their modesty and

* Part of a verse of the Koran.

judgment, was Hassan Maymendee. He was the sage vizir of Sultan Mahmood, his adviser and counseller in all his affairs.* Noor ed Deen bin Mohammed, the author of the work entitled Jamys el Hekayat, relates, that on days of vacation Hassan Maymendee spent his time in retirement, conversing with his familiar friends. On one such day he was seated in a chair with his feet bare, hanging down to the floor. Whilst thus seated, some swords were brought him for sale, and taking one in his hand, he leaned upon it as on a staff. The point of the blade came in contact with his foot; and it happened just then, that a necessitous person, thinking it a good time to appeal to the vizir, hastened into the room, and commenced relating the story of his distress. For want of observation the person leant against the handle of the sword, pressing the point of the blade into the vizir's foot; but the latter made no complaint, and bore with the pain without flinching. After the man had finished his story, the sage vizir gratified his wishes and dismissed him. The visir's foot being wounded, blood flowed from it, which one of his attendants observing, he said to the vizir, "How strange that you did not tell the fellow to be careful, and thus spare yourself this pain!" As the blood continued to run from his foot, they bound it up. Hassan Maymendee observed, "The poor man, seeing me alone, thought it would be a good time to beg a pair of shoes for his son; but had I told him to beware, he would have become confused, and unable to express his thoughts, and thus would have had to leave me in shame. The slight pain which we have experienced allowed the poor fellow to go away with a glad heart; and as so trifling a hurt to me has gained his good-will, I am heartily pleased."

Those present applauded the vizir.

Behold in this anecdote his good and virtuous qualities.

* This is evidently Mahmood, the Sebektageen, a great patron of literature. Ferdoosee was patronized by him.—A. T.

AN ANECDOTE OF THE SAME PERSON.

Among the many good characteristics of Hassan Maymendee is this—that he never ate alone. Had he even a date, he would divide it among those present. One day a man gave him three cucumbers, which were scarcely ripe. The vizir, taking one, pared it, and ate it all himself: the second shared the same fate, and likewise the third. The persons in attendance were astonished, but remained silent. He gave a present to the man who had brought the cucumbers; and after he had gone, excused himself to those about him, saying, "The reason why I ate the three cucumbers alone was this: that I found one of them excessively bitter, and so did not offer you any of it; the second and third were equally so, even more than the other; and I feared that, did I offer you any, you would remark that they were bitter, and confuse the Mussulman who presented them: so, rather than let his feelings be hurt, I preferred quietly to eat them all myself."

CHAPTER ELEVENTH.

On the subject of ease after difficulty, plenty after want, and pleasure after pain.

It is related by the Tarsonsite, the author of Serradj el Mollook, that once in the beautiful city of Bagdad, Sheik Aboo Heffez ibin Ahmed was reading with a perfumer the holy traditions, when a man entered and gave ten aktchas to the perfumer, saying, "Give me a little of a certain kind of scent." The perfumer (*attar*) arose, and gave him what he desired. He took it; but after going a few steps he let his tray fall, and all the perfume was spilt.

The man cried out aloud in great grief at his loss, so that we were much pained for him, and we said to the Attar, "Do for charity's sake give the poor fellow a little more perfume;" which he did. The man also collected, as best he could, that which had fallen, and the Attar remarked to him, "Was it proper to make such a lament over ten drachms of perfume? The Most High is benevolent, and bestows gratuitously." The man replied, "Pardon me, for you have justly spoken; but a man's patience is according to what he can bear, and my grief was involuntarily expressed. I have lately been out of my mind; the cause of which is as follows. A year or two ago, when I was wealthy and influential, I joined a caravan on my way to Bagdad, with four thousand dinars in money, and four thousand dinars more in jewels in a bag, and lost it all. I did not tell it to my companions, neither did I let them observe my affliction; for I had yet a little property left to keep me from want. But to-day a child was born to me; and besides these ten dirhems I possessed nothing wherewith to buy provisions for my family. Should I spend them, I would be left entirely destitute, and be obliged to beg; wherefore I said to myself, 'Rather let me employ it as a capital, and with its proceeds provide for my family;' and when I saw it thus escape from my hands, I became desperate, and gave way to my grief."

Whilst this man was relating his situation, a worthy person, whose house was directly opposite us, sat at the sill of his door listening. He arose and came over to us, and asked the man to go to his house with him. We supposed he was touched by the poor fellow's tale, and intended to give him something; but it was not so. He said, "When you lost the bag, who were your companions, and where were you?" He also asked many other questions about the bag, to all of which the man replied exactly as it occurred.

The worthy man then left us for a moment, and on returning brought from his dwelling a sealed bag, and asked if that resembled the one which he had lost? "Yes!" exclaimed the poor fellow, as soon as he saw the bag; "It is the very same." At the same instant, pulling the seal out of his breast, he exhibited it, and proved his claim.

The jewels of which he had spoken were in the bag; and consequently the worthy man at once delivered it over to its owner. But the poor fellow said, "Let these jewels all be yours; I freely bestow them upon you, and pray you will accept them." The man replied, "Forget us not in your prayers! the goods that belonged to you are yours once more. The Lord of the universe, by means of a slight sorrow, has turned your difficulty into facility, and your hidden treasure has been brought to light."

The lately unhappy man fervently thanked God, and with much joy and delight returned to his wife and children, his purse well filled with gold. The money he received was sufficient to set him up as a merchant of large capital. God forbid that he who confides in him for the necessaries of life, should remain hungry, or dependant upon the low and mean!

It is related in the history written by the Sheikh Amad ed Deen ibin Kethir, called "*Bedayeh ve Nihayeh*," that once a pilgrim undressed himself near the well of Zemzem at Mecca the venerated, for the purpose of performing his ablutions. On his arm was a ring of eighty miscals, which he took off and laid down near the well; when he had completed his ablutions he dressed himself and departed, forgetting his ring. After finishing his pilgrimage the man went to Bagdad, where in the course of a few years his circumstances changed, and he became so poor that his whole capital was reduced to a single piece of silver. With this he purchased a few Aleppo glasses, and having placed them on a table, he stood beside it in the market-place offering them for sale. Happening to place his foot upon a stone, he fell and overturned the table, and all his glass-ware was broken into a thousand fragments. The man, becoming desperate, gave way so loudly to his sorrow, that a crowd collected around him; and addressing them, he said, "O Mussulmans, at such a time, I was at the venerated city of Mecca, and lost, near the well of Zemzem, a gold ring of eighty miscals, which did not grieve me as much as my present loss; for now all I possessed in the world was one solitary piece of silver, and in order that I might not be reduced to beggary, I endeavored to make it a means of subsistence. It was seeing it thus at once lost to me for ever, which caused me such excessive grief."

Now among the crowd was a Mussulman listening to this man's recital of his misfortune, who, when he had ended, said to him, "Come, brother Mussulman, I found the gold ring which you lost at Mecca, and behold here is your property;" with which words he delivered the ring to the heart-broken man.

All present were astonished at the singular providence of this remarkable coincidence. Thus this man's sorrow and affliction became a source of favor from the Lord of all things, and he warmly expressed his grateful thanks. Allah is the blessed and the holy!

An innocent person of the Sheah sect was once accused in the presence of that most excellent of men the Caliph Muhtadee Billah, of the house of Abbas, of having endeavored to excite an insurrection against his government, and as being therefore worthy of punishment. The caliph commanded him to be brought before him; but the poor fellow had concealed himself, and was not to be found. The caliph, greatly displeased, promised that any one who found him and brought him before him should receive one hundred thousand dirhems. So the man was found, and, after being bound, was taken to the residence of the caliph. Whilst on the way there, they happened to meet that most generous and benevolent of persons, Maan bin Zeid. The poor man on seeing him, exclaimed, "O most excellent of men, hear me." Maan reined in his horse, and demanded why the man was apprehended. Those having charge of him replied, that the caliph had been seeking for him a long time. Maan said to them, "Release him; I will intercede for him with the caliph, and will also give you a recompense." But they refused to give him up for less than a hundred thousand dirhems; whereupon Maan took him by force out of their hands.

So they went to the caliph, and complained that they had found the Sheite whom he desired to have; but whilst on their way with him, the Emir Maan had taken him from them, and carried him off. The caliph immediately sent men to call Maan before him, and on his arrival, asked him why he had released his prisoner? Maan replied, "O Emir ul Mumaneen! five thousand of my men have been slain in your service, fighting against your enemies; and my own head also is ready to be sacrificed to you, rather than a guilty man should implore my protection in vain. Have I not sufficient interest with you to ask his pardon?" The caliph made answer, "Yes, O Maan, you have place enough in my regard for your intercession to be received in favor of the people of a whole zone, and not for one man alone." Said Maan, "O Prince of the faithful, I beg for him the honor of kissing your noble hand, and permission to depart in joy, favored also with your generous gifts." "Let him," replied the caliph, "be clothed in a dress of honor for Maan's sake, and receive a gift of one hundred thousand dirhems." Said Maan, "O Emir ul Mumaneen, let this man's gift be equal to his fault: his crime is very great, pray, therefore, let his gratuity be similarly large." The caliph commanded that one hundred thousand dirhems more should be presented to him; and when Maan had conducted the man into the royal presence, he was clothed in a dress of honor, and, after receiving the caliph's bounty, departed to his own home.

Behold the kindness and humanity which led one to peril his own life for that of another with whom he had no acquaintance, and to undertake such onerous and difficult service. This is true natural goodness. May Allah the Most High have mercy upon him!

The following story is narrated by the Judge Kazer Aboo Eumer, who lived during the reign of the Caliph Muktadir Billah of the family of Abbas.

Among my old acquaintances, was one of a respectable origin, whose condition, in consequence of misfortunes that overtook him, became greatly altered for the worse. Some time subsequently I met him again, and perceived that his poverty had been changed to splendor, and that he was engaged in extensive and important business, and possessed of much wealth. When he saw me he was greatly rejoiced, and invited me to his house, where he ordered a feast to be prepared for me at once. After some social conversation, the dinner was served up, when I said, "I will not touch your food until you explain to me what has happened to you." So he replied, "After the death of my father all I possessed was lost to me except one house. One night I retired to bed with sorrowful feelings, saying to myself, 'What shall I do?' I had a dream, in which I beheld one who said to me, 'You will have no success or fortune until you go to Egypt; so arise, delay not, but proceed thither.' I awoke, and finding that the Egyptian caravan was about to depart, I forthwith accompanied it. On my arrival there, I wandered about for two or three months without deriving profit from any one, until not a *hubbeh* (groat) remained in my pocket. Although I was hungry and in need, shame long prevented my asking aid of any one, until compelled by necessity

I went out one evening, hoping that I might meet with some benevolent person to whom I could disclose my situation. It was the Yatsee, or hour of repose; and as the governor of the city happened just then to pass by on horse-back, he, seeing me in a corner alone, stretched out his hand and struck me several blows. Addressing him I exclaimed, 'I am not the person you take me to be,' and told him all my story exactly as it had occurred, adding, 'I have come to Misr (Cairo) in search of the fruit of that dream, and this has been my lot.' Hereupon he caused me to be lifted up, saying, 'O fool that I am, it is now more than two months that I have every night had a dream in which a person appeared to me and said, "In Damascus, in a certain quarter, and in a certain house, there is a sofa, under which are hidden thirty thousand pieces of silver buried—do not neglect it." After having received so many signs and directions, shall I not act, whilst you, on the strength of a single dream, have come all the way to Cairo? what folly!' he repeated, and departed. I at once perceived that the quarter mentioned by him was the same in which I resided, and the house my own; so on the following day I joined a caravan, and reached Damascus on foot. I proceeded directly to my house; and on breaking up the sofa, a secret place was disclosed which contained two vases. On opening them, behold! I counted out exactly thirty thousand pieces of gold, which my deceased father had hidden in that spot. I found also a paper on which he had written the amount, placed in one of the vases. With this money I set up in business; my capital annually increases; every year I give the Zihiat, or alms prescribed by the Koran for the poor; and God, the great and good, increases and blesses my store." He added, "This is the fruit of the blows I received in Cairo; for which blessed be God!"

The vizir of one of the most eloquent and upright of sovereigns relates as follows: One day that great king ascended to the terrace of his residence; and on looking around him, he beheld near his terrace, in another house, a beautiful creature, fair as the rising moon or the face of the planet Venus. From gazing at her beauty he became beside himself, and he inquired of his own maidens whose house it was. They replied that it belonged to Firooz, one of his own attendants, and that the woman was his wife. "She is the daughter of such a one," added they, "very eloquent of speech, and unique in beauty." The king, quite lost in love and admiration, summoned Firooz to his presence; and giving him a letter, he commanded him to deliver it to a certain person, and collect from him the money which he owed. Firooz took the letter and returned to his house, where he prepared his arms and other necessaries, but forgot the letter confided to him, and departed. The love-stricken king arose and went to Firooz's door, at which he knocked, and was asked by the wife within, who was there. "Open the door," commanded the sovereign; and as soon as this was done, he entered, and saying, "To-day I am your guest," seated himself on the sofa. The lady, who was eloquent of speech, asked him what wind had blown her such good fortune as thus to elevate her from the dust of the earth? The king replied, "My desire is simply to pay you a visit." The lady answered, "God preserve me from this visit; for I think there is no good in it." The king responded, "I am your husband's master; perhaps you do not recognise me. "God preserve me from all evil!" exclaimed the woman, "You are welcome." She then repeated some verses meaning, "It is unworthy of you to drink from the cup out of which your dog has lapped." The king, who was greatly ashamed at the words of the woman, arose and left the house in haste, and in his confusion forgot one of his slippers. Now Firooz, having recollected the paper given him by the king, hastily returned home for it, in time to witness the king's departure. He, however, entered his house, took with him the paper, and went his way. Having seen the king's slipper, he understood why he had been sent out of the way; nevertheless, he performed the commission as he had been ordered. On his return he gave his wife one hundred golden ducats, (*sherifee,*) and directed her to go and reside a few days in her father's house; "for," added he, "the sultan has presented us with a house to which I will remove our effects." The woman, supposing this to be the case, went to her father's; but as Firooz did not visit her for several days, her brother called upon him and asked why he had thus separated from his wife. "Pray inform me," said he; "otherwise we will lay the matter before a judge." Firooz replied, "I gave her all that I was bound to do; yet if such be your desire, I am willing to appeal to the law." Accordingly, on the following day they went before the judge, whom they found seated beside the king. The woman's brother opened the case and said, "O Molana, we let this man a garden surrounded by four walls, well cultivated and without blemish, and which yielded its delicious fruit in abundance. This man, after eating the produce, destroyed its walls, ruined its well, and then returned it on our hands." The cadi replied, "O Firooz, what do you say to this?" Firooz answered, "I returned the garden to them better cultivated than when I received it." "Did you deliver it up?" inquired the cadi? "Yes," said the brother, "he did; but what was the cause of his so doing?" Firooz replied, "By Allah! I returned that garden much against my will; but once I found a lion's track in it, and fearing lest some day that royal animal's fierceness might do me harm, I concluded to compliment him by forsaking it altogether in his favor."

Now when the king heard this, he exclaimed, "Go, Firooz, enter and tranquilly enjoy your garden; for by Allah the Great, although a lion has visited it, he never raised a hand to touch a leaf in it, nor did he taste of its fruit. At a favorable moment he entered it; but filled with shame and amazement, he left it again. Never have I seen a garden with such high walls, strong gates, and pleasant cleanly walks. Go, blessed be Allah, know its value, and attend to your duties." So they left the cadi's presence, and no one among the public ever knew the true facts of the case. Firooz was greatly rejoiced; and returning once more to his dwelling, he showed more honor and regard to his wife than ever he had done before.

A STORY OF SULTAN HUSSAIN BIKRA.

Sultan Hussain Bikra was a learned and just sovereign, unparalleled for generosity and magnanimity of soul, whose noble qualities are mentioned in the book called Ahlak el Muhsaneen (or Praiseworthy Qualities.) For ardor of character he had no equal on the face of the globe; he also possessed a vizir of divine uprightness and talent, like that of Mercury, celebrated under the name of Meer Aly Sheer Nevaee. Indeed, from the time of Adam of unequalled worthiness, down to the present period, never were so just a sovereign and so pious a vizir united before. The report of their government reached the skies, and the roar of their prowess and ardor shook the face of nature, as the earth is shaken by an earthquake.

During the period of their just rule, through the protection which they afforded to science, eight hundred poets were collected at the foot of the sultan's throne, the most eminent and honored of whom, and the heads of their society, were Abd ur Rahman, Jamee, and Hussain, called the masters, who have successively enriched the world with their productions. The sultan and his vizir united in their service all who were most eminent for wit and learning; and as these patrons of talent were capable of estimating their value, those who were talented individuals had the privilege of attending in the presence of the ruler of the world.

Now it is related that Sultan Hussain Bikra held a council four times a week, in which he attended to the affairs of the faithful. Of the remaining three days, he spent one in conversation with the learned men and poets of his court, discussing and composing with them; one in company with those who were conspicuous for their talents in painting, drawing, and writing; and one in visiting the public schools of the city, where he heard the lessons of the students in the presence of their tutors, and rewarded their application to study, by giving suitable presents and promotions to each. To those who excelled he gave monthly stipends from the treasury, as an encouragement to their exertions; which had the effect also of stimulating others with the hope of like success. As a proof how excellent, benevolent, and enlightened was this sovereign, the following story is related of him:

Among the residents near his throne was a wealthy merchant, who, having divorced his wife for the third time, repented of it and desired to take her back. For this purpose he had recourse to the Ulema, who answered that there was no other way to accomplish it than by an artifice. Now the merchant, being a man of some importance and reputation, felt in awe of public opinion. But at length, not being able to support the separation from his wife, he sought out a poor man, a stranger, with whom he agreed that the latter should marry the woman, and, after the fulfilment of the holy law, again divorce her; for which service he was to present him with a hundred pieces of gold, to defray his expenses to another part of the country. The poor man accepted the terms, and was told that after the marriage he could go wherever he chose. So the woman was married to the man. They spent the night together, and became so much attached to each other, and so joined in affection, that the woman said to the poor man, "If you love me, be on your guard, and when they come to divorce us, reply that you are contented with your wife, and do not wish to part from her. I am wealthy, and we will not want for any thing. Be joyful and happy, keep firm to your assertion, and no one can separate us by force; for our sovereign is a just king."

Early on the following morning the merchant came and demanded his wife. But the poor man replied, "She is my lawful wife; why should I divorce her? I will in no wise do so." At this speech the merchant's heart leaped to his mouth. He went hastily to the cadi's; where he was informed, that if the man did not of his own free will divorce the woman, they could by no means be separated. Becoming desperate and helpless, he commenced a suit against the fellow on plea of "inequality of condition." The man was consequently brought to the court, where he was told, "You are a man of low birth, whilst this woman is of high and noble origin; you are not her equal, and therefore we will separate you by force." At this the man was greatly surprised; but being instructed by the woman to assert that he also was nobly born, he replied, "My father is a most respectable merchant in Damascus; but having disagreed with him on a certain subject, I left that city and came here a stranger." "Well, we will see," answered they, "whether your assertion is correct or not; and for that purpose letters shall be despatched to your father in Damascus, to ascertain the truth of the matter." The court thereupon granted the man a respite of forty days.

Whilst the answer was waiting for from Damascus, the fellow and his wife spent the time in pleasure and enjoyment; but when they reflected that at the end of the above mentioned period their situation would be very uncertain, they sometimes wept, and at other times laughed. At length, one evening, when three days alone remained of the forty, these two persons sat talking and weeping together over their situation. On that same night Suliman Hussain was walking incognito about the city with his tutor, as was his wont, to learn the true condition of his subjects; and as he happened to pass under their window, he heard both sobs and laughter from within. The sultan remarked to his tutor, "Whence comes it that these people alternately weep and laugh? assuredly they have some cause of complaint which we ought to know." So saying, he knocked at the door. The man within having inquired who he was, and what he wanted, the sultan replied by demanding what was the cause of their tears, and from whom they had experienced injury? The woman immediately recognised the voice of the sultan; and expressing her gratitude in prayers for his life, she said, "Under the shadow of your majesty's protection who can commit oppression that this humble servant should feel it? and yet the tears we shed are from our hearts.

"'Our sorrow is heartfelt, yet of none we complain.'"

She then related to him the whole history of their marriage; after which the generous sultan left them and went his way.

On the day following this event the sultan caused a long letter to be written to the man, as if coming from his father, saying, "My son, has time not yet taught you a parent's value, that you should leave so much wealth and riches, and go into a strange country, where you will not find a wife worthy of you? I send you as a present a few stuffs from Damascus, some pieces of silk, and other articles of value, which I hope you will receive and enjoy. Until the present time I have had no news of your condition, which I ascribed to your neglect; but *el hamdu Lilla Teala*, praise be to God! tidings of your good health have now rejoiced my heart. By the next caravan I will send you some more stuffs of this country; pray do not forget me, nor fail to write to me frequently."

The sultan gave this letter and the package of stuffs to a man in whom he could confide, with directions to inquire for the son of the head merchant of the Damascus caravan, residing in such a quarter, and to deliver the things to the person in question. The messenger did as he had been directed; and when he knocked at the door the man came out and received the letter, and the bales of silk were lowered down from the camels. The woman, who was very intelligent, called her husband in, and told him that it was all a generous act of their noble-hearted sultan. "All you have to do," said she, "is to play your part like a man." So they had the bales of silk brought in. All the city soon heard that the man had received a letter from his father. Accordingly the cadi confirmed the marriage act; and the woman's former husband, becoming desperate, gave up the contest. The fellow addressed a letter of thanks to the sultan, acknowledging the unlimited favor and bounty showed him, and asking permission to return the bales of silk to his treasury. But Sultan Hussain Bikra wrote on the back of the petition, "It is a gift made by us for the sake of God. Go, possess it, as if it had been your own father's property." Besides this he gave him other valuable presents. May Allah have mercy upon him!

It is related that once a poor and good man was travelling, and arrived at a city, the sovereign of which had a vizir whose son was unequalled for his comeliness and virtue. All the world were ardent admirers of the heart-ensnaring beauty of this youthful Phebus, but the most entranced of all was the traveller.

This unfortunate man was one day walking about in the bazaar, when suddenly he met this vizir's beautiful son, and became a captive, bound with the fetters of affection for this fair gazelle. The sovereign was also exceedingly fond of the youth, and could find no repose except by frequently seeing him; so that he would not permit the lad to amuse himself in the company of any other person, and his only recreation consisted in riding about the city. Now the unhappy traveller followed the vizir's son wherever he went, and stood to gaze in admiration wherever he stopped. Finally, in despair, he gave presents to all his servants, till they were ashamed to receive more of his liberality. In this manner he spent his all; nay, he sold even his clothes and the bedding on which he lay, to appropriate the proceeds to the same purpose; so that not even a mat remained under him, and he took up his abode in the corner of a chapel. Being now utterly destitute, he was ashamed to appear in public, and spent his time in prayer in the chapel corner. The poor man not having shown himself for three days, and his love for the vizir's son having affected the latter, he said to himself, "Let me see what has become of the unhappy fellow, and whether his partiality for me is sincere or not." So, with the desire of proving him, he inquired of his servants where the poor man was. One of them replied, that he had seen him in a certain chapel. So the youth went directly thither, and found him with his hands upraised, profoundly engaged in prayer. Going up behind him, he saluted him, and saying, "May your prayers be accepted!" embraced him. The unhappy man almost died with emotion at this gracious treatment; and when he had composed himself, the youth took his hand in his, and said, "Your affection and sincerity are well known to me;" adding, "I am your guest to-day; arise, let us go to your apartment, where we will amuse ourselves." The unhappy man, ashamed to confess that he had neither house nor room, arose, left the mosk, and exclaiming with desperation, "O Allah!" set out. Coming to a locked door, he feigned an excuse; and hoping to free himself from his embarrassment, he said, 'This is my dwelling; but my servant has locked the door and gone away." The youth answered, "After spending so much money for me, do you hesitate to break a lock?" The poor man, confiding in the All-just, broke the lock and entered the chamber.

Now this chamber belonged to a vagabond of a butcher. It was richly and comfortably furnished, and the youth, proceeding to the sofa, seated himself upon it. The unhappy and embarrassed lover was not long left in suspense; for soon he beheld the brute of a butcher, who seeing his door opened, entered, and was astonished to find it occupied by a most elegant youth, before whom stood, in an attitude of profound respect, a sorrowful and unhappy looking man. The butcher was not long in perceiving that the latter was some unfortunate, who, from necessity, had forced his door. He entered politely, begged him not to be disturbed, and added that he had fastened the door only by way of a joke. The poor fellow's heart, on hearing these words, found a little repose. The butcher arose, and setting a table, placed on it a little fruit and a bottle of wine, adding that he would go and bring some fresh roast meat. The poor man's face now showed a smile, and he began to eat and drink. The butcher departed, and soon returned with the roast; and when they were seated around the table, the youth expressed his lively pleasure and satisfaction at what he had done. Night setting in, the butcher prepared other fruit and viands for them, of which they partook; after which he made up a bed for the youth, and left them alone. The young man now undressed himself, and got into his bed; but his lover stood behind the door until the next morning with his arms crossed before him. The butcher looked in several times, and observed that the man never once changed his position. Morning having come, he again prepared their table.

Now the vizir's son had not been to see the sultan for a whole day and night, which greatly displeased him. He ordered the town criers to seek him out, and to proclaim that the owner of whatever house he was found in should be hung up without mercy at his own door. When this proclamation reached the ears of the vizir's son, he came out to the door of the butcher's house. The latter knowing that he was there, asserted that he had received him into his dwelling, in order to preserve the poor unhappy lover from shame. The vizir's son answered, "Fear not, I will go and see the padishah and return." So he arose and departed; and when he was come before the sovereign, the latter demanded the cause of his absence. The youth in reply related the sincere affection of his unhappy lover, and the generosity and humanity of the butcher. The sultan being much astonished, had the butcher brought to him, and inquired respecting his condition. The sultan then had that true lover also brought; and finding that he was possessed of very great acquirements and talents, he appointed him to be his second vizir. To the butcher also he gave the administration of a province; so that both being officers of their sovereign, the lover by his devoted affection, and the butcher by his generosity and protection, obtained their desires, and were happy to their heart's content.

CHAPTER TWELFTH.

On the right of bread and salt, showing how the observance of it has led to the attainment of elevated rank.

In the book of history it is written, that in the 250th year of the Flight of the Prophet, on whom be the benedictions of the Most High, the origin of the dynasty of the reigning house of the Zifarians, the cause of their victory over other sultans; and their own majesty and power, were simply owing to the respect which they showed for the right of bread and salt, and their close observance of justice and equity.

The cause of the downfal of the Tahiriehs, and the elevation of the Zifariehs, is this. The father of Yakoob bin Lais, in his own country gained his livelihood by daily labor; but he found that it brought him no profit, and would never enable him to amass a fortune. So assembling a number of robbers, he placed himself at their head; and one night he and his companions broke into the treasury of the governor of that time, Dirhem bin Nassir, and robbed it of many rich effects, as well as of a large sum in specie. Whilst escaping with their booty, they found on a table in a gold vessel something brilliant; and thinking it a jewel, Yakoob's father put forth his hand and took it. Wondering what it could possibly be, he licked it with his tongue and found it was salt. When he perceived by the taste what it was, his color changed, and turning to his sons and followers he said, "Return to their places the goods and money which you have taken." When they asked the reason of his command, he replied, "It is on account of the right of bread and salt, which is respected by all. Salt is necessary to every meal; and as of all favors none are greater than these two, their names are on every one's tongue. Unknowingly I have tasted of this man's salt, and to neglect observance of the right of bread and salt would bring upon us great misfortune. It was my intention to take these things; but now we will return them all, and will shortly receive a greater booty in their stead." They all submitted to his commands, returned the things they had taken, and departed.

At break of day the treasurer came, and beheld the treasury opened and the stuffs scattered about. Reflecting that this was an excellent moment for robbery, he took what he wanted and returned to his own house. Then going to Dirhem bin Nassir, he beat his garments on the ground and expressed much grief, saying, "Robbers have entered the treasury and stolen innumerable effects from it." Dirhem bin Nassir called the governor of the city, and commanded him immediately to find the thieves. The governor searched out and imprisoned a number of innocent persons. When Lais heard this, he was greatly grieved; his heart had compassion on these poor unfortunate prisoners, and banishing all fear, he went straight to the house of the vizir and informed him that he knew the robbers who had entered his treasury, and asked to be taken before the sovereign. The vizir brought him before Lais Shah, to whom he gave an exact narrative of what had occurred, and informed him that the effects were in the house of his treasurer Behram. The shah ordered it to be searched; which being done, the things were found there; whereupon Dirhem bin Nassir, becoming greatly angered against his treasurer, addressed him with reproaches, saying, "So, ill-omened wretch, you, who for such a length of time have been the recipient of our favor and were nourished by our bounty, now forget our benefits, take occasion to rob us, reject the right of bread and salt, and after taking our property refuse to return it." He then ordered the criminal to be tortured and put to death.

He next dressed Lais in a cloak of honor, and appointed him to be treasurer in the place of the deceased. Lais repented of his past misconduct, asked forgiveness for the same, and served the shah with great sincerity and fidelity. He was promoted to high trusts, became an emir of power, and was made commander-in-chief of the shah's troops. For generosity and justice his name became proverbial as far as the horizon extends.

He had two sons, named Yakoob and Eumer, whom, being brave youths, generous and manly, he educated with much care in the court of Dirhem bin Nassir. Nassir Billah gave Yakoob the drum and standard, and sent him with the rank of general against the Schismatics. Yakoob made great conquests; and as Dirhem bin Nassir had no children, and was very old, he voluntarily resigned the kingdom of Sebistan to him and his father Lais. A golden crown and girdle were sent him by the caliph; and being very powerful, he, in the 358th year of the Hedjreh left Sebistan and marched against Herat, from which place he drove Mohammed Oosee, and established his government over all Kerman, Herat, Balkh, Taberistan, and Khorasan. He always called the Abbasside caliphs his patrons; and by conducting himself with great circumspection he retained their good will. Ten years afterwards he went with his troops against Fars, the governor of which was Ismail; him he expelled, and took possession of his country. He became a sovereign, possessing a coinage of his own, and having the Khotbeh read in his name. He also passed his time in friendly correspondence with the caliph. His family continued to reign until the 550th year of the Hedjreh, and the kingdom remained in their possession three hundred years and more. The right of bread and salt, respected by them, was the chief cause and origin of this honor and prosperity, and richly was their observance of it rewarded.

It is related by Molana Asutee, that one day when Ahmed bin Tooloon was going out to view his fish-ponds, he perceived near one of them an infant laid on a sack. Having pity on it, he had it brought to his palace, where he gave it to nurses to bring up. After some years it was delivered into the charge of teachers, who taught it to read and write, and it became his most esteemed and confidential attendant.

Ahmed bin Tooloon took sick, and made a will in favor of his son, in which he also strongly recommended to his care the orphan youth. After his decease, Abool Jeesh made Ahmed his chief confidant, and begged him to serve him as he had done his father; to which Ahmed replied, "Allah be witness that I will serve you with perfect honesty and uprightness." He thus became Abool Jeesh's chief attendant, and was consulted by him on all his affairs.

Now, one day, Abool Jeesh called Ahmed the orphan to him, and said, "Go into my harem, where you will find in a certain box a jewelled chaplet; bring it to me." Ahmed departed in haste, and went into the private harem, where he beheld one of the emir's maids in the embrace of one of the harem pages. The latter threw himself at Ahmed's feet to implore his silence, and then went out. The maiden offered herself to Ahmed; but he replied, "*Naooz Billah!* Our refuge is in God, never will I show such treachery to my master;" then taking the chaplet, he brought it to the emir. The maiden, supposing that Ahmed would tell the sultan what he had seen, was greatly afraid; for she was the sultan's favorite.

About this time a maiden was brought to the Emir El Jisha for sale, who was both a poetess and a sweet singer. He purchased her for eighteen thousand pieces of gold, and in a few days became much attached to her. Ahmed Yatemee, however, was ignorant of the affection entertained for the girl by the sultan. One day she threw herself at the emir's feet and wept, complaining that the person called Ahmed the Orphan, forgetful of the benefits bestowed upon him by his master, had sought to gain her favor for himself. The emir at this news was greatly enraged; but being a most intelligent and thoughtful man, he repressed his feelings, and remarked that the matter must be inquired into. Concealing his intentions, he summoned the treasurer of his harem, and showing him a golden dish, he said, "If any one shall bring this to you, directing you by my orders to put musk into it, take it from him, cut off his head, put it into the dish, and send it to me." That day the council assembled; and as the sultan sat and amused himself with his companions under the influence and inspiration of wine, he recalled to mind the circumstances just narrated. Then sending for Ahmed Yatemee, he gave the golden vessel into his hands, and directed him to take it to the Haznadar, or treasurer, and tell him to put musk into it. According to the axiom, that safety is in fidelity, the innocent Ahmed Yatemee took the fatal vessel and entered the harem, where he found the treasurer's young man again in the company of the maiden. They asked Ahmed to be seated awhile; but he replied, "My master desires a little musk, and I must return to him." The unfaithful page said, "Let me take it to the treasurer, after which you can carry it to the sultan." So, yielding to his importunities, he gave him the vessel; whereupon the page went to the Haznadar, and asked him for some musk. The Haznadar took the page, cut off his head, and put it into the vessel, which he sealed up and sent by another attendant to be delivered to the sultan. The attendant, as directed, returned, and gave the dish to Ahmed Yatemee, who carried it to his lord. When Abool Jeesh, the sultan, saw

Ahmed return alive, and found that another had been slain in his stead, he wondered what could have been that person's crime, for which he thus had suffered death. Ahmed Yatemee exclaimed, "May the heads of all ungrateful traitors be like that of this one, who has received his just reward!" Abool Jeesh inquired what he meant by these words; to which Ahmed replied, "Some time ago, when you commanded me to go to your harem and bring you a jewelled chaplet, I found this treacherous page with such a one of your maidens; but fearing lest the scandal should be publicly spread abroad, I protected my benefactor's honor, though every day I expected God would punish the wretch's perfidy, and now he has met with his deserts." The emir arose, and had the maiden brought into his presence, and commanded her, if she wished for safety, to declare the truth. So she told the whole circumstance correctly, as it occurred, and, after she had made a full avowal, met with her just fate. Ahmed Yatamee was elevated more than ten grades higher in rank; and, because he respected the right of salt and bread, he found safety from danger through the blessing of his pure intentions.

Against that person who respects the favors of the great, glorious, and all-just Creator; and whose gratitude in submission increases, God forbid, again and again, that the door of mercy should ever be closed!

It is narrated in the history of Ibin Juzee, that once a gentlemanly person from an Arab tribe came to see the Caliph Mutazid Billah. Being most elegant in appearance, and lively and amusing as well as civil, the caliph derived much pleasure from his society; and as he considered him worthy of his intimacy, he appointed him to be one of his choice companions.

One of the caliph's Nadeems, of the rank of vizir, was a most envious person; so much so, that were it possible, he would have prevented all others but himself from ever entering the caliph's presence. The caliph, being much pleased with the Arab, treated him with great regard and familiarity; so that one day the envious vizir, under the guise of friendship, though with evil intentions, invited him to his house, where he gave him a feast. He had several dishes prepared and brought in, containing garlic and onions. The Arab liked the former very much, and ate heartily of it. After dinner the envious vizir said to the Arab, "The caliph has a great dislike to garlic; therefore be careful when you approach him not to sit too near, lest he be annoyed by the odor." The feast being ended, the Arab departed to his own house; whilst the vizir mounted his horse and went straightway to the palace, where, when he had seated himself with the caliph, the latter inquired for his companion, the Arab. The vizir answered that the low fellow was a dog, for he disliked all sociability. "Once or twice," continued the vizir, "he even had the audacity to say to me that the caliph's breath smelt so disagreeably that it was painful to sit near him; at which I was so enraged, that were it not for the dread I entertain of your highness, I would have killed him on the spot."

The caliph, on hearing this, was greatly displeased. "Let us see," said he. Just then the Arab Nadeem entered and seated himself at a distance from the caliph, fearful lest he should inconvenience him with the smell of the garlic he had just eaten. The caliph addressing him said, "Come nearer; I have something to tell you." The Arab went near him; but during the conversation he covered his mouth and nose with his sleeve, that the odor might not reach the caliph.

The caliph exclaimed, "Ha! Arab Kiafeer, (infidel,) so the vizir's words are true." His heart was full of vengeance towards the Arab; but he concealed it, and commenced joking. Finally he wrote a note with his own hand, saying, "When the bearer of this note reaches you, give him neither respite nor pity, but put him instantly to death;" then sealing it, he gave it to the Arab, saying, "Go, deliver this to such a workman, and whatever he gives you take." The Arab was greatly rejoiced and grateful for his goodness, and expressed his thanks to the caliph.

At these words the envious vizir became sick with chagrin; and after the Arab had left the caliph's presence, he went to him and said, "Come, you lucky man; sell me for two thousand pieces of gold the order which the caliph gave you." The Arab, seeing that without any trouble on his part he might make two thousand pieces of gold, gave him the order and took the money. The vizir was a friend of the receiver of revenues. The Arab took his money, and returned to the caliph and kissed his hand. The caliph, much surprised to see him return so soon, asked him the reason of it; so he explained to him how he had sold the order to the vizir for two thousand pieces of gold. "You are a polite fellow, truly," replied the caliph, "to say that my breath smelt of garlic." The Arab swore by Allah that he had said nothing of the kind. "Then," asked the caliph, "what was the reason of your covering your mouth and nose with your sleeve?" The Arab replied, "The vizir invited me to a feast in his house, and gave me garlic to eat; afterwards he told me that the caliph did not like the smell of garlic, and I therefore endeavored to prevent you from being incommoded by it." "I perceive that you have spoken truly," replied the caliph; "your sincerity has saved you;" and he repeated the Arabic proverb: "Allah punishes envy with its own recompense: it begins with its possessor, and ends by destroying him."

Bygone historians relate, says Abool Faridj Maaff bin Zikiriya of Nihirvan, as a proverb or fable, that once the king of animals, the terrific lion, was paid court to by an envious wolf and a diminutive fox. For some time, they conversed, ate, and drank together, and finally set out in company in search of prey. Some time afterwards the lion fell ill; and being unable, from weakness, to proceed further, he chose to lie still and repose. For several days the fox did not make his appearance, and paid no visit to the lion; but the jealous wolf was regular in his daily attendance, and in presenting him with a share of his prey. One day, at noon, the wolf came to the lion, and asked after his health; to which the lion replied with an angry countenance, asking where the fox had hidden his tail all this time, adding, that for many days he had not been to visit him in his illness, and had by his conduct shown himself unfaithful. The wolf thinking this a favorable opportunity to gain an advantage and throw blame on the fox, replied, "It is hard to find him now-a-days; he is seeking for game in your hunting grounds." So in this manner he cast blame on the fox to his heart's content, and the lion was filled with rage. Now the fox was informed by a private friend that the wolf had been slandering him to the lion, and had aroused ill feelings against him. The fox replied that the wolf's jealousy would prove its own punishment, since envy never blackens the object of its malevolence; so, arising, he went to the lion's abode, where the lion, addressing him, said, "Is this friendship and brotherly treatment? whilst we were sick and ready to die, you were spending your time in gay amusements." Now the fox, being a master of artifice, said, "Since you were taken ill of this complaint I have not known rest either day or night, but have been all over the world making inquiries of every physician for a remedy to restore your highness to health; at last I have been so fortunate as to discover a sure one, which is no other than a wolf's right ear. Nothing but my anxiety on your royal behalf could have kept me from your presence so long."

Soon after the departure of the fox the wolf entered, and after saluting the lion, passed on to a seat beside him; whereupon the lion put forth his paw, and with one grasp wrenched off the wolf's right ear, which he swallowed at a single gulp. The wolf fled with a howl as the blood streamed from his head, and went to the fox to make his complaint. The fox replied, that those who associate with kings should remember their fellow-courtiers with favor; in order that these in turn, being aware of their kindness, may seek to do them good rather than harm." To which he added this Arabic proverb: "If any man dig a pit for his brother, Allah will cast him into it himself."

It is related by past writers, among wonderful occurrences, that once there was a very wealthy merchant named Abd ul Semee Keal, celebrated for his fortune and station. He had moreover a lovely wife, to whom he was most warmly attached. Having arrived one day at a certain city, while making a journey on business, he saw there a fair female slave, whom a broker was crying out for sale. Being pleased with her appearance, he purchased her for five hundred dinars, and spent much pleasant time in her society. In the course of time she bore him a very handsome boy, with noble and illustrious features. The merchant, from fear of his wife, was much troubled at the birth of the child; and after the mother had nursed it for six or seven months, the ill advised merchant one night put her to death, and exposed the child on an open plain. By the incalculable bounty of God, a shepherd found the infant; and bringing it to his home, he reared it on the milk of his sheep until it grew to the age of four or five years.

At this time it happened that Abd ul Semee's road brought him to the shepherd's village, when he alighted at the latter's dwelling, and was treated by him with all the hospitality in his power. The merchant, seeing the boy in his service, inquired if it was his son. The shepherd replied by informing him where he found him, and how he had brought him up. So the merchant at once knew it was his own son, and offered to purchase the boy. The shepherd parted with him for fifty dinars, and the merchant soon after put him in a bag and threw him into the sea; but by God's mercy the waves washed the bag into the nets of some fishermen, who on opening it were astonished to find in it a fair-faced boy, almost suffocated by the water. On breathing the fresh air he came to himself, and they forthwith gave him the name of Abool Jevalik, (or Father of the Sack.) He remained in their service, and became a fisherman like themselves.

Some time after this, it happened that the merchant went on business to the town where the fishermen resided; and one day, whilst seated in a shop, the men passed by, along with the boy, carrying their fish to market. The merchant called to them, and after purchasing some fish, he inquired whether the boy was theirs; to which they replied that he was not, and related by what means they found him. The merchant forthwith recognised his son in the boy, and again purchased him for five hundred dinars.

The boy now remained in his service for a year or two, proving diligent and faithful. One day the merchant wrote a letter, sealed it, and telling the boy that it contained a recommendation in his favor, he added, "Give it to my step-daughter, and remain in her service until I return." The boy departed, and found her house. When he knocked at the door, the merchant's step-daughter came out; and seeing before her a youth of angelic beauty, she took the letter from his hand and read it. The letter contained these words: "When the bearer of this letter reaches you, fail not by some convenient means to put him to death." Now the merchant's step-daughter was in every respect a girl of much knowledge and understanding; and so taking the letter, she wrote another, saying, "The bearer is much regarded by me, and worthy. When he reaches you, give him a good reception, and immediately marry him to your step-daughter, the Saida el Mellahee. I have directed him, until I come, to take charge of all my affairs, both private and public; be careful that you show no opposition to my wishes." She then sealed up the letter, and giving it into his hands, bade him deliver it to her mother. The mother made the youth welcome, treated him with great attention and regard, and married him to her daughter.

The youth took charge of all the merchant's affairs; and when the merchant, some time afterwards returned home, he was met by the youth, and beheld that just the reverse of what he wished had befallen him. But exercising patience, he kept all to himself, and some days afterwards directed his servants to bring him some jugs of wine, and to roast a sheep. So they made a great fire; and he told them that they might eat and drink and make merry, adding, "If any one comes to you to-night, seize him and throw him into the fire, even if he should say I am Abd ul Semee himself; do as I now bid you." At night the merchant called the youth, and told him to go without and call him a servant. As the youth was setting out, his wife asked him where he was going; and he replied that her father wished for a servant. His wife would not let him go out, but said, "Let my step-father do his own errand." The merchant, supposing the young man had gone, arose; and being anxious to see how his affairs had prospered, he came to the place agreed upon. As soon as the drunken servants saw the merchant, they caught hold of him; and, although he cried out that he was their master, they would not release him, but, replying that their master had ordered them to do so, they threw him into the very fire prepared for his son, and his miserable body was soon reduced to ashes.

So the youth, by divine favor, was preserved, and inherited all the merchant's wealth; and it is a proverb handed down from our parents: "Never dig a well deeper than your own neck; so that when you have fallen into it, you may have strength to get out again." God knows what is right.

CHAPTER THIRTEENTH.

The history of the caliph of the world, Haroon er Rasheed, and the Beremikee.

There is written in the register of the times, and related by those who have recorded strange and extraordinary occurrences, the following account of that quintescence of caliphs Haroon er Rasheed, and of his vizir Jaafer the Beremikee.

Jaafer's father had been the instructor of this caliph as well as of his own son; and from the conduct of Haroon at that early age, he knew he would one day attain to great renown. When Haroon er Rasheed had become caliph, he selected Jaafer to be his grand vizir, and confided all the affairs of his caliphat to him. So attached was he to his society, that he never permitted him to be absent from him; and besides being his grand vizir, he was also his favorite attendant,—in fine, all his affairs were confided to him.

Fazel, the brother of Jaafer, was also appointed vizir to Rasheed. The splendor and éclat of this family descended from father to son, and their munificence and generosity shone from the east to the west. Their talent lay in giving strength to the weak, befriending the stranger, bestowing favors upon the unfortunate, and upraising the overthrown.

Whenever any one became worthy of their notice, he was sure to be fortunate for ever afterwards. Jaafer was the pupil of the caliph's eye, and dearer to him than his own brothers; but having at length incurred his displeasure, he ordered his head to be cut off, laid violent hands on his children and kindred, and confiscated his property to the treasury. All the public edifices erected by Jaafer, the mosks and chapels, the buildings for the accommodation of caravans, the palaces and charitable institutions, he caused to be demolished; and he even carried his resentment so far as to have it proclaimed in the streets: "Woe to that person who shall mention the name of any one of the Beremikides, or who shall visit their tombs; for whoever dares to do so shall be hung."

Those nearest related to the Beremikides, that most excellent family, were reduced to the greatest poverty; so much so that Jaafer's mother resided in a corner of the ruined palace of her late son. One of the many who had received benefits from the hand of her son having asked her what were her circumstances, Jaafer's mother replied, "Why do you inquire after my circumstances? only last week, whenever I desired to perform my religious ablutions, four hundred maidens stood ready to serve me; whilst to-day I dwell in sorrow and affliction amongst these solitary ruins." This person presented her with one thousand paras, which gave her very great pleasure; for one dirhem was then as much to her as a thousand dinars were formerly. What changes in her condition had occurred in the short space of one week is fully narrated in history, so that now it is only deemed necessary to refer to it thus briefly.

In consequence of the great anger of the caliph, no one dared to visit the graves of the Beremikees. One day Haroon er Rasheed said to one of his attendants, "I have heard that some persons go at night to the ruins of the Beremikees' dwellings, and there recite verses which they have composed respecting them. Go, then; conceal yourself near them; and should any one come there, bring him before me." So the attendants went; and some time after midnight they saw an old man come with his servant to the ruins of the palace of the Beremikees, weep over them, read from the Holy Koran, and in expression of his grief recite the following lines:

"When I saw the sword descend upon Jaafer,
And heard the crier give news of Yahiya to the caliph,
I wept for the world, and my grief for them increased,
And I said, Hereafter the world can never prosper."

After this the old man arose, and the attendants approached him and told him the caliph wished to see him. He was greatly alarmed, and said, "Pray let me have a pen and inkstand, that

I may write a farewell letter to my family; for I am aware that I cannot depend upon life for the future." So he wrote a letter, and gave it to his servant, containing these words: "Be careful never for a day to forget the benefits we have received from Jaafer." When the man was brought before the caliph, the latter perceived him to be a person of property and standing, and inquired of him, "Why in defiance of our orders do you deem it necessary to watch over the ruins of the Beremikees, and thus expose your life to peril?" The old man replied, "God forbid, O Emir of the faithful, that I should act in defiance of your will! but to forget the great kindness and benefits which I have received from the Beremikees, not to remember with gratitude the obligation of their favors, would be rebellious and insolent to the Most High; wherefore, O Emir, I have never ceased to bear them in mind. Your humble servant is named Mugaray, of the family of Numan bin Menzer, of royal descent. I formerly resided in Damascus, where I possessed influence and much property. But whilst I was one of the notables of the land, the shadow of the world's favor passed from me, and I lost all I had accumulated; and as I preferred to leave my country rather than remain in it in poverty, some of my friends sent me to Bagdad, advising me to push my fortune here: Peradventure, said they, you may meet with favor from the Beremikees. So I left them, and, with a caravan (*cafileh*) consisting of thirty-four persons besides females, arrived safely at Bagdad. I put my family in one corner of a mosk, and left them in order to seek a dwelling. On my way I remarked several persons assembled in a chapel for the purpose of reciting the noon-day prayer, after which they left it and entered a garden in the neighborhood of the chapel. 'Let me see what this means,' said I; and following them, I soon perceived among them a handsome man with a face radiant as the dawn, who took the highest seat in the company, while around were arrayed some ten young persons, his sons. Now the principal person in this assembly was the grand vizir Jaafer the Beremikee, who, addressing those around him, said, 'Be witness that I betroth my daughter Ayesha for thirty thousand pieces of gold, as her dowry, to such an one;' after which sherbets were brought in. One thousand pieces of gold in a golden dish were also put before each person present, and the same amount was given to me in a similar dish; I counted the number of those present, and found there were precisely one hundred and one persons. The Fatiha* was recited, and each individual put his dish and his gold in his breast and arose. I did the same and departed; but before I had gone far, one of the vizir's servants came after me and said that his master wished to see me. I returned; and on entering his presence, he arose, accosted me with great kindness, and made inquiries after my circumstances. I related to him what I have already told your majesty; whereupon he welcomed me, saying that I had entered the dominions of a just sovereign. 'Be not grieved,' added he; and taking my hand in his, he recommended me to his sons. 'My occupations,' said he to them, 'are very numerous; but be you attentive to this guest.' So his eldest son Ahmed took me to his own dwelling, showed me great attention, and bestowed upon me many worldly favors. Every night one of his sons made a feast for me, and presented me with a thousand gold pieces for my expenses. For ten days I had not seen my family, but on the eleventh day a servant came to me and said, 'Arise; your family are very desirous of seeing you.' So bidding Ahmed and his family adieu, I arose, and the same servant going before me brought me to a ready furnished palace. Raising a curtain I entered and perceived a splendid saloon resembling paradise itself, and the odor of aloes and amber that pervaded it entered my throat. My wife appeared before me attired in the most richly adorned habiliments. The vizir also presented me with five male servants, ten female slaves, and ten thousand dinars in money; in addition to which he gave me a deed securing to me the revenues of two villages. This great favor and kindness was

* The Fatiha is the opening chapter of the Koran.

received by me, a stranger, from the hands of Jaafer the Beremikee. I have now for ten years been living in comfort on the proceeds of his bounty; and no one knew whether I was a stranger or belonged to his family, until the time when the Emir of the faithful withdrew his favor from him and his, and they were overwhelmed with misfortunes. When Eumer bin Laid seized upon his estates, he also deprived me of my two villages, and made me return to him their revenues for the last ten years. In remembrance of the past favors of my lost benefactor, I go every Tuesday and Friday night, and, when an opportunity offers, console myself for his loss by weeping over the ruins of his former splendor, and rubbing my face against them."

Haroon er Rasheed, on hearing these words, was greatly grieved and shed tears. "Go," exclaimed he; "quickly call Laid." On his arrival, the caliph ordered him to return every thing both small and great, that he had taken from the old man, and to give him back again the revenues of the two villages. He also presented him with ten thousand pieces of gold from the treasury. On seeing this, the old man rubbed his face upon the feet of the caliph, thanked him, and said, "O Emir of the faithful, this favor also I owe to the goodness and excellence of my benefactor; for had I not been faithful even to the ruins of the Beremikees, how could I ever have had the honor and good fortune to see the caliph?" At this the caliph smiled, and ordered to the public criers to proclaim that the caliph's anger with the Beremikees was appeased, and that he pardoned their faults. Deeply repenting what he had done, he allowed their pious bequests and edifices for the public good to be made use of as before. May the Most High have mercy upon him!

CHAPTER FOURTEENTH.

On knowledge and delicacy ; on forgiveness and pardon; on restraining anger ; on receiving excuses ; and on courage and assiduity.

This story is narrated by Rebee, the servant of the Caliph Manzoor one of the Abbassides.

One day a person came and informed the caliph that a certain man held secret possession of a quantity of money and effects confided to him by the family of the Ommiades, and suggested that he should demand the same. So the caliph called me and said, "O Rebee, go find me that man." I went, and, having found him, brought him before the caliph. The latter, perceiving that he was dressed in the habiliments of a man of wealth, mildly asked him whether he had in his possession any money or effects belonging to the Ommiades, adding, "I have information regarding the property; do not therefore conceal it, but produce it willingly, and I will recompense you well." The man replied, "O Emir of the faithful, let me tell you all about it; will you be content with what is just?" "Speak," replied the caliph. So the man asked, "Are you the legal or testamentary heir of the Benee Ommiades? if not, on what grounds do you make this demand of me? The caliph replied, "I am neither their heir nor their devisee; but as they by force have deprived Mussulmans of their property, I, as the agent of the Beit ul Mâl, (treasury,) demand its restoration, for the purpose of having it returned to them." To this the man replied, "Since you have no interest in this property, and demand it for the treasury, you must legally prove that it was confided to me; for the Benee Ommiades were not people to lightly intrust to others that which they had obtained by force and oppression."

The caliph inclined his head in thought, and after a little reflection addressed me, and said, "O Rebee, this man's words are true, nothing of this can lawfully become mine; it is but just, that he be not aggrieved." So the caliph asked the man to excuse him, and added, "If you are in need of any thing, tell me." The Sheikh replied, saying, "I ask to have the individual who calumniated me brought before you." So the caliph directed Rebee to go quickly and bring him in, which he did. Then the Sheikh addressing the caliph said, "O Emir of the faithful, this man is my own purchased slave, who stole from me three thousand dinars and fled. Now I know that he has calumniated me for fear I should demand my money of him." The caliph turning to the slave, said, "Fellow, what do you reply to this?" The man could not deny it, but acknowledged the truth of the charge; so the caliph turning to the Sheikh requested that he would pardon him for his sake. The Sheikh replied, "For your sake I pardon him and give him his freedom; I also forgive him the three thousand pieces of gold which belong to me, and will add to them three thousand more as a present on my part." The caliph to this replied, "O Sheikh, generosity and goodness have found their place, but this last gift on your part is too much." The Sheikh answered, "When contrasted with your majesty's gracious words, his pardon is a most insignificant thing. The caliph's bounty is wide; pray then excuse the gift."

Behold what a religious sovereign was this, who did not go beyond the Holy Law, nor deviate from equity. *Naooz Billah* we seek our refuge in God. The present date is the year one thousand and thirty-seven, on which we have just entered. Were a similar occasion and opportunity to occur to the men in power of this age, they, after taking from the Sheikh all his goods and property with the supposition that he secretly possessed more, would torture him to death, and give the calumniating slave to the public crier for sale.

Never was there, in the olden times of Islamism, a period of so much oppression and injustice as in Egypt, where, when a Mussulman dies, they seize upon his property, and leave nothing to his unhappy children. For the Holy Law they have no respect, and it has become a by-word in their language.

Muhtadee Billah, one of the caliphs of the family of Abbas, was a very pious sovereign, exemplary for his attention to the Law of God and a protector to his people. The most learned men agree that after the forty caliphs, Eumer ben Abdul Aaz of the Ommiades, and Muhtadee Billah of the Abbassides, are to be counted as next in worthiness. He was a sovereign that watched over his charge day and night, and who did not love oppression or the workers of sedition, but personally attended to the affairs of the poor. It is related by Mollana Eskiaffee, "I spent a night once with Muhtadee Billah. In the morning a man came to him, saying that he had a claim on the caliph's son, and demanding that the cause should be tried. The caliph called his son, listened to their argument, and condemned his son to pay the man his due, thus impartially judging the case." The Molla also relates, "Once during the month of holy Ramazan, I, in company with Hashim bin Kassim, was the guest of Muhtadee Billah. Three dates were presented to him; one of which he put before himself, one he gave to me, and the other he presented to Hashim. We recited the evening prayer, and then seated ourselves at table. One or two pieces of bread and a little salt and vinegar in a cup were placed before us. They ate of it, and asked me why I did not eat;" adding, "Is not to-morrow the fast? We have nothing more than this." I replied, "O Emir of the faithful, the good things of this world are permitted to you, why not therefore partake of them?" The Emir replied, "Allah be praised for the benefits which he bestows; rather let Eumer ben Abdul Azziz of the Ommiades be mentioned for his abstinence and piety. Shall not he who was the uncle of the prophet and the descendant of Abbas be participators in his blessings and favors? As for me, I have no taste for the good things of this life; and God be praised that I have chosen this path, and am withdrawn from the enticements of the world." He then showed us that the shirt he wore was of a coarse stuff. In his whole life he never was addicted to drunkenness or pillage, but spent his means in preventing oppression, and in affording protection to the humble. May Allah have mercy upon him!

RELATION OF MUTASIM BILLAH'S CAMPAIGN AGAINST, AND CONQUEST OF ANKORA.

Mutasim Billah, a caliph of the family of Abbas, was a brave and generous sovereign, who was much occupied in making religious wars against infidels. One day, when amusing himself with his attendants, a Mussulman prisoner who had escaped from his infidel captor brought a letter and presented it to the caliph. A full cup had been served to the caliph, and this he held in his hand at the moment when the letter was delivered to him. He put down the cup, opened the letter, and read in it, written three different times, "O Mutasim, O most perfect of men!" Mutasim cried with a loud voice, "Take away this enjoyment, and bring it to me no more until the voice of that complainer reach my ear." He called his vizir, and informed him that he was about to undertake a march against Ankora; and he ordered the troops to be ready in three days' time, with forty thousand cavalry distributed among them.

Now a woman of the family of Hashem had been taken prisoner; and it was she who wrote the letter to the caliph from the city of Ankora, asking if, during his caliphat, it was creditable to his honor that she should remain in captivity. Inspired by these expressions, on the following day he set out from Bagdad, and made directly for Room, the brave soldiers having departed one day before him as his avant couriers. Soon they reached Ankora, surrounded its walls, and prepared machines for throwing stones against them. The place was besieged on all sides, no quarter or mercy was shown, and its citadel was taken by force. The conquerers entered the city and possessed themselves of untold wealth.

The governor of the city was brought prisoner before Mutasim Billah; and when the caliph questioned that infidel bey respecting the persons confined in his prisons, he had them all released and brought before the caliph. On seeing them, he asked which among the females was of the Hashemite family; whereupon the woman who had written the letter presented herself and said, "May Allah recompense you with good, O Emir el Mumaneen, prolong your life from day to day, and augment your majesty." The caliph gave the choicest of the infidel captives as a slave to this Hashemite woman, as well as the best of the dwellings in the place; and to the other Mussulmans who accompanied him he gave the best of the captive women in marriage, locating them in that city. He appointed a number of troops, sufficient to protect the city; and his soldiers became immensely wealthy. He gave the command of the city to one of his own slaves, and married the Hashemite woman to him; after which one blessed and lucky day he set out on his return to Bagdad. On his arrival, all the grandees and notables of the city came out to meet and conduct him to his palace, when he recommenced amusing himself among his attendants, and said, "Now bring me that full cup, and let me drink it." So magnanimous and benevolent a person, and so valorous and brave a sovereign was he!

THE STORY OF MUKTAFEE BILLAH AND ABOOL AENEE OF MEKKA.

Muktafee Billah, a caliph of the family of the Abassides, was a most benevolent and naturally mild sovereign. During his caliphat he was accustomed to seek amusement among the learned and pious men and poets of his time. He was also a very generous person; so that his attendants became wealthy and powerful from his liberality. One of his courtiers, named Abool Aenee of Mekka, was gifted above all the rest with a melodious voice and an unequalled talent for music, and was likewise an admirable poet. He was nearly related to the caliph. When he first came from Mekka he was not so wealthy as the other courtiers; indeed, in comparison with them he was a poor man.

One day Muktafee addressed his attendants, and told them he would give them leave of absence until the hour of *ikindee;** adding, "Go and amuse yourselves in such manner as you please; but return after the *aser*, as I intend to-day to take some remedies for my health." Abool Aenee arose on hearing this, and begged leave to ask a favor of the caliph: it was, that he would allow him to act as his door-keeper for that day, and let the regular door-keeper go with the rest of the attendants. The caliph granted his request, and retired to his private apartments. Abool Aenee then took his post with the rod of office in his hand, and performed the duties of door-keeper, all the other attendants having left the palace. The caliph took the medicines recommended him, with the desired relief; and about the hour of *ikindee* he came out of his apartments in good humor.

At that time a person came on the part of his sister to inquire after the health of the Emir el Mumaneen, and received from Abool Aenee the good news of its improvement and the good spirits of the caliph. When this news was taken to the Saidet el Nissah she was much pleased, and sent Abool Aenee as a token of her satisfaction a roll of money amounting to the sum of one thousand dinars. Just then the grand vizir likewise sent to inquire after his master's health; and he also sent Abool Aenee an expression of his

* The time of afternoon prayer is called in Turkish, *ikindee;* and in Arabic, *aser*.

joy, amounting to one thousand dinars. The chief ministers of the caliph's government sent to make the same inquiries, and in return for the agreeable reply gave Abool Aenee a handsome sum of money.

The next day the caliph took his seat on his throne, and all his ministers and attendants were present. Abool Aenee had counted the amounts received, and placed them in the closet of the door-keeper, which he sealed. He gave the ordinary door-keeper five hundred dinars, and, delivering to him his staff of office, went into the presence of the caliph, whose feet he had the honor to kiss. The attendants commenced conversation, and the caliph, addressing them, said: "You have all been amusing yourselves, whilst Abool Aenee was on duty," and he presented him with one thousand dinars. Abool Aenee arose, and after expressing his gratitude to the caliph, replied, that the gains of the day spent in his majesty's service as door-keeper were greater than the profits of an Indian commerce. The caliph was pleased, and smiling, asked him what he had received; to which Abool Aenee replied, that the Fahr el Mahzarat (the vizirs) and the principal persons of the state had given him, as expressions of the delight they felt on hearing the news of his gracious majesty's improved health, each a present according to his rank, and that the whole amounted to sixty thousand dinars.

The Emir of the faithful was much pleased, and commanded his treasurer to give to Abool Aenee ten thousand dinars more, saying, "His saddle is new, and may his horse not be lame; and since his services were perfect, let the sum be even seventy thousand." The greatness and majesty of the Abasside caliphs may be imagined from such noble generosity and glory as this.

The following is related of Jaafer Beremikee, the generous without calculation, the celebrated and renowned by all the tongues of the world, against whom Haroon er Rasheed, by the malicious denunciation of enemies, became incensed, and whom he put to death. Although he repented of his deed, "repentance profits not after destruction," and what was done was done for ever.

It happened that a poet of the desert, named Aboo Attar ibin Addee Artah, of the tribe of the Benee Tayee, was in the habit, every year, of composing a Kassedeh, or Poem, which he then took with him to Bagdad, and presented to Jaafer, the Beremikee. When, on visiting Bagdad as usual, he learnt the downfal of the Beremikees, and the cruel death of his patron Jaafer, he wept over his tomb forty days, composing stanzas of lamentation to his memory, and otherwise expressing his grief. While complaining against the heavens of injustice, he thus wept and exclaimed: "How many years is it now since I annually cut short the space and distance of this desert to enjoy his noble generosity, and return to rejoice my wife and children with his favors. Now, alas! rather than go back to them helpless and broken-hearted, let me die upon the road,—better had I never lived to see this misfortune;" and so saying, he threw himself down in despair. Overwhelmed with affliction, he fell asleep and dreamt as follows: "I saw," said he, "Jaafer, the Beremikee, in paradise, surrounded by the Hoorees and Gholams of that abode of felicity; and I ran and threw myself at his noble feet, pressed my face upon them, and inquired after his health and condition. He gracefully replied, 'O Aboo Attar, be not grieved for us, nor forget us in your prayers. The most high and all-just Deity will, with unbounded mercy, pardon in the garden of satisfaction (heaven) the sins of those who are of good qualities and natures, and who have been generous and liberal. Allah be praised, every year during my life I used to give you for your children, in God's name, three thousand pieces of money. You would then depart with a light heart; but now, after undergoing so much trouble and travel, it is not generous to allow you to return to your wife and children, afflicted and heart-broken. Do not imagine that this dream is futile and profitless; but place your confidence in God, and at noon mount your camel, and go to the city of Bussorah; there seek the street called Sook el Herraz, where resides a friend of ours, named Abool Fadel Medjed ed Deen, a native of Mosul; give him our greeting, (salaams,) and tell him that I have sent him the possessor of the Amar (token) of the last bean, to whom he must give three thousand pieces of gold. Should he ask you,' added he, 'what kind of an Amar, tell him it is that of the Bean;' and like a spirit he disappeared from my sight. It was something between dreaming and waking," continued Ibin Adee, "and when I awoke I began to think what it could be, and concluded, confiding in God, by feeling sure that it was another good deed of Jaafer. So I set out for Bussorah, and on arriving there dismounted, tied up my camel, and searched for the street named Sook el Herraz, which I found filled with all that is rich and beautiful. I asked for the person named to me, and found seated in his shop a sedate, dignified, and good-featured man. Approaching, I saluted him in a respectful and dutiful manner; to which he replied in a considerate and attentive tone. I informed him that I was a poet of the desert, named Aboo Attar bin Addee, son of Adde ibin Artah, sent to him by the possessor of the token, with the request that he would pay me three thousand filooree (ducats). He put his hand to his head, (in acquiescence,) replying, 'To hear is to obey;' and for his own security asked, 'What kind of a token is it?' When he was told it was that of the Bean, he bade me welcome as a friend; for Jaafer had been his benefactor, the source of his prosperity, the tree of his well-being, and the fountain of his ease and possessions. He embraced me, and kissed my face, and brought me to his own dwelling, where he showed me every kind of respect and attention."

Abool Attar went on to remark that Abool Fadel's dwelling was a large palace (*seray*) with innumerable servants, and all his domestics were clothed in black.

An apartment was immediately got ready for Abool Attar, who addressing him, said, "O Abool Fadel and Jood, (Fadel signifies excellence, and Jood liberality,) I have a question to make to you. I have observed that your children and all your attendants are dressed in black, for which there is necessarily a cause. Has any of your offspring, or one of your near relations, or some other one dear to you died, that you should be so enveloped in mourning?" When Hodjah Abool Fadel Medjed ed Deen heard these words from Ibin Addee, he sighed, and tears fell from his eyes like water from a fountain. At length he replied, "The cause is, that that most noble and generous person, the source of all my prosperity and distinction, that descendant of the companions of princes, through the intrigues of certain faithless persons, became the object of Haroon er Rasheed's anger, and was compelled by him to drink of the cup of martyrdom. We have for some time been clad in this garb of mourning and affliction; and now for the story of the token of the Bean, the sign of which you brought me. It occurred in the dwelling of Jaafer bin Yahiya, and it has never become known to any individual but myself. I am very anxious to learn who informed you of it. Explain it to me, I pray."

Ibin Addee replied: "O Abool Fadel, I am from the country of Kahtan, the tribe of the Benee Tay, and from the sons of Addee bin Artah. Both my father and myself are well known to great and small among the Arabs, as two of the principal desert poets. Every year I composed a Kassedeh, and went from the Benee Tay to Bagdad, where I presented it to Jaafer, and received from him as a recompense one thousand pieces of gold, with which my wife and children were rejoiced and made comfortable for a whole year. This year, when as usual I went to Bagdad, I learnt the downfal of the Beremikees, and for forty days mourned over the tomb of Jaafer. Rather than return in despair to my family, I, reproaching my luckless star, laid myself down to sleep, when behold that benefactor appeared to me in all his glory in a dream. I asked about himself, and he replied: 'O Ibin Addee, the caliph, through the calumnies of my enemies, has put me to death; but God, who knows that I was much attached to the family of the Prophet, has had mercy upon me, and placed me in glory and honor. He also inquired after my circumstances, condoled with me, and sent me to Bussorah, to see and speak with you. He told me to do so with the Amareh (token) of the Bean, which I have done.' So now, O Sidi, since Allah has sent me for some wise purpose from the Benee Tay to this land, he has also destined this conversation with you; do, therefore, I pray you, explain to me the circumstances of the token of the Bean, given you by Jaafer, that it may be remembered and told to the tribes of the desert."

Now when Abool Fadel heard this, and saw the urgency with which the request was made, his eyes filled with tears and he replied, "O Ibin Addee, this is the account of what occured between the deceased and myself.

"I am from among the inhabitants of the country of Jaaber, near Mosul. Once I was reduced to great poverty and indigence, through being robbed by soldiers who invaded the country. Having a large family, I was helpless and unable to procure food for them; so I chose to leave my native place, and conduct my wife and children to the residence of the caliph at Bagdad. As a means of support for my family I purchased a small quantity of beans, which, after roasting them, I sold again in the bazaars. My capital consisted of only a single *oka* of beans; but by re-selling them and purchasing others, I managed to gain a livelihood. It happened that about this time the city of Bagdad was visited by a great deluge, in consequence of which the Tigris and Euphrates overflowed their banks.

"One night we were near being drowned. I had soaked the beans which I intended for sale on the morrow; but the flood filled the streets with water like so many rivers, and it was impossible to go out. I was amazed and knew not what to do, and could not help thinking what would become of me, if my little capital should be lost. Early in the morning my wife said to me, 'Arise;

confide in the blessing of Allah; roast your beans; and as usual, if God pleases, a door will be opened to you by that Opener of doors without keys. Whatever is necessary to the subsistence of your wife and children will be given you.' So I, encouraged by these words, placed the bean-tray on my head, and set out. All the streets were filled with water, and it was almost impossible to pass them; yet I strove, with an almost despairing heart, to get along as well as I could. It happened that the water had reached to near the palace of the deceased Jaafer Beremikee; and he, in company with his harem, was seated outside of his dwelling looking at the flowing deluge. It happened also that his eyes fell upon me, as I wandered about in the water endeavoring to dispose of my beans; and pointing me out to his wife he said, 'Behold that man, who, whilst the streets have become like the sea, still persists in wandering through them, with the water up to his mouth. Should it be only for the purpose of gain, his avarice merits contempt; but if he is compelled thus to provide for the subsistence of his wife and children, through love of that great God who makes sovereigns of his humble servants, I will do something for this poor bean-seller which will prevent his ever again scenting the odor of poverty and indigence.' I then heard Jaafer call to me from his palace, saying, 'Ho, fellow! the vizir wants you;' and obeying his summons, I went to the palace, where on my arrival I stood confounded. Coming up to me he bade me welcome in a most friendly manner, and told me not to be abashed. Then with great kindness he inquired why in such a deluge I was engaged in the employment of a bean-seller. 'Do not deceive me,' said he, 'but speak the truth.' He asked my name, what place I was from, and what were my circumstances. After some hesitation, I gave him a true narrative of my past life, and how, after my arrival in this country, I had to gain a livelihood for my children by purchasing an *oka* of beans, which I soaked at night and on the morrow sold in the streets; I also told him how, notwithstanding the deluge, I had been encouraged by my wife, who urged me to rise, saying that Allah provides for the subsistence of all his servants, and out of his treasures would supply the daily wants of our humble selves. 'So,' said I, 'putting my confidence in Him who orders all things, I withstood the fatigue and difficulties of the weather, hoping to gain sufficient to furnish food for my family; and this, my lord, is the truth of my condition.'

"When the deceased heard my story, he smiled and said, 'O Medjed ed Deen, be not grieved; the Most High will provide for all your wants.' He then ordered room to be made in the balcony where he sat, and immediately after called out for all the members of his family and his attendants to assemble near him. Then addressing them, he said, that whoever among them really bore him one atom of pure affection, or observed the right of bread and salt, would take a handful of my beans, and recompense me for the same according to their generosity. So each took a handful, for which some gave me a purse of gold, and others costly jewels and rich dresses, until the hall of reception was filled with them; and only after all the beans in the tray were taken, did they depart. The deceased then turning to me, said, 'O brother Medjed, the servants have all taken their share, and there is nothing left for the master of the house.' I, ashamed, looked into the tray, and found remaining only one small bean; this I placed before him, and requested him, though it was little, to consider it as much. He was pleased with my reply; and taking the bean, he gave the half of it to his wife, and kept the remainder for himself. He then asked her what they should give. She replied, 'A thousand pieces of gold.' But the deceased answered the chaste lady and said, 'This benevolence of yours is not worth the price of a penitential robe.' To this Abbassah his wife replied, 'Whatever you give I will give also.' The deceased then said, 'Good! here are a hundred thousand gold pieces;' upon which Abbassah offered an equal amount. When I saw this, I thought, 'Can this be real, or is it a dream?' And whilst I was reflecting, he ordered a servant to carry all the effects, money, and clothes to my house.

When my wife saw them she exclaimed, 'What can this mean; have you seized upon some treasury, and sent home its contents ?' I replied that they were the blessings sent us by Allah in return for the prayers which she had made, and related to her all that had transpired, telling her of the benevolence and generosity of Jaafer Beremikee. My wife exclaimed, 'A hundred thousand blessings on the heart of him who has bestowed upon us at one gift so much wealth! But it is better that we leave this country and go to another; for as all the world here knew of our poverty, they will be jealous of our prosperity, think us proud, and perhaps bring upon us by their calumnies some great misfortune.' Her advice seeming to me good, I left the city of Bagdad, and came with a cafileh to Bassorah; here I established my residence, and by engaging in trade have increased my fortune, and obtained great wealth. Hence all that you see me possessed of is derived from him whose generosity and benevolence were unequalled, Jaafer the Beremikee. To me, who received such immense riches and favors from the deceased, what are three thousand gold pieces that I should not hasten to obey his orders?" He then gave me three thousand gold pieces more, adding, "I swear by the greatness of God, that if you come to me, I will every year present you his usual gift of one thousand gold pieces out of what the deceased gave me; and I beg that you will not forget either him or myself in your prayers."

He who, after their decease, prolongs the kindness and benevolence of those who have been generous in their prosperity, merits grace and favor, and will surely obtain divine assistance and aid. May God have mercy upon them all!

Mutamid Billah bin Abad, the sultan of Merakesh and Kurtubah, was unsurpassed as a poet and composer, and eminent for his acquirements in literature; he was likewise celebrated for his generosity, and for courage and bravery was a very lion. He treated with great favor and liberality the learned men and poets who resorted to him, and acquired the eminent character of being the most bountiful sovereign of his age.

In the history called Hezanet et Tarikh by Ibin Taid ibin Helkhan, it is narrated, that this sultan had a wife named Remekieh, one of the most beautiful of women, of unequalled skill in poetry and composition, and otherwise eminent for her learning. She bore him a beautiful daughter, who was also gifted with a character of great liberality, sincere and upright in disposition, and of quick intellect. She was equally celebrated for her acquirements in poetry and composition. One day, as Ibin Abad records in his history, the sultan was seated with his wife on a lofty place which commanded an extensive view, when by God's will a heavy rain began to fall, the roads fast filled with water, and the mud became so deep that people were obliged to wade through it with legs bared to their knees. When Remekieh saw this, she declared that it made her envious to see these people thus wading in the rain, and that she longed to do the same. Ibin Abad, with the view to satisfy her, commanded his vizir, saying, "Scatter before your palace thirty or forty thousand gold pieces worth of ambergris, musk, and other odoriferous things; and let the watermen pour rose-water upon it and stamp it into mud." Then turning to Remekieh he said, "Arise, go with your maidens and satisfy your desire." So she went as commanded; and she and all her maidens and other attendants bared their legs, and, filled with mirth and hilarity, collected the scattered objects. After they had finished their sport, Ibin Abad gave permission to his people to fall upon the remainder; and every one got what he could collect, snatching from each other. The historian states that Remekieh sometimes offended the sultan by asking "What have I ever experienced from you but severity?" Ibin Abad once replied to her reproaches by saying, "What! will you not even except the day of the mud?"

Remekieh at this question was ashamed, kissed his hand, and begged him to pardon her petulance.

Thirty or forty years were spent in such affectionate acts as the preceding, until by divine providence Yusoof bin Tashfeen appeared in that country, and conquered the sultan's dominions. One day he suddenly made an excursion, and, after taking the fortress of Merakish, captured the sultan. Both of them ended their lives in the prison of that same castle.

Now, it happened that during the period of the sultan's adversity, his daughter, named Sebeseh, so celebrated for her beauty and amiability, was taken captive by a man of her condition and given to a *dellal*, or auctioneer, to be sold in the streets of her father's capital. A merchant of respectability bought her and brought her to his dwelling. This person had a most beautiful and captivating son, to whom he was desirous of giving her as an *odalik* (concubine or mistress); but when he mentioned it to the unfortunate sultan's daughter, she replied that religion required him to know her condition and who she was, that he might act according to the principles of the true faith. "I am not a slave," said she, "but the daughter of the sultan of Merakish, Mutamid Billah bin Mutazid Billah, and, on the day of my father's misfortune, during the pillage of our palace, was taken captive by the individual who sold me to you. If you wish to marry me legally to your son, write a letter to my father, agreeably to the requisitions of the Holy Law, and ask his permission; for otherwise I would rather my head were cut off than to give my consent." When the merchant heard this from the girl, he respected her, and said, "You are our benefactress; you command us; and it is beyond our power to urge you. Be it as you will." So the girl herself addressed a letter to her father explaining her condition and beging his permission to be married, and dispatched it to the castle of Igmat by a courier. Ibin Abad and the girl's mother had been day and night in tears for the loss of their daughter, wondering where their delicate and tender child could be, and how she was situated. So at a lucky time the courier of fortunate footsteps kissed their hands, and handed them a letter from the object of their solicitude. They immediately recognised her hand-writing, and learned, with great satisfaction, an account of her circumstances. They offered a hundred thousand thanks to Heaven, and blessed the All-Just for his goodness towards their daughter; they then called two witnesses from among the prisoners, and before all the Mussulmans in confinement betrothed their child to the son of the merchant. The news was carried back by the same courier; and soon after his arrival the sensible merchant made a great wedding, and had these two unequalled jewels united. Their after lives were spent in happiness, and they were the parents of many children. The excellent daughter never neglected to be of use and assistance to her parents. The following is a correct copy of the letter which she wrote on the occasion of asking their permission to marry:

"Hear my words and listen to my discourse on the subject of my conduct, which is irreproachable. Do not deny that I was a slave, and that I was a daughter of the prince of the Benee Abad. He is a great sovereign who reigns over his age; but times have their revolutions and seditions. God desired to send division amongst us; and whilst in abundance of sweets, he made us to taste only of bitterness. Sedition rose up against my father's throne. We became separated, and he lost his good desires. I fled, and my condition became debased; yet my mother no longer could regain her own. I was sold away as a slave; who could then save me from misery? A good man received me as his wife, he was a handsome and noble man; he cheapened my price, and was pleased with his bargain. I told him that he surely would lead me in the good road. O father, tell him of my true condition—of my birth and family; this is all I can ask of your friendship and good will, and I hope that the princes of the Remekieh will receive me benevolently and respectfully."

ACCOUNT OF THE KINDNESS OF HAROON EL RASHEED TO THE IMAM ABOO YUSOOF.

It is a fact, well known, that the Imâm Aboo Yusoof was once the cadi of Bagdad. One night he became possessor of the sum of fifty thousand miscals of gold, and the following is an account how this occurred.

The Emir of the faithful, Haroon er Rasheed, one night became enamored of his brother Ibrahim bin Mehdee's maiden slave, and asked him to sell her to him for thirty thousand pieces of gold. But Ibrahim swore that he would neither dispose of her nor give her to him; and rising from his seat, he left the caliph's presence. Subsequently he became greatly alarmed lest his refusal should offend his brother the caliph, and took council on the subject with Aboo Yusoof. The Imam advised him to give one half of her to his brother, and sell him the other half; whereby he would avoid breaking his oath. Ibrahim followed the Imâm's advice; and giving one half of his maiden to the caliph, he sold him the other half for fifteen thousand pieces of gold, the moiety of the sum which had been offered him. When the money was paid over to Ibrahim, in gratitude for his escape from his brother's anger and power, he presented the whole of it to Imam Yusoof.

Now Haroon er Rasheed, being greatly enamored of the maiden, was desirous of consummating his purchase that very night, but was prevented by her illegal condition. So he had recourse to the Imâm, and inquired of him whether there was any remedy for the matter. The Imâm replied, "Marry her to one of your slaves, and let him divorce her without touching her; after which approach her." The caliph followed his advice, for which he gave him five thousand pieces of gold, and married her to one of his slaves; but her husband, after the marriage, refused to divorce her. The caliph offered him ten thousand pieces of gold as an inducement; but still he refused. So he again had recourse to the Imâm's advice. The Imâm recommended him to make a present of her to the slave, which would render the marriage contract invalid. Haroon er Rasheed followed this council, giving the Imâm ten thousand pieces of gold as a token of his regard. After this he approached his maiden; and as an expression of the pleasure he experienced on seeing her face again, he gave the Imâm ten thousand pieces of gold in addition to what he had given him before. The maiden also presented him, out of the dowry which the caliph had bestowed upon her, ten thousand pieces of gold. And thus in one night the Imâm Yusoof became the owner of all these sums.

This tale is related in the Sharki (Commentary) of the Makamati Hariree by Mehdi Bedly Isa bin Jaafer. May Allah have mercy on them all!

CHAPTER FIFTEENTH.

The following is an admirable dissertation on the subject of the versatility of worldly affairs.

Let us, in the first place, inquire what is the cause of the decrease of the power and prosperity of great and mighty sovereigns in this fading and temporary world; and how it is that a foreigner, by effort and bravery, is enabled to attain to sovereign power and place.

God, the Master of all masters; the Creator of the world, the Opener of all doors; the Cause of all causes, who exalts his glory above all doubt, allots destinies from his treasury of subsistence, in immeasurable quantity facilitates the innumerable hopes which exist in the circle of existence of every being, and in the best possible manner provides for the wants of all. Once in every age (*kuroon*) he accepts of a great and glorious sovereign as meriting the exhibition of his power, and deems him worthy of the concealed treasury of his favor. And therefore it is the duty of that greatly favored sovereign to acknowledge the value of the divine grace bestowed upon him, by showing respect and regard for the men of talent and excellence who appear during his reign. Let them refrain from teaching their subjects with force and oppression; for such was the custom of the ancient sovereigns.

During the sway of the sultans of the house of Othman, from the reign of Othman Ghazi to that of Selim bin Suleiman Valee, no unlucky hands were ever applied to the skirts of royalty, or the betrothed of the empire (i. e. the Sultan). They governed with justice and equity; never deviated from the principles and statutes of the Othman rules of Suleiman; and regarded the laws of their ancestors as if they were the words of the Eternal, and as twin brethren of the Holy Law of the Prophet. Hence the pillars of the state were firmly supported, and the regulations and laws of the government were executed with vigor and impartiality.

On the decease of Sultan Selim Khan, Sultan Murad Khan succeeded him on the throne. The grand vizir, Mahommed Pasha, acted in conformity to the ancient rules, and did nothing inconsistent with them. When Mahommed Pasha became a martyr, those who succeeded him in the grand viziral chair followed in his footsteps, and, like him, never went beyond the statutes of the realm. The country was, therefore, prosperous; the forbidden goods, called bribes, never entered the purse of a sovereign of the house of Othman, and the property of the *vakufs* (pious bequests) and the inheritance of orphans they carefully abstained from touching.

It is asserted that Shemsi Pasha changed the name of bribes to that of "gifts," or "presents," and persuaded Sultan Murad Khan to accept them, and to recompense those who gave them with high and important offices; a practice in which he soon was imitated by his ministers. From that time the offices of the state have been sold to the highest bidder; and persons of obscure origin and abject condition have become possessors of the highest offices of the government; whilst the descendants of the most distinguished and faithful servants of the Othman family have been dismissed from public employ, and ignominiously degraded. These modern office-holders show no respect to the conduct of their predecessors; they elevate all, without discrimination, who can pay for their favor; whilst the experienced and talented, if without money, they knowingly debase. Thus, all distinctions of right and worth being withdrawn, the condition of the world becomes daily more troubled and confused, and the enemies of religion and the state are strengthened on every side.

Sultan Murad Khan, a gifted and excellent sovereign, was well acquainted with the condition of his empire; and when his fortunate star arose, he did not remove one step from the place where he was, but contented himself with learning all its affairs from east and west. He appointed one of his servants to the command of an army against Persia, and conquered the best parts of that kingdom. After these conquests, he personally watched over the affairs of his empire and government; and as he made himself well acquainted with all its interests, both private and public, he was able to aid those of his own servants, who were in the way of duty. His vizirs, in particular, were all men of great talent and capability. Sinan Pasha, Othman Pasha, and Rasheed Pasha, were persons of strict religious principles, and well versed in public affairs. It was Rasheed Pasha who took the son of the Shah of Persia prisoner, brought him to Constantinople, and made the capture a bond of peace between the two countries. "When a sovereign," he would say, "is attentive to what is occurring around him, and all his officers and other servants are filled with awe and fear of him, there is but one gate to the government, and those who have not the entrance to it do not interfere in the affairs of state."

After the decease of Sultan Murad Khan, rebellion broke out on all sides, and the enemies of religion and the state burst in upon us. The evil-minded Kuzil-bashes attacked us on all sides, and raised their hands to the skirts of the kingdom, until much evil fell upon it. In the centre of the country of Anatolia rebellious Tellalees arose in arms; and for ten years one hundred thousand muskets were employed in their hands to injure the country, until it was reduced to ruin and poverty. Many crowned and royal personages were made headless; and these things continued until the time when the comet of glory, the Sultan Ahmed Khan, shone out and illuminated the universe. He appointed his predecessor's prime minister, Murad Pasha, to be his chief vizir, and gave him command of the army against Persia; and whether he turned his hand against the infidels or the evil Kuzil-bashes, by God's aid they were crowned with success, particularly in Anatolia, the seat of the Tellalees, who were all put to the sword, their evil-infected bodies effaced from off the world, and the district purified of their unclean association. May Allah the High have mercy upon him!

After the decease of Murad Pasha, those who occupied the seat of grand vizir had their affairs interfered with by others; their full powers became curtailed; and the Ottoman offices, like the articles sold in the Pit Bazar, (old clothes market,) were vended by public criers from door to door; while those who had not admittance to the grand vizir, had no attention paid to them. Other ministers of state took no part in the more important affairs, and the principles and laws of the government were wholly disregarded. A number of men with new traditions, by means of bribes in money, verified the adage, *Deulet ul irgal afet ul rejal*, or "place to the low is ruin to the country," and it is now more than forty years that the Ottoman empire has been thus reduced and ruined, while those excellent officers of state who, in the space of twenty or thirty years rose from one employ to another, have been dismissed by the said individuals, from their charges. Those persons who possess a knowledge of the true condition of the empire are slighted by those who had supplanted them by virtue of money. The great aim of these latter is to despoil their fellow-subjects of their property, and thus reimburse themselves for the sums expended in obtaining their places; whilst the good name and character of the country is deemed of no value. They dispose at will of the subjects of the sultan, who is become only a punisher, whilst they amassed all the wealth of the land. May the Most High recompense them according to their deeds! May they not enjoy either their ill gotten wealth, but give out their light like a glowworm, and may their lives be extinguished in the same length of time.

VERSES.

"Stretch not forth thy hand to the public store, even if it be of the purest gold; for it is the poison of a snake, and the wound that it makes will go on increasing."

"The light which is fed with fat from the entrails of the poor, is the fire-fly of oppression of the state. Be not envious at beholding the redness of the Prince's *pillar*, for it is the blood of his heart and the tears of his eyes."

It follows from the preceding, there is no man brought up by the state who has not received as many as ten camel-loads of bribes; and the reason of the ruin of all good order is to be found in the frequent changes in office. When these are sold over twice a year, how can any wealth remain in the country, or subjects be found in it? and how can any other state of things exist, when the sovereign remains ignorant of the state of his affairs, and is unacquainted with the good or evil condition of his people. Sovereigns give full power to their vizirs, and should therefore watch after their conduct, and ascertain whether they act for the interest of the state, and perform their services with zeal and effect; and whether their people are in the enjoyment of a peaceful tranquillity, and free from sedition and rebellion. At the present period, A. H. 1036, the practice is, whenever a man becomes the governor of a province, to strive to ruin its inhabitants by extortion and oppression. If there be any appeals to justice, they show a great regard for the law, since litigation is to them a rich source of profit. Indeed, it seems a blessing that money will influence their hearts; for pity without a bribe is an impossibility. They thus become possessors of great wealth in this world, for which they must suffer in the next. The sovereign will have to answer for these deeds, and for the oppression which they have shown to his rayahs and poor subjects; and he must stand in this account in the presence of the All-just. The result of this conduct is, that nothing is blessed at the present time.

Have you not often remarked, that a man from the lowest ranks of life, in a short time, through the bribes received by him, attains to the grade of vizir? yet, in the course of five or ten years, his good fortune is turned to naught by the chagrins which came upon him, and his career is cut short by the sovereign's sword. We pray God that those who under the Ottoman dynasty have attained to favor and rank, and yet know not what fidelity in service is, who neither care for the sovereign's good name and reputation, nor regard the holy laws, may ever meet with misfortune. The present article is written simply to offer evidences of the divine Unity, to testify in favor of God and his Prophet, and to excite zeal for the true faith by me, who am the recipient of the high favors of the Ottoman family. From the time of Adam, down to the present period, oppression of the people has ever been the cause of the injury and decline of the sovereigns of the world. One of the sons of the sultan of the land of Persia, who lived after the prophet Adam, on whom be peace, was Sihak-Mar. At that time Jemsheed reigned with justice and equity; he lived one thousand years, and reigned five hundred, until tempted by Satan the accursed, he aspired to be a god. Sihak, whom the Most High sent against Jemsheed, was originally in the service of Shadad, of the tribe of the Benee Hamir, as a Tehaush (messenger). After reigning as a powerful king one thousand years, he marched against Jemsheed, took all his countries from him, and put him to death. The sovereign power then passed into the hands of Sihak, who reigned for two hundred years, in equity and justice. At the end of that time, Satan cooked a savoury dish of food, which pleasing Sihak, he declared that any thing he might desire should be granted him. Satan then asked leave to kiss the Shah's shoulders, which he was permitted to do; whereupon the forms of two serpents appeared on them, and commenced paining him. Satan then assumed the character of a physician, and appearing before the Shah, he advised him to use men's brains as a remedy. Two prisoners were taken out of his jail, and killed, and their brains rubbed on the painful spot. Each day two innocent persons were sacrificed for this purpose, until no more victims remained in the prisons; then lots were cast for individuals in the city, and those on whom they fell were made use of. In this way, some hundred of thousands of men were put to death. At length the son of a person named Kiavai Ahenker, a smith, was seized upon for a similar sacrifice. A year or two later another son was taken; on which the father, maddened with grief and rage, fastened the skin which he used as an apron to the summit of a pole, and called upon all those who were consuming with the cruelty of the tyrant, to assemble round the standard of their faith. Some of the population went out merely as spectators; but others took up arms with him, and with cries of "Allah! Allah!" broke into the dwelling of the governor of Isfahan, cut off his head, and exhibited his clothes to the populace. They next marched against Sihak, and put him to flight; they overtook him, however, and cut off his head; and then finding a person of the race of Jemsheed, named Feridoon, they placed him upon the vacant throne. Kiavai, who became the vizir of Feridoon, preserved the standard of the apron, adorned it with different kinds of jewels, and gave it the name of Derefshi Kiavany. In the conquest of Adjem (Persia) by the Moslems, (under the Caliph Omar,) this standard was captured, and distributed in pieces amongst them.

Sihak was a disciple of Harut and Marut, and was well acquainted with sorcery, and reigned one thousand years with violence; but, on account of his tyranny, the All-just permitted a smith, one of his own rayahs, to defeat all his troops, and cut off his head. Power and might were useless to him; for the Most High is all-powerful.

CHAPTER SIXTEENTH.

On the the fall of the Mussulman power, and the diminution of the rule of the Sultan as Caliph.

The upright caliphs, on whom be the peace of God the most high, namely, Aboo Beker, Omar, Othman, and Ali, reigned for a period of thirty years as caliphs; and the cause of the loss of power after the Flight, is as follows: Ali, the executor of the Prophet, on whom be peace, was the most learned, excellent, and benevolent of them all; he was unequalled in having possessed the full confidence of the Prophet, and was the chief register of the inhabitants of Arabia. In his time Mooavieh was Hakim of Syria. Having determined on his dismissal, he took council with Ibin Abbas, who said, "It is not now the proper time; for Mooavieh is greatly attached to office, and has near him Omar, and Ibin Azz, who are men of penetrating minds. It is therefore better to dissemble for a while; and after you are firmly fixed in your caliphat, do as you please." Ali replied, "I would not for the whole world do any thing underhanded, and shall therefore certainly dismiss him now."

Mooavieh rose up in opposition to the caliph's orders, and held out against him; and the wars which ensued between them are well known. During Ali's time, he was unable to effect every thing; the Imâm Hassan resigned his charge of his own free will. The great Sheik Mohayed ed Deen Arabi relates some of the sayings of Mooavieh, one of which is the following: "Raise your empire and eminence, so as to reach the goal of your wishes. I, though of humble extraction, have by force and effort elevated myself, until I reached the place I desired. As to Ali, he is not a caliph, he is only an emir; for the glory of the universe (Mahommed), on whom be the peace of the Most High, declared that the caliphat would commence after thirty years." The author of the work entitled Jaami el Hikayat, or 'Collection of Tales,' says: "The cause of the dissension between the Lion of God (Ali) and Mooavieh, and of the dispute about the Imâm Hassan, was the advice which he received from Omar bin el Azz. The discord gained ground from his not strictly following the advice of that most intelligent of men, Ali bin Abbas, who hastened the dismissal Mooavieh. The decline of the empire and authority of Ali, and the greatness of Mooavieh, were owing to the intrigues and treachery of Omar bin Azz."

CHAPTER SEVENTEENTH.

On the decline of the Empire of the Beni Ommiya, and the increase and rise of the Abbaside Caliphs.

The first of the sovereigns of the Beni Ommiya, and the last of the Mooavieh's, was Mervan Khamar. They comprised fourteen individuals, who made Damascus the seat of their throne (capital). Their empire extended to the countries of Adjem, Arab, Mekkah,

Yemin, and Magreb; and their majesty, and glory, and power, were celebrated from east to north. The cause of the decline of the dynasty is as follows:

Mooavieh attained to the government (Imaret) in the forty-first year of the Hedjreh; and his dynasty terminated at the death of Mervan, in the year one hundred and thirty. The cause of the accession of the family of Abbas, is this: Hashem bin Abd el Malek, the thirteenth of the Benee Ommiya, who became caliph, was a low and bad man; and whilst he was particularly affected with the evil passion of amassing wealth, his troops and people were left in misery. The generosity of Mooavieh and Yazid, as well as of the other princes of the same family, was well remembered; but Hashem's lowness and vulgarity were so disgusting, that his own princes and other officers deserted him, and intrigued against him. If any one in his presence spoke of death, or of any evil disease, he would stop him and reproach him, for he did not like to hear of such things. After Hashem's death, his son Walid ascended the throne. He was a tyrant and a wicked man, and frightened the people with his oppression. At length they killed him, and his son Yazid succeeded him. This sovereign lessened the pay of the troops, and received the name of "Yazid the Senseless." He was avoided by every one, both great and small; and when he died, his young son, named Ibrahim, took his place. He reigned two months, when Mervan the Red made his appearance, who put Ibrahim to death, saying he was but a child. The Most High, however, had destined the empire to the Benee Abbas. Mervan, who experienced much trouble in his reign, was a merciless and cruel person, who showed no favor to the learned and good, but governed them all as if they were no better than his rayahs, and intrigued against them. He was of a bad disposition, and unclean. Up to the time of Hashem, the government had been carried on systematically and in good order; for all his predecessors were men of knowledge, and gifted with generosity and liberality. After Hashem, each succeeding member of the dynasty became worse than the rest, and more tyrannical. The public deserted Hashem, and his rayahs and other subjects were impoverished and ruined. Enemies arose on every side; and at this interval, in the one hundred and twenty-fifth year of the Hedjreh, Mohammed bin Ali bin Abdallah, of the family of Abbas, began secretly to excite the people against the caliph. On Abdallah's death, which occurred soon after, he willed his claims to his son, the Imam Ibrahim; and in case of his death, they were to descend to his second son, Abool Abbas, the Imam Seffah. In the year one hundred was born Abool Muslim Khorassanee, called Abd er Rahman, whose destiny it was to call to the true faith both Arabs and Adjems, as was predicted in the holy tradition.* Ibrahim came to this person, and with many praises appointed him Imam, at the same time presenting him with a banner, to which he gave the name of *Raiti Zull*, or "The Flag of the Shadow." He told him to go and begin with Khorassan. Abool Muslim assembled thirty or forty thousand men, when Nasser Sear was the general of the filthy Ommaviehs: him he marched against and defeated. When the news of this defeat reached Mervan the Red, he sought out the Imam Ibrahim, and put him to death. His brother, Abool Abbas Mansur, and his other relatives, took flight; but in the one hundred and thirty-second year of the Hedjreh they made their appearance again, and ascending the mosk of Kufah, proclaimed to the people Mervan's oppression and the ruin he was bringing upon their country, and exhorted them to submit to the rule of the sons of Abbas. All present agreed to do so. Their star thus once more found strength to rise; they conquered the whole of Adjem, and in one year subdued Egypt, Syria, Aleppo, and all Irak and Arabia, and their empire reached even to Yemin. His uncle's son, Abd Allah bin Ali, was his general; he sent him against Mervan, whom he defeated near Mosul, and dispersed his

* "Certainly God will send every hundred years a sovereign to avert the errors of the people."

army. Mervan fled to Egypt, pursued by the general, who, having overtaken him in the neighborhood of the village of Aboo Sair, cut off his head. Now it is seen that there were fourteen sovereigns of the Benee Ommiyah, whose united reigns lasted nearly one hundred years; and that they attained a high degree of power and distinction, their empire extending over Arab, Adjem, Yemin, and Aden. From Hashem to Mervan, two or three individuals only showed respect for the world; and the cause of the downfal of their dynasty, was their hatred of the learned and virtuous, and the cruelty and oppression which they practised towards their rayahs and other subjects. Behold, in this narrative, abundant instances of examples to be shunned.

AN ANECDOTE

Which shows the greatness of the majesty and glory of the Abbasside caliphs, and the cause of the decrease and overthrow of their empire. So great was once their glory and power, and the splendor of their reign, that the Sultans and Hakims of the neighboring countries came to visit their heaven-like capital in Bagdad, and would often pass a whole year in waiting for an audience, sometimes obtaining that favor, and sometimes failing to do so. According to the account written by that sultan of traditioners, that most correct historian, Ibin el Juzee, entitled "Montazim," and "Mizan Shahi Saad Edden Kermani," on the subject of the grandeur and splendor of their reign, their wealth and treasures, and the number of their troops, the following may be considered a true picture.

In the time of Muktadir Billah, one of the caliphs, and in the three hundred and fourth year of the Hedjreh, ambassadors came from the kings of Room to offer him magnificent presents. They were introduced to the vizirs of the caliph, the chief of whom, Ibin Said, lodged them in some dwellings of his own, where he feasted them bountifully. When they had sufficiently recruited themselves, they asked to be presented to the caliph. Their request was made known, and orders were issued for their presentation. On the day following, the ambassadors mounted, and went to the palace of the vizir, and all the principal authorities of the government likewise paraded to the palace of the caliph, where each one took his appointed station. The ambassadors with the grand vizir, on their way to the palace, passed through the midst of the city, and visited the principal bazars and streets of Bagdad. On arriving at the palace, they found eight thousand door-keepers, in caps of gold, stationed at its gates, all ranged in files, and each holding a rod in his hand. On either side of the gates valuable horoscopes were suspended. Passing these, they entered the court of the caliph's own palace, called the "Dehlizi Azem," and found both sides of the way lined with attendants. The court itself was lined, right and left, with the officers of the government, completely covered with gold, and arrayed in embroidered garments, who were sent to meet and salute the vizir. A historian named Sulee says, "I saw on that occasion, stationed on both sides of the way of the imperial gate called the *Dehlizi Azem,* sixteen thousand soldiers, and besides these, one thousand pages belonging to the guard, appointed to serve in the royal palace, all dressed in golden sashes, with embroidered clothes and scimitars of gold. At the door of the palace were one hundred private keepers, standing near the entrance; and on either side of the way were the sultans and the Beyler Beys, waiting with the Ojak Beys to be introduced to the caliph. Over the private entrance was a window of gilded lattice-work, from which hung a sleeve of black velvet, worked in jewels of different kinds, five cubits in length. When the Hakims and Sultans, who came to be presented to the caliph, had had their audiences, it was the custom to kiss this sleeve, and then ask permission to retire.

When the vizir and the ambassadors had reached this place,

they respectfully kissed the sleeve, and then continued on to the palace of the caliph. The private attendants of the caliph next met them, and saluted them as they passed. After this, they met the caliph's eunuchs, seven thousand in number, four thousand white and three thousand black, who were drawn up in rows on either side, and saluted them as they passed by. According to the history entitled the Merati Zaman, from the northern entrance to the palace of the caliph, and from the outer gates to the castle of the caliph, besides the other valuable objects on either side of the way, were thirty-eight thousand horoscopes. When the ambassadors beheld these places thus richly ornamented, they inquired if they formed the residence of the caliph. Each place was then named and described to them. They came next to the palace called *Dar esh Shedjreh*, where the caliph's cuirasses and other arms were hung up, the former amounting to ten thousand, and the latter to eighteen thousand pieces all adorned with jewels; besides which there were innumerable other curious and rare articles. At the *Dar esh Shedjreh*, ranged on both sides of the way, were one hundred lions confined by golden chains. Passing on between them, they proceeded to the place of the caliph's throne, called *Dar el Ferdoos*, or the "House of Paradise," having in front of it a large reservoir, in which grew a tree of pure silver, its leaves being of gold, and its fruit of divers hues. When the wind blew, different tunes proceeded from the branches; and birds of various plumage were perched upon them here and there, each of which sang with a different note. The ambassadors beheld all this as they proceeded from the *Dar el Ferdoos* to the place where the caliph was seated on a throne of ivory and ebony richly jeweled. They rubbed their foreheads on the throne; and then retiring they took their station in a place distant one hundred cubits' length from him. The vizir, with crossed arms, stood before the throne, and a Terjuman interpreted his words to the caliph. He caused the ambassadors to be invested with robes of honor, and presented each of them with twice one hundred thousand aktches; after which they returned by the way they came. The vizir showed them the caliph's own palace, where more than a hundred enormous elephants were exhibited to them; after which they returned to the *Dar el Khelifeh.* There they each received another robe of honor, and departed by the Bab Shems. Beyond the palace was a street called *Sook es Selaseh,* a celebrated high road which runs through the heart of the city; and also a place called *Zat el Menaie,* where were more than a thousand Minarets. Just as they had reached it, the mid-day prayer was being proclaimed from them by the Ezzâns. The ambassadors were puzzled at hearing so many voices crying out the *Allah Ekber* at once, and asked what it meant. "Are these the columns of Islam?" they inquired; and some of the ambassadors, acknowledging that the Mahommedan religion was a good one, made a profession of it. In this way they returned to their houses, praising the power, greatness, and glory of the caliph.

To what a degree of might and majesty did the preceding caliphs attain! and what a comparison it offers with the age of the caliph Muktadir Billah, during which the enemies of the government appeared every where! The empire of the family of Abbas was a fabric of majesty, which produced thirty-seven caliphs, who for five hundred and twenty-four years held the reigns of government, and ruled from east to west. The cause of the decline of their power, was their disregard of the laws of their ancestors, and their having deserted the royal path of justice. When the caliph Mustassem Billah attained to the caliphat, he took possession of that paradise-like residence of Bagdad, and, being without experience, was inclined to dissipation and self-indulgence. He left the affairs of his government to his grand vizir; whilst his favorite pages, eunuchs, and other servants were each vizirs themselves. Whenever the vizir complained against them, the caliph's favorites would put him down by replying that their sovereign wished to reign alone. If the vizir for a moment neglected his charge, the other authorities would commit oppression and tyranny over the rayahs. The Hakims and Beys who had long administered the government were dismissed, and young and inexperienced persons put in their places. Thus, every one became disaffected; and the neighboring enemies of the government, hearing of its internal dissensions, and knowing that the caliph was not an upright man, stirred up a bitter enmity between him and Menkoo Khan, one of Jenghiz Khan's sons. All the dissimulation of the vizir was ineffectual; the quarrel increased, and Menkoo Khan sent his brother Holagoo Khan, with four hundred thousand Mogul troops against Bagdad, who beseiged the city and plied their battering-rams against its walls. At last, when the caliph was reduced to extremity, he, with his son and three thousand of the noblest of the family of Abbas, mounted their horses, and left the castle for the camp of Holagoo, in order to make their peace with the conqueror. The caliphs and his sons were admitted; but the Emirs and Ayans were kept outside.

Having shown a friendly face to the caliph, Holagoo ordered the city gates to be thrown open; which being done, the Moguls entered the city and took possession of it. On the following day the caliph and his three sons were thrown into prison, and the inhabitants of the city were put to the sword to satisfy the fury of these conquering troops. Holagoo next cut off the heads of the caliph's sons. He caused the caliph himself to be wrapped in a green ox-hide and exposed to the sun, where he expired under the feet of the passing infidel Tatars; and this was the end of the family of Abbas. May the Most High have mercy on them all!

So, from being a great empire, they were stripped of wealth, troops, and possessions of every kind. The cause of this downfal was the young caliph's giving himself up to dissipation and amusement, and leaving the direction of his government to a few youths and eunuchs; his ignorance of the consideration due to men of learning; and his having displaced those officers who possessed wisdom and experience, and appointed young persons in their places, without talents or knowledge of governing, who oppressed the world.

His subjects having been disappointed and exasperated by such treatment, when the enemies of his government made their appearance, the country was yielded up by them without much resistance.

CHAPTER EIGHTEENTH.

The downfal of the Gergany kings, and the rise of the sun of felicity of the Delmean (called the family of the Boiyas).

According to Mir Khond Shah, the head of the Delmean dynasty was Aboo Shejaie, a man sprung from the middle class of society. He had three sons, Ali, Hassan, and Ahmed. One day Aboo Shejaie paid a visit to an astrologer, to consult him about a dream he had had, and to ask for its interpretation. "I saw," said he, "in my dream, a fire, which increased as it burnt, and by degrees consumed the whole country. It consisted of three parts, from each of which there proceeded a great light; and before it stood an immense crowd of people, with their hands crossed before them." The astrologer was a man of talent, and hesitated to tell the young man the signification of the dream. "If you do not give me," said he, "either a horse, a piece of gold, or a robe, I will not explain it to you." To which Aboo Shejaie replied, "Vallah! in all my life I never owned a horse, nor have I ever seen ten pieces of gold together at one time; moreover I have but a single cloak. But pray accept my best prayers, and explain to me my dream, whereby you will confer on me a great favor." The astrologer replied, "Be it then good news to you; for know that you are destined to have three sons, who are to reign upon the earth, each one of whom will be a powerful sovereign. When that time arrives, I pray you to have me in remembrance." Aboo Shejaie answered, that he must be making game of him, and laughed; but the astrologer declared it was true, and would not retract a word of what he had said. Amed ed Dowlet, the elder son, went to the city of Meravedy. Its governor, who resided in the town of Kerieh, was a very brave and generous person; and on account of his intelligence and good management, and his liberality to all those who visited him, they never would leave him. Many persons assembled around him, and more than a thousand went with him against Ispahan; but then Ibin Yakut who had ten thousand horsemen, made war against him, and drew him off. He went to the kingdom of Orkhan, and conquered it; and as he continued, his army and power increased in strength, and he became exalted and honored. After this he sent his brother Ruken ed Dowlet, and conquered Kiazroomi. Subsequently, he made Ispahan the capital of his empire, and the governors in that neighborhood began to fear him; he also became possessor of many troops, and went on conquering. In the twelfth year he defeated the forces of Ibin Yakut, the governor of Shiraz, and thus mastered the whole country. He gave up the city to the soldiers; but not so much as a mustard-grain or a crumb of the booty was taken by himself. He entered the palace of Ibin Yakut, wondering where he could obtain the means of paying his soldiers; when suddenly a snake thrust its head out of a hole in the roof of the palace, and drew it back again. As it did this several times, the general took its conduct as a sign to himself, and ordered Amed ed Dowlet, the servant of the harem, to go out and see what the serpent was about outside of the roof. The servant went, and on examining the spot found a number of boxes filled with gold; some of which he brought to Hamed ed Dowlet, who, with thanks to God for the gift, immediately commenced distributing it to his troops, and making merry.

VERSE.

"No one has power without trouble and anxiety. In seeking for a serpent, you find a rich treasure. Who would not like to seek for a serpent, and find a rich treasure?"

After this he inquired for an expert tailor to cut him out some clothes. A deaf one was found, who had been in the employ of Ibin Yakut. When Amed ed Dowlet saw him, he exclaimed, "Bring me an ell measure," which is called in Persian *tchob.* The deaf tailor, hearing only the word *tchob,* replied, "What can a man of fortune and wealth want with a tchob? I do not deny that there is need of a measure; for I have a box of stuff belonging to Ibin Yakut, which ought to be cut up. If you desire, I will bring it." Amed ed Dowlet thanked God, and ordered it to be brought in. So the tailor departed, and soon returned with the box of choice stuff, out of which he cut a suit worthy of a sovereign, and dressed him in it.

The power of the family of the Boiya became so great, that it ultimately conquered Bagdad; and Amed ed Dowlet appointed his brother Moaz ed Dowlet to be governor of that city. For a long time money, was struck and prayers read in their names, joined to those of the caliph. They resided sometimes in Shiraz, and at other times in the *Dar el Malik,* at Bagdad. There were nineteen sovereigns from this family, all of whom governed with justice and equity. They respected and protected the pure, and the learned, and the poets. "Wealth," said they, "is not lasting; rather let our name remain on the page of the universe." They therefore took no care to amass money, but freely bestowed it upon the worthy, and thus endeavored to acquire a good reputation. God be merciful to them all!

ANECDOTES TAKEN FROM PROVERBS.

An upright and good man was once asked what were the signs of a man of talent, and the connexion existing between them. He replied, "There are three things which show a good understanding: namely, first, the faculty of expressing one's ideas in a few words; for many words cause sorrow, and blame." "If," asked they, "the individual is absent, from what can his talents be estimated?" "From three things," was the reply: "from the character of the person he sends on his business, from the manner in which his letters are written, and from the kind of present he may send; for the person he sends must be the representative of himself, the letter which he writes must be of the same quality with his conversation, and the degree of his benevolence and good favor will be known from his present."

It has likewise been said that one of the strongest proofs of talent, is the faculty of disguising one's thoughts from others (dissimulation), good behavior in society, and an unassuming deportment. This last trait arises from the good characteristics which are bestowed upon man by his Creator. A good disposition is considered as the most glorious of all divine gifts and benefits; so much so, that the greatest of prophets, on whom may Allah bestow his blessings and peace, has said, "He who does not use dissimulation, will not find the aid of others."

The following is imputed to Ibin Anwat, known as Habeeb Allah Hafiz. "Once a man appeared in the presence of the Prophet Suliman, on whom be peace, and represented that during the meeting of the people a goose disappeared. Suliman ordered that the congregation should meet again at the Mejid (chapel); which being done, he mounted the pulpit, and asked, 'Is it right that you should steal a goose from one of your brethren in the faith, and put its feathers on your head, when you come to chapel?' When the person who had taken the goose heard this, he immediately clapped his hand to his head to feel for the feathers; and the Prophet seeing it exclaimed, 'Behold the man who has taken the goose;' and in fact so it turned out to be the case."

In the four hundred and sixtieth year of the Hedjreh, an Idam sultan, named Asad ed Dowlet, reigned with great power and distinction, and was celebrated for the care he took of his government. During that period a merchant, a stranger, who had formed the intention of making a pilgrimage to Mecca, arrived at a town in the empire of Asad ed Dowlet, where he put up. When the time of the pilgrimage arrived, the stranger did not know with whom to deposite the money he had with him, which was more than was necessary for the journey, and amounted to a thousand pieces of gold. So he concealed it at the foot of a large tree which grew without the city; and, supposing that it would be safe there, proceeded on his way. On returning from his pilgrimage, he visited the place where his money had been concealed; but not finding it, he was greatly distressed and wept with grief for his loss. Meeting with a friend, he was advised to petition the sultan on the subject, which he did; and when the sultan had read his petition, he was requested to have patience for a few days. The sultan next called all the pilgrims of the city together, and asked whether any of them, during the year, had administered as a medicine the root of a certain tree? One of them, replying in the affirmative, said that he had done so to an officer in his highness's service. The sultan accordingly had this individual brought before him; whereupon he acknowledged that when digging for the roots of the before mentioned tree, he had found a sum of money, amounting to a thousand pieces of gold, which had been concealed there. He then handed the sultan the sum found by him, which was forthwith delivered to its owner. The latter returned his best thanks and prayers for the restoration of his lost property, and set out for his own country. All those present extolled the talent and intelligence of Asad ed Dowlet; his great name is written on the leaf of time, with praise for his good acts; and his excellence and benevolence are widely celebrated.

AN ANEDDOTE OF AN EVENT WHICH OCCURRED BETWEEN THE SULTAN ALAI ED DOWLET DELIMEE AND THAT CHIEF OF PHYSICIANS, THE SHEIK ABOO ALI BIN SINNA (AVICENNA).

When Ibin Sinna was in Ispahan, in the three hundred and ninety-eighth year of the Hedjreh, that powerful person, Alai ed Dowlet Aboo Jaafer Delimee was its governor. At that time, distinctions and marks of regard were bestowed on Aboo Sinna without ceasing. One day the sultan took from his waist a rich and valuable belt, and bestowed it upon that excellent Sheik. This the latter afterwards gave to one of the sultan's own attendants. The sultan observing it on the individual, inquired how he came by it. The man replied, that he had received it from the Sheik as a present. The sultan was greatly displeased, and rebuked the attendant severely for having accepted it; at the same time he swore to take the Sheik's life for caring so little for his gifts. But one of the Sheik's friends giving him information of what had occurred, he acted on the proverb which says, "Separate from him whom you cannot withstand," and forthwith departed from that country in disguise. On coming to another city, and dismounting at a caravanserai, he walked to the market-place in search of provisions. Whilst thus engaged, he observed a youth of talent and science, around whom a crowd of people were collected asking him for remedies. The youth in turn showed to each one the remedies for his complaint, and the means of recovery from his malady. Presently a woman made her appearance, bearing a white vase in her hand, which she showed to him. The youth said that the vase belonged to a Jew; which the woman confirmed. Afterwards he said, that she had eaten that day half an egg and some curds; and this the woman also avowed. The young man next asked if the woman did not then reside in a filthy part of the city; and the woman answered affirmatively. Aboo Sinna, observing the youth's superior talents, was astonished at his language and the remedies which he prescribed. The young man's eyes happened to meet those of Aboo Sinna; and making him a secret sign of recognition, he addressed the Sheik with deference and said, "You are he who has received that divine science, and are that unequalled and most perfectly excellent person, the Reis Aboo Ali bin Sinna, who fled from Ispahan through fear of the Sultan Alai ed Dowlet, and are come to this place with the intention of residing here." Then feeling kindly towards the Sheik, he left all his business, kissed the Sheik's feet, took his hand in his, and led him to his own house. After receiving from the young man all the usual attentions of a servant, the Sheik asked him whence he had drawn his conclusions, and how he knew that the vase belonged to a Jew. The youth replied, "I observed the old woman's tunic, and knew from its marks that she was a Jewess; and I judged that the vase also belonged to one of the same people. Her dress was soiled with eggs and curdled milk; and I knew that she must have eaten of both these things. Moreover, knowing that the Jew quarter at this time is a filthy place, I remarked that it was unclean." "But," said the Sheik, "How did you become acquainted with me and my profession?" The youth said in reply, "Knowing the envy of Alai ed Dowlet, the circumstance of your having fled from him is a proof of the renown of your excellence, and that your sagacity and mental powers must be as bright as the sun in the heavens. I have heard too of the good qualities with which you are gifted, and I beheld on your noble front the characteristics of those traits, which beamed upon me like the midday sun; from all of which I felt assured that you were the celebrated physician Aboo Sinna. I likewise knew that the sultan could not bear to be separated from you for a moment, and therefore was convinced that you must have left him by your own desire and against his will." The young man next bent the knee of politeness before the Sheik, and thanked God for allowing him to meet with such a man. The Sheik then said, "What have you to ask of me? tell me your wishes, and, as far as my destiny permits, I will endeavor to promote them." The intelligent youth replied, "It is impossible that you should remain separated from the sultan; and what I ask from you is, that when you again appear before him, you will relate the occurrence which you have witnessed, and obtain me a place in his service, even as one of his most humble attendants."

Some days after this, a man came to the Sheik on the part of the sultan, who begged his pardon for the past, and invited him to return to his palace. The Sheik took the youth with him, and on reaching the sultan, related what he had witnessed respecting him; wherefore the sultan forthwith appointed him to be one of his own pages.

CHAPTER NINETEENTH.

On the condemnation of folly, the rarity of talent, and on evil characteristics.

The great Sheik Muhid ed Deen el Arabee, of Saliheh, near Mecca, on whom be peace! asserts that folly is a disease, for which there is no other cure than death.

VERSE IN ARABIC.

"Every disease has its remedy, except for folly; that alone is incurable."

The Prophet, on whom be peace! has likewise said, "Folly is the commonest portion of mankind."

The characteristics of one possessed of folly are as follows. His head is long; because the part from which a man's folly issues is his brain, and length of head is owing to smallness of brain, and little brains denote little intelligence, which is the cause of folly. A man's character may be known by his acts: by his never looking to the termination of his affairs; by his never changing his opinion; by his never gratifying the wishes of others; by his being self-willed; by his pretending to know what he does not know; by his having no desire to learn; by his disclosing his secrets; by his telling every one all he knows, as well as what he does not know; by his inattention to the rules of society; by his precipitancy in replying to what is said by others; by his ignorance of science; by his haste and negligence; and by his ill-timed laughter in company, which resembles the braying of an ass.

The following anecdote is narrated by Esmaee,* one of the best men of his age.

I once saw a powerful man of Bassora, who was seated in front of his door, dressed in splendid clothes, and surrounded by elegant looking attendants, and was engaged with them in conversation. Now, this man had a very long and thick head. Observing this, I asked myself whether this characteristic of the man was a proper token of his mind; and with a view of learning the fact, I saluted him and asked him his name. "My name," replied he, "is Aboo Abd er Rahma Rheem Meliki Yevm ed Deen."† I smiled and felt convinced of the weakness of his mind; for the man had showed me the smallness of his understanding and the extent of his ignorance.

* The author of the Arabian novel called *Antar*.

† These words generally commence chapters of the Koran, and are quoted incorrectly.

It is related that once two fools set out in company to go from one village to another. Whilst on their way one of them said, "Come, let us have a talk together;" so they sought out a comfortable place to sit down in. In the course of conversation one of them said, "I should like to own a flock of sheep; so that I might eat when I chose of their meat, or drink their milk, or make clothes of their wool." The other replied, "I should like to have a pack of wolves; that I might turn them loose among your sheep, to devour them, and tear their fleeces in pieces." The first speaker asked of the other why he wished for so evil a gratification; and presently proceeding from words to blows, they beat each other as long as they had strength to stand up. At length they stopped, and agreed to refer the subject of their quarrel to the judgment of the first passer-by and be governed by his decision. It happened that a man passed along driving an ass loaded with two skins of honey, which he was taking to the city for sale. So accosting him, they related what had occurred to them, and asked him which of the two was foolish. Now this man was a greater fool than either of them, and taking off the bags of honey he gave one to each of the disputants, saying, "Beat each other with these, and I will see which of you is the greater fool." They did so, and he looked on. With the first blow the skins burst open, and the honey ran over the ground. When he saw the honey flowing, "Vallah!" exclaimed he, "may my blood flow like this honey, if either of you have any sense; you are both fools." What a wise decision for one who was forgetful of his own hurt!

ANECDOTE OF SHABOOR, THE DOUBLE-SHOULDERED, AND THE KAISER OF ROOM.

One of the ancient and powerful kings of Adjem (Persia) was

a famous sovereign, of a just and equitable character, he was distinguished for generosity and liberality, and was known by the name of "Shaboor, the double-shouldered." One day he called his vizirs, and said to them, "I have occasion to ask your advice. I purpose making a journey, and visiting the Kaiser of Room, to learn something about his circumstances and conduct; what do you say to this?" The vizirs all counselled together, and afterwards replied to their king: "The idea which your majesty has conceived is certainly dangerous; for a sovereign cannot easily travel about in the world alone as he may choose. We therefore counsel that, by all means, you forego your intention." Yet, notwithstanding their endeavors to prevail upon him to change his mind, they were unsuccessful. At length he asked the advice of one of his vizirs who had held the office from the time of his father, a most talented and learned person, so much so that he was regarded as a philosopher, and as one acquainted with all religions and all languages. From him the Shah received the same reply, namely, that it would be better to forego his design. Still he determined to make the journey. So telling the vizir that he had the following request to make of him, namely, that he would favor his project, and provide means for performing the journey. The wise vizir then begged Shaboor to permit him to go first to the country of the Kaiser of Room, where he would be ready to forward his views and wishes on his arrival; and the vizir, having received the royal consent, immediately commenced putting on robes, and attiring himself in the guise of a monk. He was learned in the science of medicine, and in the prescribing of remedies, and in surgery. In that science his abilities were great, and he carried with him Chinese ointments which had the quality, if rubbed upon the flesh, of curing wounds in a very short time that had otherwise proved incurable, as well as of immediately assuaging the pain arising from them. For his services he never accepted compensation from any one.

This personage set out, as we have said, for the kingdom of

the Kaiser of Room, where he soon acquired great celebrity, and his reputation spread over all the world. He became celebrated among religious people for his piety and self-denial, and even obtained great renown among the patriarchs and priests of the Nazarenes. The best of these latter, including their famous chief named Abool Abad, soon became very intimate with the vizir. Abool Abad always acted on the vizir's advice, took his council and opinion, and yet surprised the vizir by his own learning and intelligence. In fine, the vizir was so much pleased with his company, that he forgot Shaboor, until one day there was a great feast at Constantinople to which all the public, both great and small, were invited. Now Shaboor had set out on his journey incognito, and arrived at Constantinople; where, with the view of not being known, he dressed himself in his worst clothes, and mingling with the crowd at the feast partook of the food prepared for them. Now the Kaiser of Room, besides having Shaboor's form portrayed on the walls of the city, had had his likeness painted and put up in all the public places; so that whoever stopped to see them should learn to recognize him. He had him also painted on all his cups and other vessels. It so happened that Shaboor was looking intently at one of the portraits of himself which the Kaiser had had painted, when an intelligent man's eyes happened to fall upon his person; then looking at the portraits he recognized Shaboor, of which he forthwith gave information to the Kaiser. The latter looked at him attentively, and likewise recognized him. Shaboor, however, denied himself; at which the Kaiser said that if he was not indeed Shaboor, he resembled him exceedingly, and so ordered him to be executed. Shaboor observed the merciless executioner approaching him, and was fain to acknowledge his identity to save his life. So they took him before the Kaiser, who showed him every respect and attention, and was astonished that a victorious enemy should come to him of his own accord. At length, however, he cast Shaboor into prison, and proclaimed war against his country; then getting ready his armaments, he set out with an innumerable host. For Shaboor they made an elephant of bullock's hide, forty layers thick; inside of which was an apartment with a window like that of a magazine, so that the people outside might look in upon him. The feet of the elephant were made like the wheels of a wagon, that it might be drawn about; one hundred stalwart men were appointed to be its guards. In this way Shah Shaboor was carried towards his own kingdom; and because he refused to follow the advice of his wise men, he became a victim to this gulf of danger. He now repented of what he had done, lamented the fatality which had come upon him, blamed himself as its cause, and sought relief from the difficult position in which he was placed. He wondered where he could find a salve for his incurable wound, and resigned himself to the providence of the sovereign Lord of all, saying, "To whom shall I tell my complaint; from whom shall I seek relief?" As to the Kaiser, he entered into the territory of Persia; and at every halting-place he had the elephant in which Shaboor was confined brought near his tent and that of his patriarch, where it remained with a tent pitched over it, surrounded on all sides by his guards. Every day a province of Shaboor was subdued, its trees cut down, and ruin carried wherever they proceeded; whilst Shaboor's wise vizir passed his time in a tent pitched for him near that of the patriarch, planning means to liberate his master. Every night he spent in the society of the patriarch, relating to him curious occurrences and news; by which means his voice reached Shaboor, and consoled his afflicted heart by the appropriate tales which he told. Shaboor understood, from the subject of his vizir's discourse, that the latter's intentions were to procure his release. The Kaiser arrived at the province of Fars, cutting down the trees, wasting the country, and spreading ruin and devastation at every step, until he finally reached the site of the throne and the capital of Shaboor, which he commanded to be besieged day and night. His engines weakened its walls, until Shaboor became apprehensive that the place would be captured.

HEMISTICH FROM HAFIZ.

"I acted according to my inclination, and in the end acquired a bad name."

"To whom," exclaimed the Shah, "shall I complain against this affliction? my own hands have brought it upon me."

One night, being excessively troubled, he said to the attendants who brought him wine and food from the Kaiser, "Envy and affliction have made a deep impression upon me. If it be your desire to prolong my life, loosen a few of my strong chains; either stop my breath at once, or restore my wasted frame, by loosing this collar from my neck, and these chains from my body." The faithful attendants had pity on Shaboor; they mentioned his name to the patriarch, at whose side the vizir happened to be; and the latter understood that Shaboor had cut off all hope of the thread of life, and was desperate. The vizir, seeing that it was time to answer the affliction of his master by going to his assistance, and that the aid of Him who nourishes all was near, that night addressed the patriarch, saying, "I have a singular story to tell you, if you will listen to it." The patriarch replied that it would give him great pleasure to do so; adding that his hearing would be charmed and his understanding embellished by the vizir's wisdom. So the vizir commenced, and related the following story, intending it as an example to console Shaboor:

O patriarch, once in our country there were two young creatures, beautiful as Perees, and of good and benevolent qualities. One of these young persons was named "Aiyin el Ehel," and the other, the female, "Saidet en Nar." These two fair creatures were united and formed one, and never for a moment were separated from each other. One day Aiyin el Ehel was engaged in conversation with some friends, when one of the latter spoke highly in praise of a lady who was beautiful as Zahrah, (Venus,) the envy of the Perees. When Aiyin el Ehel heard this person spoken of in such flattering terms, he became enamored of her, heart and soul,—so much so, that he asked her name; to which the speaker replied that she was called Saidet ez Zeheb, and that her dwelling-place was Arabia. The youth could no longer control himself, but forthwith set out in search of her. Having reached her and beheld her beauty, he saw that she was a sweet and lovely creature, but not more so than his own wife. And yet, according to the nature of man, longing for the enjoyment of something new, he began to desire the beautiful Saidet ez Zeheb. But Saidet ez Zeheb also had a husband, who, becoming acquainted with the meeting of these two, seized and carried off Aiyin el Ehel to a dark and solitary house, where he confined him, placing over him an ugly old woman, who had but one eye, and whose ears, nose, and hands had been cut off. Aiyin el Ehel, now knowing the extent of his misfortune, and that he had brought it upon himself, commenced weeping and moaning. His lamentations reached the hearing of the old woman, who, seeing Aiyin el Ehel in tears, was attentive to him, and said, "Pray what is the cause of your being confined in this wild and distant place?" Aiyin el Ehel replied, "O, pitiful mother, I am an innocent youth, ignorant of any crime." The old woman said, "Your story is like that of the run-away horse, who said, I was seduced by a hog. The horse at first lied, but when at last he took up the skirt of faithfulness, and disclosed the truth, he was freed from his misfortune." When Aiyin el Ehel heard these merciful words, he said to the old woman, "O mother, pray tell us something about what occurred between the escaped horse and the hog." So the old woman related as follows:

"It is said that there was once a handsome man, who possessed a horse swift as the wind, of which he took very great care; and not confiding in his own servants, he used to give him all his fodder himself. In the morning he arose early, and mounting his horse, rode him over hill and dale, to where there was a green spot; then alighting, he unbridled and unsaddled him, and let him graze upon whatever vegetation he could find;

afterwards, putting on his saddle and bridle again, he returned home, walking by his side. These were the attentions he showed to his horse. One day, having done as before mentioned, he took the animal out where there was some green pasture, and dismounted to let him graze for some time. Suddenly the horse sprang away from his master, and fled across the desert, carrying with him his saddle and bridle. The master sought every where, but in vain; the shades of night surrounded him, the beast still fled on and was lost from sight, and at length his master returned home. All night long the horse had borne the saddle and bridle: being fatigued, and overcome by sleep and hunger, he wanted to feed, but was prevented by the bridle; and when he wished to lie down, the saddle and its stirrups prevented him. The second and third day he was troubled in this way; and in the hope of finding relief, he went off in a particular direction. On the way he met with a river, which he crossed, though with great difficulty; but the bridle on his head, and the saddle on his back, got wet; and at noonday the sun's heat increasing, it became tightly bound around his waist, and he suffered greatly. Hunger also made inroads upon him, until he was no longer able to walk or stir. Just then a sharp-tusked hog came by him, and, taking him for an unexpected prey, ran his tusks into his side; then stopping, he remarked that it was a poor faint horse, consisting only of a few bones.

VERSE.

'With eating and drinking it had nothing to do; so hunger reduced it to skin and bones.'

Going nearer, the hog inquired the cause of his leanness; and the horse replied that it was occasioned by the hunger he suffered in consequence of his saddle and bridle. The hog then asked what was the cause of his present dangerous predicament, and of what nature was his fault or crime. The horse answered, 'I am not conscious of having committed any fault.' But the hog said, 'You certainly conceal some wrong you have committed, and are therefore reduced to despair of life; come and speak truly, for "safety is in sincerity," and you will be freed from the chains of misfortune.' So the horse, scenting the odor of compassion from the language of the hog, related to him all that had happened to him, and his own treachery. When the hog had learnt all about the horse, he said to him, 'You have been lying from head to foot; how can you say you are innocent? After receiving so many benefits from the hands of your master, you have made him a base return, and have met with this affliction as a punishment for your ingratitude. Had you returned to your master before it came upon you, you would have escaped this misery: but you persisted in your fault, and continued in your evil conduct; so that at length you have received the recompense of your evil deeds. What can I do to assist you? I had another design upon you; but since you have experienced so much sorrow, and suffered such adversity, as an act of charity I will free you, and give you your life.' So with his tusks he at once cut loose the horse's bridle and saddle; and the latter, being freed from his ties, with a light and swift foot fled away across the plain."

When Aiyin el Ehel heard this tale from the old woman he disclosed all his own history to her, acknowledged his faults, and with humility and submissiveness begged of her, saying, "O mother, the merciful hog, which was but an impure animal, had pity upon the horse, and freed him from his confinement. Is it proper then that you, who are gifted with human feelings, and are elevated in nature above that animal, should allow me to remain here in affliction? Leave me not here in confinement and sorrow, but be generous; free me from the gulf of misfortune into which I have fallen, and you will receive many favors in return for your goodness." To this the old woman replied, "Since you were tempted to sensuality by the seductions of Satan, and have acknowledged your fault while still but a youth; make yourself in every respect worthy of pardon and forgiveness, strengthen your good intentions, let the cord of request leave your hand, be constant in your patience and submission, and, please God, I will find the means of freeing you. 'Let loose the arrow of destiny; for it always reaches its target?'" When Aiyin el Ehel heard these benevolent words from the old woman, he said, "It is better for the imprudent to be silent, and leave others to remedy their errors;" and after that held his peace.

Now the vizir spoke these words to the patriarch, but so as to reach the ears of the person for whom they were intended; and again addressing the patriarch, he continued, "Let this story be finished here to-morrow night; we can then give a good and perfect conclusion to it." The patriarch considered the vizir's words as good; and the latter, rising from his seat, retired to his place of repose. The place where the preceding conversation had been held permitted Shaboor Shah to hear the words of his vizir. From the story he understood that it was a parable intended for himself; that Aiyin el Ehel meant Shaboor Shah; that Saidet en Nar (Nar signifies fire) was the kingdom of Persia, to whose inhabitants he alluded on account of their being fire-worshipers; by Saidet ez Zeheb was meant the country of Room; Zaib, Saidet ez Zeheb's husband, was the Kaiser; Aiyin el Ehel's desire for Saidet ez Zeheb was his own desire to visit and see Room. In the old woman with the hands cut off he recognised himself, powerless and tormented; and the whole story meant that he should be patient, and his vizir would without fail endeavor to bring about his deliverance. Shaboor listened, and was somewhat consoled by his remarks. When night came on again, and with it the time for the fulfilment of his promise, the patriarch begged the vizir to conclude his story. The latter recommenced and said,

"Aiyin el Ehel was for some time in despair. When each night the old woman lighting her lamps would tell him to have a little more patience, he repeated to her the Arabic proverb: "He knows not the sorrows of a prisoner who has himself never suffered confinement;" and said, "It is not easy, O mother, to have patience; if you have any means of releasing me, pray let me know it." To this the old creature replied, "How headstrong you are! Where is your prudence? Is this manly courage? If you are a prey to the ravages of time, be patient.

VERSES.

'Patience is bitter, but bears sweet fruits; though you are subject now to the sorrows of time, be not hopeless of better fortune.'

'There are many locks without keys; the Opener comes, sees, and forthwith opens them.'

To console you," continued she, "I have composed a story to suit your case." Aiyin el Ehel prayed her to relate it; whereupon she commenced as follows:

"Once in times past there was a merchant of wealth and generosity, who had a talented daughter pure as a Peree. The garden of his existence had produced no other fruit than her. One of his friends brought her a heart-seducing beautiful gazelle. The merchant's daughter, having no worldly troubles, loved this gazelle to such a degree that she was never without it for a moment. She had a collar made for it richly worked in gold; and for its support she kept a fat cow. As the gazelle daily grew in stature, two little horns made their appearance on its head, at which the merchant's daughter was greatly astonished, as if she expected to see it next take the colors of the chameleon. One day the girl inquired of her companions the cause of the two horns which had appeared on her gazelle. They told her that similar one's grew on the male of this same species of gazelle, and attained to a greater length than any other of its members. The girl forthwith repeated this to her father, and begged him to procure a gazelle for her, of good size and full-grown horns. The parent ordered his huntsmen to catch such a one; and when they had done so, it was brought to his daughter. The girl saw that each of its horns was more than a cubit long, and that branches grew out of them here and there; its eyes were black as *kohel*, and its form was perfect. The fair young girl adorned it with rich and costly ornaments, and provided for it whatever it could possibly want. The small gazelle and the larger one being kept together, they soon showed a liking for each other; and one day the former addressing the latter said, 'Before I saw you, I thought there was nothing existing with my form.' To which the large one replied, 'Away on the plains there are an infinite number of animals like us, increasing and multiplying in countless numbers.' The young gazelle, in accordance with its nature, desired to see those of its own species, and asked the elder one to conduct it and show it the world. It so anxiously pressed its request, that the latter replied, 'You should know the value of the food which you find ready prepared for you; pray, therefore, forego your desire to visit the distant mountains and plains, where every path is beset with danger, lest you repent of it when too late.' But the younger animal persisted with such urgency, that the other at length yielded, and they both arose and set out for the wild plains. The young gazelle was delighted with its travels, and associated awhile with those possessed of the two horns; until one day it happened to get separated from the flock, when it wildly ran about on the plains. Meeting with a gully produced by a torrent, it fell into it, and notwithstanding all its endeavors was unable to get out itself, for the gully was very deep. So it had to remain there, and begged of the larger gazelle to deliver it from this dilemma; which the latter was unable to affect, and could only cry and lament its lot.

"In the mean time the merchant's daughter was heart-broken for the escape of her favorites; and the merchant, pained at the sight of his child's distress, urged the huntsmen, with many gifts, to go in search of the lost gazelles. He sent several of his own servants with orders to find them and bring them back. They searched for some time, and at length perceived at a distance a man driving a gazelle before him. They went towards him, and then observed that a huntsman had taken a large gazelle, and having bound its feet, was about to cut its throat with his knife. Looking attentively they perceived that it was the largest of the two gazelles of which they were in search; so taking it out of his hands, they asked where were its ornaments. He replied, 'Here they are.' 'How did you take it?' added they. He replied, 'I had prepared my nets, and was watching them, when this one and a doe were the first to come near; the former was caught in my net, but the latter fled away over the plain.' The merchant on hearing this, said, that if he could catch it also, he would give him the dress which he held in his hands. So the hunter, making every endeavor to succeed, got on the track of the doe, heard its voice, and finally, upon coming up to it, perceived that it was the merchant's. It was in a narrow ravine; so hastening on, he caught it and conveyed it to the merchant, who recompensed him properly, and returned to his own mansion with both the gazelles. There finding his daughter still in great grief, he put the animals into their accustomed place. But the doe showed an aversion for the large one, and would not associate with it, avoiding it whenever it came near. Many means were employed to overcome its dislike, but without effect; until, one day, when by chance the doe was asleep, the other gazelle drew near and gently accosting it, reproached it for the groundless aversion it had manifested. The doe replied, 'And are you not that unfaithful and perfidious creature who in time of pleasure was my devoted friend, but who, when I was a prey to misfortune, did not come to my assistance, but thought only of your own gratification and enjoyment?' To this the other replied. 'O light of my eyes, refrain from such words, I myself was a prey to misfortune in the hands of the huntsman; otherwise I would never have forgotten the rights of companionship. From this the doe knew that her companion had been caught like herself; she therefore changed her ferocity into familiarity, and they ever after remained as good friends as before."

Aiyin el Ehel, having listened to the old woman's tale, learnt from it that she was unable to bring about his deliverance, and refrained from asking her any more questions.

STANZA.

"Every discourse has its time, and every deed its hour."

It is narrated that when the wise and pleasant-spoken vizir had reached this point, he became silent and excused himself, saying, "Pray, pardon me; for Inshallah! the work of the past night yet remains undone." The intelligent patriarch replied, "O man of pure faith, do not ask to be excused; pray amuse us with your comfort-increasing discourse, and apply a remedy for my afflicted heart with your truthful speech." So the vizir, again commencing, said,

Now Aiyin el Ehel, in his sorrowful night, drew his torch toward the aurora; and early the next morning the merciless Zaib beat the unfortunate prisoner with severe blows, and frightened him by adding that he would soon kill him. So he lost all hope of life, and increased his lamentations. Again night came on; and the old woman not arriving as usual, the prisoner became yet more alarmed. At midnight she came; and he addressed her, saying, "O loving mother, what is the cause of your delay?" She replied, "O young man of broken spirit, the observation which you made last night, censuring me with the remark, 'No one knows the sorrow of one who is in confinement,' has touched me; and were I to tell you all the contempt which I have experienced, and all the afflictions I have gone through, you would forget yours, and no more reproach me.' Aiyin el Ehel replied, "Up to the present time shame has withheld me from asking you any questions; but now I beg you to tell me a little of your history." So the old woman related as follows:

"O youth, I was once the favored wife of one of the favorites of a sovereign, by whom I had several children. One day that sovereign, who was a tyrant, becoming displeased with my husband, put him and my sons to death, and sold me and my daughters in the public market. It happened that my present tyrannical owner bought me, and brought me to this place, where I became reduced to feebleness by his exactions and the never-ending work which he gave me to perform. I bore with this treatment for seven years, until I could support it no longer, and ran away. He found me again and cut off my nose. I served seven years more, with the same sorrows, and fled away again. Again he recovered me, and then put out one eye and cut off my hands. I served him yet seven years, and once more fled. He found me out again, and this time cut off my ears. I now am tired of life; and have determined this night to free you from the tyrant's prison. I know that he will not suffer me to live; but death to me will now be a comfort!" She in fact forthwith cast off Aiyin el Ehel's chains, and said to him, "Now go, your way is open." She then took a khonjar and placed it in his hand; but he caught her arm, and addressed her, saying, "It is not proper that you should die at my hands; come and be free with me. If death be in this path, let us meet God's decree together." The old woman replied, "I am now feeble and aged, and not favored with sight." The youth answered, "Allah is benevolent; pray make haste. When you can go no further, I will take you on my back; and I am strong." The old woman said, "Since you offer me so much aid, I yet hope, that with your encouragement, I may not be an impediment to your escape. But tarry not; let us depart." In a short time they reached Aiyin el Ehel's dwelling, where he showed the old woman many marks of respect, treated her as his mother, and recompensed her richly.

Here the vizir ended his story, the afflicted Shaboor having heard all he had related. He also understood from the fable which it contained, that by the doe he meant Shaboor; by the excursion of the doe and the gazelle over the plains, Shaboor's amusement with his vizir; by the captivity of the doe, Shaboor's imprisonment by the Kaiser; and by the disgust of the doe for the gazelle, Shaboor's want of faith in his vizir. When he heard the vizir speak of the project to release Aiyin el Ehel, namely, that if he was unable to walk he would carry him, his hopes and resolution were strengthened. In fine, the night of the enterprize to free Shaboor had come. The wise vizir by some means got into the patriarch's kitchen, and put an inebriating drug into the food there preparing. At night the patriarch as usual went to his supper, and the vizir retired to his own tent. An hour afterwards the patriarch and all his attendants were sunk in a profound stupor; when the vizir saying, "Now is the moment of action," arose, went to the tent in which Shaboor was confined, opened the door of his prison, knocked off his chains, took him out, and stealthily left the Kaiser's camp. They approached the foot of the citadel, and cried out to the watchmen on the walls, that their Shah Shaboor was free. Immediately cords were let down, and they were drawn up into the castle, where, though the soldiers were weakened with the long siege, the sight of their sovereign gave them new heart and strength. The vizir addressing them said, "The Kaiser is now negligent, supposing you too weak to fight. He is filled with pride, his troops are all drunk and overcome with sleep; come, let us sally forth and surprise them." The proposition being approved of, Shaboor's soldiers marched against the Kaiser's camp, routed his troops, and captured all they possessed. They took the Kaiser prisoner and brought him before Shaboor, who went out to meet him, paid him great respect and honor, treated him kindly, and addressed him thus, "In the time of your power you did not put me to death; therefore, now it is my turn, you shall meet with no harm from me. For it is said,

PERSIAN VERSES.

'Whenever your enemy falls into your hands, treat him not with severity; the punishment of his own feelings is sufficient.'

In thankfulness to Him who from his great kindness, whilst I was a captive, gave me power to overcome you, I will let you go free. I will not recompense you with cruelty; but, I demand of you, that you restore peace among those of my provinces where you have excited rebellion; that you rebuild such of my walls as you have destroyed; that you plant trees in the place of all those you have cut down, and cultivate their growth; and moreover that you free all the prisoners you have taken, and send them back to me." The Kaiser agreed to all these demands, and became responsible for their due accomplishment. Shaboor then made a great feast for him, and they spent many days in amusement and in pleasure, after which the Kaiser set out for his own kingdom. To the day of his death he was tributary to Shaboor; and they ever afterwards observed the laws of friendship towards each other.

THE STORY OF NAAM BINTI TEVFIK AND NUMAN BIN REBIEH BIN JABER.

In the times of the kings of the family of the Beni Ommieh, there resided in the city of Cufah a very respectable merchant, named Rebieh bin Jâber, a man possessed of excellent feelings and kindness of heart. He had a son who was also of a good natural disposition; and as the close of the father's life was drawing near, all his hopes and desires became centred in this his only child. He named the boy Numan, paid great care and attention to his education, and taught the fair youth to read and write; so that he soon became possessed of the accomplishments of pleasure and knowledge. He purchased a maiden slave, of angelic features and uncommon beauty, in short every way worthy to be the companion of his son; and her name was Naam binti Tevfik. The master who instructed them did all he could to teach that *reshki hoor*, (object of jealousy of the Hoories of paradise,) who was a tender maiden, such as the eye of the world had never beheld, nor the ear of the son of man heard of. Together they learnt to read and write, and in the course of time had acquired all the information necessary for them; and when they arrived at the years of maturity, both, like the sun and moon, in pure brilliancy and light, were equal in knowledge and accomplishments, particularly in the talent of music and song. In the garden of beauty they were like two cedars.

VERSE.

"If ever there was one being unique in the world,
A second like which sure never was seen,
It was she, it was she.
Whenever that woman made melody,
Those who heard her became lost in love."

Their wealthy parent had erected for them a palace, like that of *Aram Zat ul Amad*, or the gardens of Paradise, which he had painted beautifully, and richly furnished, and where his son and his cedar-shaped Naam were sent to spend their evenings in pleasure and enjoyment.

One night when he was disposed to make merry with his slave, she took a lute in her hand, and with a sweet expression of countenance sang a harmonious air. Whilst they were thus engaged, by chance the governor of the city of Cufah, the cause of much sorrow, Hedjadj ez Zalim, or "the Cruel," passed by the house. Hearing the melodious sound of the sweet creature's voice, he sighed involuntarily; and after listening for some time, he praised her eloquent tongue, and the taste with which she played upon the instrument, adding, "If this slave's face and person are equal to the delicacy of her voice, I will give whatever may be demanded for so priceless a jewel. Go see," said he, "and bring me news whose she is; for as there cannot possibly be found any thing better, I will buy her for a present to the caliph." So calling the chief of the city police, and confiding the accomplishment of the affair to him, a master of intrigue, he recommended him to be diligent and expeditious. This man next morning very early called to his aid a cunning old woman, and said to her, "Help, O mother of praise-worthy conduct, Hedjadj the cruel and unmerciful has need of you: you must inform me to whom this girl belongs, how we shall be able to obtain possession of her, what arrangement must be made to bring it about, and what promises will deceive her." The artful old woman made reply, "On my head and eyes be it! if the object of your desires be in the skies among the Pleades, under the earth, or on the face of the earth, I will make it my duty to find her; and so you may consider her as already in your service."

VERSE.

"She was the sorceress of the day, that artful old wretch; she was expert in all ways of deceit, and could vex even Harut;* she was a fox for cunning, and could teach that animal tricks."

The officer conducted the old woman to Hedjadj the Cruel; and when she was introduced to him, Hedjadj said, "Go to the dwelling of Numan bin Rebieh; and if you find that slave worthy of being presented to the caliph, do whatever may seem best to you, and render yourself worthy of my liberality." Then that old wretch attired herself in the habit of a *Sofy* a hundred years old. Taking in her hand an iron-shod ebony stick, she put a shawl on her head; and seated upon her ass, bending it almost double with her weight, and making that unfortunate one weep to God, she sat out on her way, saying in a loud voice, "Allah is one God, O inattentive people!" and thus reached Numan bin Rebieh's dwelling. The simple-minded people who met her on her way embraced her hands and feet, and implored her prayers.

At noon she reached Numan's dwelling, but, on wishing to enter it, was prevented by the door-keepers. The old witch said to them, "I am a servant of God, who have deserted the world, and have no other desire than to acquire knowledge and offer devotion; what then will it profit you to prevent my entrance?" Whilst they were engaged in discussing her request, a servant from within made his appearance, and the old woman addressed him, saying, "Wherever I bend my steps they bring good fortune; and as every one profits by my prayers, is it proper for

* An angel condemned to eternal punishment.

these door-keepers to obstruct my entrance?" The simple-minded servant said to the door-keepers, "Disturb her not, let her come in;" and placing himself before the old woman, he conducted her to Naam, Numan's comfort, with whom he left her, thinking thereby to merit her prayers. Naam, being likewise deceived by the woman's appearance, showed her every mark of respect and honor, and invited her to be seated, that she might enjoy her conversation. The old woman was scarcely seated before she exclaimed, "Let prayer-time not be forgotten; show me a retired place where I may perform my devotions." Naam, like the waving cypress, hastened to serve her, and spread her carpet in a retired place with her own hands. The old woman prolonged her prayers from noon to *ikindee*, and from then till nightfall, without once rising from her carpet. Thus, by her great show of piety, she gained not only Naam's heart, but also the hearts of her attendants, who all knelt around her and implored her blessing. Every night the old wretch told Naam's maidens stories about pious people; until early one morning she arose, and asked permission to depart. When Naam asked her where she was going, she answered that she wished to visit some holy persons who resided in the vicinity; and she so praised them, that Naam begged to be allowed the privilege of accompanying her. "Let me change my dress," said she; "and I will go with you, to benefit by the prayers of the good people." The old woman said, "If the recompense of your holy visit is written on your forehead, it will be easy; be not grieved, you will in due time meet with the full accomplishment of your wishes." So they disguised themselves, left the house, and departed on their way. The unfortunate girl put faith in the old woman's words; and soon they reached a door-way, the portal to the palace of Hedjadj ez Zalim, which they entered. Then putting Naam in a vestibule, "Remain here," said she, "whilst I go and see whether the holy man is alone." So, going in, she informed Hedjadj of her success; and then the accursed creature departed by another door. Hedjadj came to the vestibule; and beholding the beauteous girl, he saw that she was a most graceful creature, resplendent as the moon in her fourteenth day, illuminating the whole vestibule with her splendor.

VERSE.

"A pure maiden unequalled,
With the world a slave to her ringlets,
She is a fresh rose from the garden of fidelity,
And a thousand philomels are her lovers."

Forthwith he ordered his steward to take a sufficient number of soldiers, and conduct the maiden to the caliph. The officer immediately got ready a litter, and, putting the unfortunate and wretched Naam into it, set out for Damascus. Poor Naam now knew something of the cruel misfortune to which she had become a prey; her suffering heart was tortured with anxiety, and her eyes wept tears of blood, at being separated from her lover and home. In thirty or forty days they reached Damascus, and entered the palace of the caliph, when the steward presented Hedjadj's letter, and delivered up the maiden. Now when Abd el Malek saw the maiden's heart-ornamenting and world-embellishing dove-like loveliness, he acknowledged her to be a perfect beauty, whom the Painter of creation had drawn on the page of existence, such as the eye of observation had never seen, and of which the ear of imagination had never heard.

VERSE.

"She was well made, graceful, delicate, and fresh,
From head to foot ornament and splendor:
Limpid water never reached the clearness of her lips,
No cord could encircle her delicate waist;
Her teeth in brightness could make the stars envious,
Her smiles are profiles in the eye of the soul;
Rose-buds open when she smiles,
Jewels are scattered about when she speaks."

Involuntarily the caliph became lost in love for the beautiful creature, and the thread of control (over himself) escaped from his hand, so that he became enamored to the core of his heart. He approached the maiden, and conducted her into the interior of his harem, where he ordered the attendants to prepare for her apartments worthy of her beauty, treat her kindly, and be attentive to all her wants.

The caliph, in his glee and satisfaction, said to his sister Abbassah, a lady whose beauty was incomparable and whose mind was world-captivating, "O lady of ladies, Hedjadj has done me a service such as could not have been equalled, for the pleasure it gives me, had he sent me news that he had subdued to my sway a whole province. His present is one truly worthy of acceptance." Abbassah replied, "May your pleasure be everlasting; what kind of present is it that he has made you?" The caliph gave Hedjadj's letter to his sister, wherein he stated he had bought for twelve thousand pieces of gold and sent to him a maiden worthy of his honorable acceptance. His sister then said, "With your permission I will go and see her, and gain her good will and friendship." The caliph went abroad; and his sister went to Naam, where she saw an angel indeed in human form. "May Allah aid you," said she; and asked after her health.

VERSE.

"'With so much beauty are you a moon from the skies;
Or a new species of humanity, as yet unseen?'

Truly if one gives his heart to so precious a jewel as you, you merit it; one look of yours is worth twelve thousand pieces of gold, and most cheap at such a price. It was the good luck of my brother, the caliph, that sent you to him."

Now Abbassah's beauty was celebrated all over that country; but when it was brought into comparison with the union of Naam's charms, the moon appeared eclipsed. That lady of ladies inquired after her health, adding, "Your head was fortunate indeed that you should become the companion of so great a sovereign." But poor Naam only uttered a sigh, and addressing Abbassah, asked her, saying, "O fair of front, inform this thy hand-maiden who sold me, and for whom was I taken; to whom does this abode belong? tell me, I beseech you, in the name of your own beauteous person, the cause and source of my affliction." Abbassah was greatly astonished at this interrogation, and asked what it meant. "Do you not know who sold you, that it was Hedjadj, governor of Cufah, who bought you for twelve thousand pieces of gold, and sent you to the caliph; that this is the palace of the caliph; and that I am the caliph's sister?" When Naam heard these words she burst into tears and wept bitterly, so as to wound the heart and liver of Abbassah.

VERSE.

"The fountain of her source overflowed;
Her liver was branded like tulips,
And her tears fell like morning dew."

Abbassah was a woman of intelligence, and she perceived that there must be some secret connected with Numan; so, after some words of consolation, she arose and went to the caliph, and said to him, "O Emir of the faithful, a few days repose must be given her; delay awhile before you go near the maiden, until she becomes familiar with the other slaves. She is now in low spirits; leave her to herself." The caliph seemed displeased, and said, "Pray let a physician be summoned to the maiden." Abbassah answered, "On my head and eyes be it; let us see." So she began to ask every where for a physician. But let us leave Naam and her unfortunate condition, and return to the unhappy Numan.

When Numan had the misfortune to be separated from his mistress, and found that his faithful girl and beloved one did not return that night to his dwelling, his heart beat and his eyes wept as he bewailed her absence; and his aggrieved father lamented with his son the loss of his mistress. The rose-cheek of Numan's beauty faded like autumn leaves; and the afflicted parent, with the hope of obtaining relief for his son's complaint, sought a physician. If divine wisdom guide the humble servant, the desire of the afflicted will be accomplished, and the object of his hopes be attained. Thus whilst the distressed father, Rebieh bin Jaber, was seated overwhelmed with grief, suddenly a voice reached his ear, saying, "Let him appear who needs an expert physician, an able astrologer, versed in geomancy and the other hidden sciences." This was a man who, according to the custom of the country, proclaimed his calling in the public street. Rebieh at once ordered his servants to bring in the man; the servants did as they were bid, and conducted the physician before their master, who showed him more than common attention, and begged of him a remedy to soothe the affliction of his son. When the expert physician had felt Numan's pulse, he knew that no medicine was needed, and said to the parent, "Your son has not an atom of disease; but I perceive he is feverish from the passion of love." Hereupon the father related the whole circumstance of his son's condition, and added, "Tell me, is my son's mistress dead; or if she is alive on this earth, to whose skirts has she become a prisoner, and is there any means by which she can be freed from this affliction?"

Now the physician was an adept in the science of geomancy. So taking some sand in his hand, he scattered and divided it, looked at its meaning, and twice bent his head; he once more threw the sand, again spread it, and perceived that she was in Syria. He then answered the father, saying, "Good news to you! for the close of this trial is united with luck, although it bears heavily upon you. After your maiden left you, she did not pass the night in this city, but departed from it." The old man answered, "Since you are sure she is in Syria, throw once more, that we may know in whose house she is, and who holds her in confinement. The physician did as he was requested, and threw the sand again. On examining it he smilingly said, "Good news, good news! your maiden has been sent by the governor of this country to the city of Damascus, and is now in the palace of the caliph. With divine permission we will loosen this knot." The old man was greatly rejoiced at this news, and gave the physician large and valuable presents, assuring him that all he possessed was at his service, if he would only find a remedy for his son's affliction. The physician replied, "You must provide whatever is essential for the journey; we will proceed directly to Damascus, where we will see what God will show us." The father gave the physician a thousand pieces of gold, then got ready a number of horses, and set out for Syria. After some days they reached the city of Damascus; and taking lodgings in the centre of the city they opened a shop, which they stocked with jars from Kishan for drugs and liquids. For some days they treated the sick who visited them for their complaints with suitable remedies; and soon the name of the physician became celebrated throughout the city. Poor Numan, with the hope of finding relief from his grief, sat opposite the physician, consuming away like a taper and wholly submissive to his orders.

One day, unexpectedly, a female slave of the caliph's palace gave information to Abbassah that an expert physician from Irak had visited their city, who cured the afflictions of all who applied to him, and prescribed remedies for every manner of disease. So Abbassah ordered her to describe to the physician poor Naam's condition. "Let us see," added she, "what he will do for her." One of the harem attendants named Cahrmanah proceeded to the physician's shop and said to him, "I am a servant of the inner palace of the caliph. One of his most favored maidens is in ill health; and if you can provide a remedy for her, you will be fortunate, and worthy of great favor and recompense." The physician replied, "On my head and eyes be it." After questioning Cahrmanah, he assured her that the maiden had no natural disease; "but," said he, "tell me her name." "Stranger," answered Cahrmanah, "are you a giver of medicine to the sick, or a seller of girls?" The physician replied, "Pardon me; the reason why I asked the name of the sick person is, that I may ascertain its number, write some holy appropriate names on her star, and then undertake the necessary remedies." Cahrmanah exclaimed, "May God bless you! your knowledge has been manifested in every science; the maiden's name is Naam, and her father's Tevfik." At this the physician said, "Inshallah, if God pleases, his assistance (*tevfik*) will aid us."

When poor Numan heard this conversation, scalding tears fell from his eyes, and involuntarily he uttered a plaintive moan. The physician spoke to him in his own tongue, and said, "*Fash makun, hamush bash* (divulge not, and be silent); rise, and hand me that vase of medicine." Numan obeyed; and after the physician had wrapped a piece of *majum* (electuary) in a paper and poured some liquid into a jar, he told Numan to tie up its mouth tightly with paper, and write with his own hand this direction, "Mix every morning a little of the liquid with water, and drink it." This Numan did as directed, and then delivered the jar and paper to Cahrmanah.

When Naam saw her lover's handwriting, she immediately sprang to her feet; and having hastily mixed and drunk the sherbet, she said to Cahrmanah, "Your goodness has been recompensed: my heart finds great relief from this medicine; and if my complaint can be relieved, it will be by means of this. What kind of a man is this physician?" continued she to Cahrmanah. The latter replied, "He is just arrived from Cufah, and is a man of extraordinary talents.

VERSE.

To discover dispositions and natures
He knows every kind of science.

He has in his employ a youth;" and as she went on to describe his beautiful form and dress, Naam's eyes filled with tears, and she understood that without doubt it was her lover.

Whilst they were thus engaged in conversation, the caliph

came to pay the maiden a visit; and Cahrmanah said to him, "O Prince of the faithful, an expert physician has come to our city; from him I obtained some medicines which have been most beneficial to her." On hearing this, the caliph was greatly rejoiced, and putting into a purse five hundred pieces of silver he gave it to Naam, and bade her send a portion of it to the physician who had benefited her. "His labor is not lost," continued the caliph; "only let him be diligent and attentive." Naam took one hundred of the pieces and gave them to Cahrmanah. She put the remainder into a purse, with a scrap of paper, on which she wrote with her own hand, "The greeting of Naam, who is separated from her beloved friend, her country, and her home." Then sealing it up she delivered it to Cahrmanah, who conveyed it to the expert physician, saying, "Thanks and blessings upon you; for, Inshallah, your remedies have proved beneficial to our sick one, and she has regained her color and strength. Her heart is rejoiced, and she has sent you this purse." The physician gave the purse over to Numan, who opened it; and when he perceived the maiden's handwriting his senses left him, and his cypress form, like a shadow, strewed the ground. The physician threw rose-scented water in his face; whereupon his senses slowly returned, and tears flowed from his eyes. When Cahrmanah beheld this, her heart was touched; she wept, and much grieved thus addressed Numan, "O part of my liver, may they never smile who make you weep; what, pray, can be the cause of your tears?

VERSE.

O joy of the heart and light of the eyes,
The envy of Perees and jealousy of Hoorees,
This must be a strange condition for you,
This is no common sorrow; for
On the mirror of your heart is the dust of grief,
And it seems there is a sorrow in your breast."

Numan replied, "I have found you more piteous and tender than my parents. I am the unhappy being whose companion Hedjadj ez

Zalim, governor of Cufah, by means of a deceitful old woman, enticed away and sent off to the caliph. This is the grief which has separated me from my home and country, and sent me into a sorrowful exile." On hearing this Cahrmanah involuntarily shed tears, and said, "Your words are true, the affliction of that beautiful creature is caused wholly by her separation from you."

The physician then offered the purse to Cahrmanah, saying, "I have no need of money or gain; but I implore you by my gray hairs to favor our cause, disclose not our secret, and if in this affair you do us a service you will be remembered until death in our prayers." He moreover presented to Cahrmanah, for her attentions, the humble gift of five thousand pieces of gold. Cahrmanah promised to peril even her life in their cause, and to bring the two lovers together.

VERSE.

"No one should eat sorrow, for God will give aid;
Perhaps a remedy may be found for each ill.
I will aid you as long as I live,
And weep until I see you smile."

So taking with her some medicines, she went to Naam; and when she began to converse with Naam on the subject of her history, she soon found verified all that Numan had said. Naam wept and said, "My fate under God's providence is in your hands, and my prayer is that you will conceal our secret." Cahrmanah asked, "Do you not desire to see your lover, that unhappy one who has been captivated by your locks?" Naam replied, "Do you ask the sick if he wish for health? Let me once more behold his beauteous form, and I can die content." Cahrmanah then said, "Arise, and bring me a suit of clothes." Naam did as she was desired; and Cahrmanah, taking the garments in her hand, proceeded to the dwelling of the physician. When she asked Numan if he desired to see the maiden again, he answered, "Yes, be it only to look and die." "Arise then," said Cahrmanah, "dress yourself in that female attire, and let us be gone; the All-just alone has power to accomplish your desires." She then dressed Numan in a woman's guise, saying, "Now offer up prayers for success." Taking leave of the physician they departed and went to the entrance of the palace. The eunuch stationed there asked who her companion was, adding, that he could not permit her to enter. Cahrmanah replied that she was the sister of Naam, the new favorite of the caliph; and so he suffered them to pass. When they had come to the gate of the inner court of the Harem, Cahrmanah said, "I cannot pass beyond this, and will await you here. This passage has two sides, each of which has ten rooms; take the right hand, count the rooms as you pass, and remember that the ninth is Naam's, whilst the tenth is that of the caliph's sister Abbassah. Do not mistake, but enter the ninth room; and after seeing your mistress, return to this spot." Numan passed on, counting the apartments as he went; but terror and embarrassment caused him to miss a number, and he entered that of Abbassah. In it stood a rich throne-like sofa, and the sides of the room were ornamented with brocade and silk. It was empty; and the unfortunate Numan, almost lifeless with fear, threw himself on the sofa, supposing it to be the apartment of Naam.

Presently a stately and noble person, like the world-adorning Phœbus entered the apartment, and beheld seated there a woman who from fright did not rise to her feet. Abbassah (for it was she) exclaimed, "What foolish woman are you, who without permission thus enter my apartment?" Then acting on her Hashemite generosity of character she added, "What kind of person are you? let us know." Poor Numan threw himself at Abbassah's feet, and rubbed his face and eyes upon them in humility. Abbassah, on beholding this, was touched with pity, and said, "Be not afflicted, you are in a place of safety." She then uncovered Numan's face and breast, and seeing he was a man, exclaimed in a tone of pity, "Unhappy man, what secret cause has reduced you to this disguise: what misfortune has befallen you? speak with candor and let me know the truth, for safety is in sincerity. Who you are and where your home is, is known from your disguise?" Numan replied, "I am a wretched man ever in trouble and sorrow; I have seen much affliction; my heart is grieved and my spirit groans."

Numan's tears flowed from his eyes as he related all his history, with the eloquence of natural feeling, until Abbassah's also fell upon her angelic mirror-like bosom, and she exclaimed, "O Numan, you are now in a place of safety; be happy." She clapped her hands together and called her maidens; and when they were come, "Hasten," said she, to one of them, "prepare me a seat;" and to another, "Go, convey my salutations to sweet Naam, and invite her to come alone and see me." The maiden departed, and did as she was directed; and Naam, replying, "On my head and eyes be it," arose, and came to Abbassah's apartment.

Abbassah having told her maidens to make place for her, led Naam into the apartment, where, as soon as Numan beheld her, these true faithful lovers rushed into each other's arms, and fell senseless on the floor. Abbassah threw rose-water into their faces, and recalled them to their senses; and they both cast themselves at her feet, offering up many prayers for her benevolence. The maidens who attended upon Abbassah were greatly rejoiced for their companion's sake; they took their instruments and played a joyous air, accompanying themselves with their voices; even Naam forgot her past sorrows, and taking a lute in her hand, sang an air appropriate to the occasion of her reunion with her lover.

During this display of delight, lo! the caliph himself unexpectedly came to visit his new maiden; and hearing the sound of music and song, he approached on light steps his sister's door, saying, "Barik Allah! what sweet voices are these?" When Abbassah became aware of his approach, she threw a shawl over Numan's head and advanced to meet her brother. The latter, as soon as he was seated, said to her, "Whatever your pastime may have been, pray continue it, and let us be a partaker of your joys." So Abbassah immediately handed her brother three cups, brim full cf ruby liquid, which he drank; and after it had given him pleasure, she addressed him thus, "O Emir of the faithful, this is our story: In past times there was once an old man who had a heart-binding son, who was brought up with great delicacy; and for him he had purchased a maid, who studied with his son, was his constant companion, and who, in fine, for knowledge and accomplishments became the wonder of the world. One night as these two were amusing themselves, the governor of the city in which they lived, an unjust and tyrannical man, happened to be making his rounds, and passed by their dwelling, where he heard the sweet voice of the maiden. On the following day, by means of an astute and intrigueing woman, he deceived the maiden, got her into his power, and sent her to the sovereign of the age as a present. The youthful owner of the maiden became greatly distressed on being separated from his beloved mistress, and devoted his life to seeking her out. By some means he obtained admittance into the palace where she was confined, and there they met. In the midst of their rejoicings, and the mutual recital of the sufferings they had experienced during their separation, the sovereign himself suddenly entered the room; and on beholding them he, without delay or asking any questions, drew his sword and put them both to death on the spot. This is all we can expect of an ignorant sovereign who never inquires into the merits of an affair; but what do you think he should have done?" The caliph replied, "What a strange and ignorant fellow he must have been; the two unfortunate persons were excusable, he should therefore have learnt their story, aided the accomplishment of their desires, and prevented tyranny. But he was of a bad nature and an ignorant man."

Abbassah then exclaimed, "O Emir el Mumeneen, generosity and benevolence are an inheritance of the tribe of Koraish. Tell me; should such a circumstance occur in your reign and under your empire, by the souls of your noble forefathers, what would you do?" The caliph replied, "I swear that were I convinced that the condition of the individuals was such as you describe, I would bestow many gifts upon them, send them back to their country, and punish the governor who, whilst it was his duty to prevent injustice to Mussulmans, did the reverse."

Abbassah thanked and blessed the caliph, kissed his hand, and said, "May the shadow of your justice and penetration never pass by the innocent." Then suddenly throwing off the shawl from over Numan, "Behold," said she, "O Prince of the faithful, the afflicted youth, the subject of my tale; and this is the maiden who was so cruelly separated from her lover. Hedjadj ez Zalim treated them as I described; and is it proper that he should endeavor with a lie to cause your noble self to commit sin? power is in your own royal hands."

The caliph, overcome with surprise and emotion, suddenly arose, and taking the maiden from Abbassah's hands gave her up to Numan, dressed him in a robe of honor, and placed him in the rank of his military officers. He dismissed Hedjadj ez Zalim from his government, and appointed the physician in his place; and after learning from him his true condition, said, "Blessed be God; how dear must truth be to you, seeing that you chose to incur difficulty and danger for its sake." He also questioned Cahrmanah; and finding her faithful and true, he bestowed on her one thousand dirhems. Under the shadow of the caliph's favor she never knew adversity, and the pity which she had felt for the two lovers was converted into joy. As for Hedjadj, on being dismissed from his office he soon sank into poverty and wretchedness.

CHAPTER TWENTIETH.

On the subject of those who are perfect in the talent of epistolary correspondence, and excel in good breeding.

It is related that one of the Arab kings, a prince of humble extraction, named Melek ibin Mehleb, appointed the celebrated and brave Emir Hedjadj ez Zalim his general in chief, and sent him against the tribe of the Khavaridj. The benevolent Emir subdued that evil band, killed the greater part of them, and captured their wives and children. He also took an incalculable amount of booty, to inform himself respecting which the Melek sent him a messenger of much eloquence. This person having arrived, Hedjadj inquired of him, "O brother Arab, how did you leave the Emir Melek ibin Mehleb?" To which the other replied, "I found him thus,—his friends in the greatest mirth possible, and his evil wishers overwhelmed with sorrow and grief." Hedjadj asked how he behaved toward the troops. The man answered that he was moderate in his disposition, and on very kind terms with their officers. Hedjadj then asked what was his affection and regard for the Rayahs; and the messenger answered, it was just like that of parents for their children. Hedjadj next inquired how he behaved in time of battle; and the messenger replied that he did not know either bodily pain or the sensation of fear. Hedjadj then said, "How does he conduct himself in seasons of relaxation?" The messenger replied, "The world in his eyes is less than a rose-leaf, and he values riches no more than the dust." Hedjadj again asked, "In short, what is the nature of his mind and capacity?" The man replied, "It is like a circle, of which the beginning and end are unknown, and whose head and feet are not to be found." Hedjadj praised the brevity of the ambassador's replies, and remarked that he was a magazine of secrets. Then addressing those who were with him, he said, "This man's sharp and subtle language has amazed me. He has raised roses in the garden of my heart, in favor of him who sent him; and his ready wit gives me a perfect idea of the modest and superior intelligence of Ibin Mehleb." He then expressed to the envoy his high opinion of him, and clothed him in a dress of honor besides presenting him many other gifts.

AN ANECDOTE OF ALEXANDER AND A PHILOSOPHER.

An account of a conversation between a philosopher of India and Alexander of the two horns, (Alexander the Great,) a monarch distinguished for his equity and justice, unrivalled for wisdom and intelligence, and a sovereign well versed in the knowledge of the true and practical Aristotle. This learned master was a disciple of the divine and equally learned Plato. It is related by him that Alexander's father Philip temporized with Darius, who at that same period was also a great sovereign, and, to prevent any dispute and war between them, annually sent Darius a thousand eggs of gold of a certain known weight, through which gifts he kept up a good understanding between them. When Philip quitted this life, his son Alexander ascended the throne. His mind and intelligence were perfect, and for knowledge and courage he was unique in his age, so much so that his renown daily increased, and spread over the whole world. As he did not send to Darius the tribute which the latter had received from his father, Darius sent him a messenger, demanding the cause of the delayed remittance. Alexander wrote to him in reply, that the hen which had laid the golden eggs was dead; but that her son who held her place, being deeply versed in the arts and sciences, would not fail, if Darius desired it, to present him in their stead with some jewels made of brilliant Damascus steel. When the messenger with this answer reached Darius, the fire of his rage becoming lighted, he exclaimed that it was necessary to teach Alexander his limits, and to punish him for his audacity; and with this view he marched a large army against him. Thus war was waged between them, which ended in the death of Darius. Alexander becoming victorious over his father's old enemy, no one remained to oppose him; so that he extended his empire and dominions over all the adjoining parts, and their inhabitants submitted to his sway.

When Alexander had concluded the war with Darius, and had conquered his kingdom, there was a great sovereign reigning in India, named Keebed, to whom Alexander addressed letters containing these demands, "Submit to me, and send me every year a fixed sum of money as tribute; by which means you will enjoy most perfect quiet and tranquillity. Be also ready to do this forthwith, so that I may point you out as an example to others."

Now when Alexander's letter reached Keebed, he read and comprehended its contents; for he was a wise and good sovereign. He well knew Alexander's power and worth; so he showed regard and consideration for his messenger, and to his missive replied: "The probability of our not submitting to the great ruler of the universe, or standing in opposition to him, is deferred." So he sent him some presents, such as were never before known to be collected together by any one sovereign. Among these was a most beautiful Peree-like maiden, the like of whom has never been seen since the sun of the world commenced his revolving course. Another was a philosopher of most remarkable wisdom, of an eager disposition and generosity of character; who, in consequence of the fineness of his mental structure knew the contents of another's mind before making any inquiries of him; and who could give correct explanations of another's thoughts. Another present was a most learned physician, who, for his power of preserving health and curing diseases, followed next to the Messiah. He was a most perfect master of the science of medicine; the remedies which he applied for the most difficult of diseases brought aid and relief to every ailment but that of fate; and the very dust of his feet was worthy of being a crown for the most learned sage. Another present was a cup, which remained ever filled. All the creatures on the face of the earth, perhaps even the army of Alexander, in fine all mankind and the Perees, might drink out of it without lessening its contents one drop. All these objects he offered to Alexander, as a mark of his respect, and sent them each in charge of one of his own attendants, over whom one was appointed as their chief. When the Indian Sultan's messengers reached Alexander, he gave them a flattering reception, and lodged them in a rich palace. On the following day they had the honor of delivering the presents to Alexander. He had assembled all his principal men, ministers, and committees of state in a great divan; and before these the Indian Sultan's messengers presented their gifts. The maiden was first offered; and all present, having once fixed their eyes upon her beautiful features, were unable to remove them to any other object. Even Alexander became greatly enamored of her; he appointed her to be over all his other maidens, and his whole household of girls became submissive to her.

Then that unique king ordered the erudite philosopher to be tried before being brought before him: he had him lodged in a high dwelling, where the trial was to take place. For this purpose he had a large cup filled to its brim with clarified oil, so full that not another drop could be put into it. This cup he had sent to the Indian philosopher, who, when he saw it, put a thousand needles into the oil, and returned it to Alexander. Alexander ordered the needles to be melted, run into the form of a globe, and returned to the philosopher, who changed the shape of the globe, and casting it into the form of a pure mirror, sent it back to the sovereign. Alexander next put the mirror in a plate of pure water, and sent it to the philosopher. The latter changed it into an unequalled bottle; and putting it into the dish filled with water, it floated on its surface. This he sent to Alexander, who emptied the bottle of its water, filled it up with earth, and returned it to the philosopher. The philosopher, on seeing it, changed color and wept; and, full of grief and despair, returned the bottle to Alexander just as he had received it.

On the following day Alexander assembled a great divan, and called together all his learned men. He also sent for the philosopher, who presented himself before the honored assembly. As he was approaching, Alexander fixed his eyes closely upon his form, and remarked that he was a man of tall stature, large frame, handsome countenance, and of large hands. He thought to himself, "This figure being inconsistent with science, his handsome form shows a character for perspicacity, ardor, and spirituality." As he revolved these thoughts in his mind, the philosopher observed him attentively, rubbed a ring against his cheek, and afterwards placed it against his nose; then with a quick step approaching Alexander, he offered him such compliments as are addressed to sovereigns. Alexander showed him great respect and attention; and bidding him be seated, they entered into conversation. He inquired of the philosopher what was the object of his rubbing the ring upon his cheek as he approached him, and afterwards placing it against his nose. To which the philosopher replied, "I observed that your majesty noted my personal appearance in a manner which seemed to say, 'They have sent me this man on account of his insinuating form, for it is rare to see knowledge combined with such fair proportions.' I, for this reason, and to verify the accuracy of your judgment, intimated by my gesture that I was truly one of a hundred, even as there is but one nose on a face.*

The Zul Karnain (possesser of the two horns or ruler of a period), greatly pleased with the philosopher's wise explanation, said, "I sent you a cup filled with pure oil; what was your idea in putting needles into it?" The philosopher answered, "You observed that I was so filled with divine sciences that there was no room for another atom; and I answered, that I judged you were both filled with my wisdom, and instigated by many excel-

* In Turkish the same word (*yooz*) means both "face" and "hundred."

lent examples, just as the needles found a place among the pure oil."

Alexander then asked, "When I sent you the same needles formed into a globe, what was your object in returning them to me shaped and polished like a mirror?" The philosopher replied, "You had said that the destruction of life and the shedding of blood had surrounded your heart with the rust of affliction, and there was no longer any thing left you besides the love of science. I answered that I would change your sensible character, through good and pleasant means; and that the bright mirror is to you, what an atom is to the sun."

Alexander next remarked, "I had put the globe under water; whilst you flattened it out and gave it a concave form. You then placed it on the same water, there turned it, and thus returned it to me. I poured out the water, filled the vessel with earth, and sent it back to you; and when you beheld this, not being able to do any thing more, you commenced weeping, and sent it back to me untouched. Pray what was the cause of your weeping?" The philosopher replied, "Your idea in putting the globe into the dish of water and sending it to me, was to show that the days of your life were drawing to a close, and that I understood how difficult it was in the days of ease to acquire many sciences. Now, great lord, let it be known to you that much may be done, by proper means, in these days of ease, and in a short space of time. This is seen by the globe, which, being put under the water, came to the surface, floated, and shone brightly there." Alexander spoke and said, "But what is the answer to the earth?" The philosopher replied, "Your object relative to the earth was evidently to show that the end of all things is death and corruption, and you asked whether there was any way to prevent it. But as I could propose no remedy, I wept involuntarily to think that every soul that places his foot on the temporary palace of this life must drink from the hand of destiny and pass away into the other world. Fortunate is the person who spends a few days with ease and comfort in the great house of this fleeting world; and whose good deeds are mentioned and his memory spoken of with pleasure after he is gone."

The great and powerful Alexander praised the philosopher, and would have given him innumerable presents; but he refused them all, excusing himself thus, "Were I in the least degree to seek after worldly goods, I should lose my possession of that divine knowledge which is a gift from above. Now having accomplished my duty to Alexander, I have but a word or two more to say." "Speak," replied Alexander. The philosopher continued, "O sovereign of the world! you are the master of the persons of all the dwellers in the habitable quarter of this globe, who have submitted to your rule. Now, do whatever is your will, but be careful that you are master of their hearts also; for that, you must know, is the possession in which true royal power and wealth consist." Alexander, in return for the philosopher's council and advice, made him sit on a silver throne at his side, strewed him over with pearls, and made him a thousand excuses for the poorness of the gift. May the Most High have mercy upon him!

STORY OF THE FAITHLESS KEPEUK KHAN, WHO WISHED TO DEBASE RELIGION AND ISLAMISM; AND OF THE VICTORY SUSTAINED BY THE TRUE FAITH.

Kepeuk Khan, of the ill-omened family of Jenghiz, after the the death of his father Oktay Khan, ascended his throne in the month of Rebia el Akher and the six hundred and forty-third year of the Flight. Having joined the Isavian* (Christian)

* Isavian, from Isa (Jesus).

religion, he endeavored hard to propagate that abolished rite,* and Nasarinism (Christianity) daily strengthened itself in his heart. The iniquitous Nasarin priests collected around him ; and while he debased the professors of Islamism, he exalted and aggrandized these blasphemers. One of these priests, who had much influence over him, constantly labored against the Islamites, and devised measures to ruin the white nation of the Prophet, which may the Most High preserve from sorcery and divination. He kept urging Kepeuk Khan utterly to destroy that people. But the Khan did not adopt his advice ; for he knew that they were very numerous. At length he one day came to that accursed Kepeuk Khan and represented to him that he had devised a new plan. Kepeuk Khan inquired what it was ; and the graceless fellow replied, that it was to make eunuchs of all the Mussulmans and their sons, so that they would naturally cease to be a people, and thus the creed of Isa, on whom be peace, would prevail. Kepeuk Khan approved of this plan, and for its execution caused a decree to be sent on the subject throughout the country over which he ruled. That odious Khan one day assembled a numerous divan (or council). All the priests who had planned the affair took up the orders which had been proposed, inquired what they contained, read them, and, after sealing them with the *tamghá* (sign manual) of Kepeuk Khan, left the divan in great joy. The Khan was about to expedite the persons who had been appointed to convey the said orders to Iran and Tooran, when divine zeal and a prophetic miracle evinced itself according to the holy verse of the Koran : "Their pride upon this earth and their iniquitous fraud,"† and the tradition of the prophet, on whom be peace : "O God send one of your dogs upon him." A dog suddenly rushed upon him, which first tore up the orders that were in his hands, and then mutilating him in a shameful manner with his teeth, fled away over the plains and disappeared from sight.

* It will be remembered that Mohammed abolished all religions but his own.

† Koran, 35 : 41.

Verily he that draws a dagger against another shall receive its point in his own breast.

THE STORY OF MUMIN ZADEH AND THE MOGUL.

Says Sahibi Tabakat, In the year six hundred and forty-eight I was travelling on business of a commercial nature, from Khorassan to Hindustan, in company with the master Reshid ed Deen, and the Hakim of Belkee, a most learned person. On the way I asked him to relate to me something strange which he had seen or heard during his travels; and the Khodjah told the following story.

" A son of a Mussulman, an inhabitant of Termuz, became a prisoner in the hands of an infidel Mogul. The boy by reading the glorious Koran became possessed of a most noble exterior; and the Mogul, observing his ingenuousness and capacity, spared no pains in his education. When he had reached the age of puberty he confided all his affairs to him, giving him such full authority that he became the envy of his equals; so much so that the Mogul's relations and friends spread the seeds of destruction upon the soil of envy for that tender Mussulman plant. They waited patiently for an opportunity of satisfying their evil intentions; until at length the Mogul died, having ordered in his will that several of the prettiest girls in his Seray (palace) should be interred with him alive. 'When you bury me,' said he, 'put them in my grave with my body, and close up the door.' Up to the time of the Keuzghun sovereign's being blessed with the true faith, this rite was performed; but he abolished it. Now the Mogul's envious relatives, having hidden their vengeance in their breasts for such a length of time, were all united in the design of interring the youth in the place of the girls; and he, being helpless, performed the *ghoosool* (rite of ablution) and with great grief was put into the tomb. Its door was closed up, and his satisfied enemies, leaving the wretched youth to his lot, departed. The young man rubbed his face upon the earth, and in deep affliction asked aid of Him who supplies the wants of all mankind, as it is written in the holy Book: 'Say, who will save you from the darkness of the land and sea?'

"Aid was sent him from above; for suddenly a light appeared in one corner of the cave, and two frightful figures with burning torches in their hands came to the deceased infidel and struck him, so that the fire from their torches was scattered about the vault. A spark of the size of a pin's head struck the wretched young man's face and burnt him; upon which one of the two beings cried out, 'There must be a Mussulman here;' and asked, 'Who are you?' To which the young man replied, 'I am an unfortunate Mussulman, who fell a prisoner into the hands of an infidel.' He who had addressed him struck one corner of the cave with his torch; and a hole opened, through which it was easy to escape. Then turning to the youth, he made a sign for him to go out. He did as he was bid, and found himself in the plain of Termuz, which is distant from the place of burial three month's march of a caravan travelling day and night."

The rayah added, "I became acquainted with that young man at Termuz, and heard this story from him, without the intermediation of any third party; and, in fact, I saw the burnt scar on his face."

THE STORY OF THE SULJOOK SULTAN MELEK SHAH, AND PIRA ZAL DAD KHAH.

It is narrated that once when the great and generous Suljookide sultan Jelal ed Deen Melek Shah bin Arslan, was hunting in the neighborhood of Ispahan, he alighted from his horse at a most beautiful spot covered with verdure; where amusing himself with his companions, each one set out in a different direction in search of game, until they perceived several unfortunate calves grazing on the plain. Meeting with a cow, they wounded, flayed, cooked, and ate her on the spot. Soon afterwards the noble sultan, being in great good humor, mounted his courser and returning to his royal residence, arrived with all his troops, officers, and attendants at a bridge, over which he intended to pass. He there beheld an aged man seated on the bridge, who, as soon as his eyes fell upon the person of the padishah, arose, crossed the road, and taking his horse's reins in his hands, commenced crying out aloud, "O just sovereign and sultan of good character, your humble servant has several young orphan children, for whose nourishment he possessed a cow, which has been hunted down and eaten. A whole day and night my children have been crying for food; but having no longer any strength left, I know not what to do for them. If you, with all your power and glory will be just, defer not what is my right and due until to-morrow; else when you come to the *Serati Mustakim* (a narrow bridge over which the faithful must pass on the judgment day), I will lay hold of your skirt, overwhelm you with shame and contrition, and demand justice in the presence of the Eternal Avenger for the way in which you have dealt towards me." The old man wept as he uttered these words, and his tears wounded the hearts of all the padishah's troops. The Sultan Melek Shah dismounted from his horse, and excusing himself, said, "O venerable man, I declare that I had no knowledge of the injustice done you." He then replaced the old man's cow, with seventy others, each of which gave milk. Having thus with the hand of benefit gained the good will of the old man, and received his prayers in his behalf, he remounted his horse and returned to the city.

Some time after this, when Jelal ed Deen Malek Shah departed from this transitory world for the palace of eternity, the same old man came to his tomb, accompanied by his orphan children; and overwhelmed in tears and grief, they rubbed their faces upon its earth. Then raising his head, with fervent heart and weeping eyes he thus addressed that court where want is never felt:

STROPHE.

"O God, I swear by thy path, which is the true one; by thy faithful ones who are now servants in thy court; by the tears of innocent orphans; by the sighs of the aged and oppressed; by that submission which is obligatory on us; and by thy great bounties, which are not promised in the Book.

O King and Most High, and O Sovereign who decreases not! on the day when your servant Melek Shah, fearful of your punishment, had pity upon our condition, and answered our petition for justice by releasing us from the oppression we had experienced, he changed our grief into joy. We therefore implore thee, O thou who art the most piteous of the pitiful, that through the incalculable treasury of thy grace he be not excluded from admission into Paradise, but with great mercy be pardoned and made happy."

By Divine will, some of the most glorious of the saints afterwards seeing Melek Shah in their dreams, they asked him how he was in the other world, and how he stood in the presence of the All-just; and they say that the happy sultan, thanking and blessing God, replied, "The prayers of that old man have gained me the blessing and pity of God; for it is written in the holy traditions:

"God shows mercy to those who are merciful; do therefore mercy to those who are on the earth, that those who are in heaven may be merciful to you."

STORY OF TWO BROTHERS, THE ONE EMINENT FOR HIS JUSTICE AND LIBERALITY, THE OTHER INFAMOUS FOR HIS OPPRESSION AND EVIL MINDEDNESS, WITH THE RECOMPENSE THEY BOTH RECEIVED.

It is related that in the time of the Benee Israel (Israelites) there were two brothers of great celebrity. Each one was the sovereign of a separate country. One was a paternal and just governor, possessed of a good disposition and pure faith; whilst the other was so very tyrannical and oppressive, that thorns sprang up in place of roses, and his bitter words were as so many snakes. In the days of these two sovereigns there was a prophet engaged in inviting mankind to his faith, and in pointing out the true religion. The Most High had also granted to this prophet the knowledge that the just sovereign who followed in the ways of God had but thirty years longer to live. The good prophet gave information of the divine decree to the subjects of this king. All of them were in consequence in great grief: their hearts burned with sighs and sobs, and they were much afflicted, and felt pity for him. Whilst those who had the misfortune to be under the rule of the merciless tyrant wept with the others, and prayed to Allah that he would not permit them to suffer thirty years more of his oppression. Finally the subjects of those two kings assembled together, and separated all the sucking infants and other children from their mothers; so that both parents and children lamented the infliction to which they were exposed, and begged that the life of the just king might be prolonged, and that of the tyrannical one cut short. They spent three days in this manner, praying to the All-merciful. On the fourth day the great and glorious God made a revelation to the same prophet, and commanded him to give the good news to the aggrieved, that, according to his usual mercy towards his servants, he had accepted their prayers, and had given thirty years of the tyrannical king's life to the just one; also that he had given the former three years of time to prepare for death. At this all the people were rejoiced, and offered up innumerable prayers and thanks to God for his mercy. Three years afterwards the soul of the merciless sovereign was called away to Jehennem, (hell), and found a place there for his excessive oppressions. The just king lived yet thirty years, which were taken from the life of the former, comporting himself well, and being finally placed in an exalted position in the other world. The protection which he showed to the poor and weak was the cause of his felicity, both in this world and in the other.

PERSIAN VERSES.

" O heart attached to justice strive to execute it; strive to refrain from all falseness and hypocrisy; hang out the banner of justice on the roof of the palace of accomplishment; lead thy steps into happy lands and ways. The learned, so as to bind the fate of nations, taught this to Alexander (the Great), namely to acquire a knowledge of all scents, that he might be able to distinguish the false from the true, and thus find out the real state of every matter."

ANECDOTE

Concerning the submission to the commands of the Lord, the respect shown to the Law of the Prophet, the regard paid to the rights of Mussulmans, the zeal for Islamism, the religion, and the equity of Sultan Selah ed Deen bin Ayoob.

On the decline of the Fatimite dynasty, the reign of Sultan Selah ed Deen bin Ayoob, a prince unrivalled for piety and justice, became most eminent in Egypt and Damascus. After the martyrdom of his paternal uncle, Noor ed Deen, he became an independent sovereign, and reigned with the above mentioned qualities over Mosul, Haleb, Damascus, Egypt, and Yamin. He was a strict observer of the Holy Law. In the history entitled Tarikh er Ravzetaïn fi Akhbar ed Devletaïn, it is stated by the chief judge Shaffay, that a slave belonging to a merchant residing in Diar-Bekir escaped from his master, and was sold from one hand to another until he was brought at last to Egypt, and was disposed of to the Sultan Selah ed Deen. He was employed in the sultan's service; and becoming a favorite with the sultan, he attained the rank of vizir, in which he died. As he had no children, his inheritance fell to his master the sultan. He left a fortune of eighty thousand pieces of gold.

Some time after his death his former master heard of it. Taking the proper documents with him from Diar-Bekir, he travelled to Damascus, where he exhibited his proofs and receipts at the holy Mehkemeh, (court or tribunal of justice,) and, having had them properly authenticated, continued on to Egypt. He went to the residence of the chief judge of that period, entered his reclamations, and exhibited his titles. The judge told him that his claim was a good one, and returned the documents to him, adding, that though his adversary was a person of high rank, he was one who devoutly respected the laws of the Holy Book. "Come to-morrow," said he, "and present your statement before the council in the castle, and let us see what will be done." The man departed; and on the day following the judge went to the divan, where, while engaged in conversation with the sultan, he informed the latter that a legal adversary had just appeared and filed a complaint against him. The man himself now entering the divan, the judge arose from the sultan's side, and, after pointing out the individual as his adversary, left him, and seated himself in his own place. The claimant presented his petition to the sultan, who read it, and saying to the man, "Let us subject the matter to the Holy Law," left his seat and repaired with him before the judge.

They both stood up before him; and after the judge had listened to the suit, he thus addressed the sovereign: "O Molana Sultan, a slave belonging to this man fled from him. Having subsequently heard of him, he has produced his papers in this court and proved his claim." The sultan replied, "The slave acquired all his goods and wealth while with me. What says the Holy Law on the subject?" "During all that time," replied the judge, "the slave was the property of this man;" and he cited the verse of the Koran which says: "The slave can possess nothing but by his master." The sultan acquiesced in the holy justness of the sentence, and returning, he seated himself in his own place, where he ordered that the whole of the property left by the deceased slave should be delivered to the man.

All those present blessed the sultan. This man possessed two freehold estates (*mulk*). These the sultan purchased of him for eight thousand dinars, for the purpose of converting them into pious foundations (*vakoof*), and paid the money for them. But he afterward presented them again to the man, saying, "The public may possibly say that the property was worth more, and that the sultan obtained them at too low a price; and as what occasions discontent does not suit me, I have returned them."

Behold what a just sovereign, and firm supporter of equity and religion; and see in this, an instance of the degree of submission which is due to the Holy Law. May the Most High have mercy on them all!

A TALE ABOUT A WEALTHY MAN, AND A DERVISH WHO LIVED IN HIS NEIGHBORHOOD.

It is related that once among the benevolent men there was a wealthy merchant, who lived in the neighborhood of a patient, self-resigned Dervish. One day a young son of the merchant went into the Dervish's dwelling at a moment when the latter was taking a meal with his wife. The boy, child-like, looked on as if he expected to be invited to join them; but this not being done, he returned weeping to his home. The merchant inquiring of him the cause of his tears, he replied that he had been at the house of the Dervish whilst he was eating, and wanted some of their food. The merchant much pained arose and went to the Dervish's house, where he asked whether it was right for him whilst eating not to ask a child that stood by and saw him, to taste a morsel of his meal. He added, "Had you satisfied his desire, he would not have wept in the manner he did, nor have given me pain." The Dervish excused himself, saying that a secret not worthy of being told was the cause of his not asking the child to partake. The merchant, not considering himself fully answered, asked what the secret was. "Let us know it;" said he. The Dervish replied, "For the sake of Allah pardon us, and bring not the veil of our honor to the dust." But the merchant insisting the more, the Dervish continued, "Pray be not the cause of exposing our secret;" and recited these verses :

PERSIAN VERSES.

"O thou who mountest a delicate animal, beware lest thou become feeble in that mud and water. Desire not fire from the house of the poor man; for the smoke from his windows is the grief of his heart."

The old man was greatly troubled, and replied, "You must certainly let us know it." The Dervish now desperate, said, "The food on which we fed is *hallal* (legitimate) to me and my wife, but forbidden to all others; and that is the true reason why I did not offer any of it to your son." The merchant replied, "*Subkhan Allah!* Blessed be God! Can a meal then be legitimate to one, and forbidden to another?" The Dervish answered, "Yes; for these three days past I have not had sufficient strength to gain food wherewith to support nature. But going out this morning with an empty hand, I found on a certain pile of ruins the dead body of an ass. I cut off and cooked a piece of its flesh; and whilst I and my wife were eating it, your child came in. This is the real cause of our neglect.

PERSIAN VERSE.

'Thou passest the night in pleasure and joy; but how knowest thou how our nights are spent?'"

When the old merchant heard this from the Dervish, he threw himself at his feet and wept. "*Ayvah!*" said he, "if the Most High at the day of judgment and repentance asks after him who lived under the same shade with me, how shall I answer him?" He then took the Dervish's hand in his own; and leading him to his own dwelling, he divided his wealth with him, giving one half to the Dervish, and keeping the other for himself.

That night the merchant saw the Sultan of prophets, on whom be peace, in his sleep. He told him that the intercession made in his favor by the prayers of the Dervish had been received at the court of eternity; that his wealth in this world had been blessed to him; and that in the other he would enjoy half the felicity of his neighbor the Dervish.

Now the sultans and exalted hakims, as well as others in office who have it in their power to do good, are required to inform themselves of the condition of their subjects and the poor; and, by attending to their wants, to endeavor to lessen and assuage them with a sufficiency; so that on the morning when secret things are made public, in the presence of that Judge who asks not what has been done, they be not exposed to the fangs of punishment and torture.

STORY CONCERNING NOOR ED DEEN SHAHID OGLOON, AND THE MELEK SALIH.

It is related of that just prince, the king of Damascus, Melek Salih, that every night he went about the city in disguise, inquiring into the condition and circumstances of the poor. One very cold night, when every one was frozen with the snow and rain that fell, he heard, as he was making his rounds, a voice proceeding from a convent. On approaching it he perceived a naked Dervish, trembling with the cold, and crying out, "O Allah, the sultans of the world, and the governors over the sons of Adam, make their innumerable gifts the source of selfish happiness; and whilst surrounded by their power, pride, and enjoyment, they seek not to know, but neglect thy poor and needy servants. If, at the last day, these insolent people should, through thy glory and grandeur, enter Paradise, and be counted worthy of its tranquillity, I seek not nor do I desire to set my foot therein."

Melek Salih ed Deen approached this poor Dervish with weeping eyes; and sending for a purse of silver and a dress, he fell at his feet and conciliated his good will, and said, "It is certain that dervishes at the last day (lit. to-morrow) must be sovereigns in Paradise; therefore let us in our princedom associate with you to-day in this world. We now come to you in peace; and it is our hope that to-morrow you also, when in the enjoyment of your sovereignty, will not close the door of amity against us, but, bestowing your favor upon us, will treat us with peace and affection.

PERSIAN VERSE.

"I to-day made peace again; you to-morrow do not oppose me. I am not one who becomes proud of his numerous attendants. I am also not one to turn my face away from the unfortunate. Do not act badly towards me; for there is trouble even in Paradise."

CHAPTER TWENTY-FIRST.

On the subject of great benevolence, delicacy of character, nobleness, and pride.

It is related of one gifted with the characteristic of great benevolence, namely, Omar bin Hamrah, that one day he visited Mansoor, one of the Abbaside caliphs; and whilst conversing with him, a man came in to complain of his condition. Mansoor said, "*Men zulmek,* who has oppressed you?" He replied, "Omar has seized upon a village belonging to me, which he has pillaged and keeps possession of." Turning to Omar, the Prince of the faithful commanded him to rise and stand up with his adversary. Said Omar, "If the village belongs to him, I have no cause of altercation with him. If I am in the right, be witness to the fact: for I now present it to him for nothing; let him therefore go and take possession of it. I prefer to give up a hundred such villages, or even resign every present which the Prince of the faithful has done me the honor to make me, rather than rise up to contend in his presence." *Barik Allah!* God be praised! this is the way to show the respect due to rank, and the regard that belongs to those who are in high places.

One day the caliph Seffah was conversing with Omm Selmeh on the subject of the delicacy and benevolence of Omar bin Hamrah; when Omm Selmeh asked that he might be sent to her, so as to give her an opportunity of seeing him. "I will give him," said she, "my jewelled chaplet with fifty thousand dinars. Let us see whether he will accept it. If he does, he has no delicacy of feeling, and we will ascertain the fact." So Seffah sent Omar to Omm Selmeh, who, during the interview showed him every mark of regard and respect, and asked him whether the chaplet which she held in her hand would suit him. "If it does," added she, "pray accept it from me." She then offered it to Omar, who, from motives of civility, did not decline it: but when he arose to go, he left it behind him. Omm Selmeh, supposing he had forgotten it, sent it after him by one of her people, who, having found him, delivered it to him. Omar took it in his hand, and made a present of it to the servant who brought it. When Omm Selmeh learnt this, she praised Omar's great benevolence, and purchased the chaplet back again from the servant for five thousand pieces of gold.

It is related that when Abd Allah bin Tahir became governor (*walee*) of Egypt, one of the nobles of Egypt sent one night as a present to the former one hundred maiden slaves, each carrying a plate filled with gold. Ibin Tahir read the note sent with the present, and then wrote on the back of it, "A present from you which can be received at night, can be also received during the day;" adding also, in Arabic, "What God has given me is better than your gift; perhaps your gift has occasioned you more pleasure than to me." And thus he refused the offering.

It is said that Ahnef bin Kais was possessed of a most excellent temper. One day a person asked him, "From whom did you receive your disposition?" To which he replied that he learnt it of Kais bin Asim. "One day," said he, "I was at his house, as a guest, when dinner was brought in. Kais had a young son seated by his side. A maiden came in, having in her hand a dish; in placing which before Kais she by accident let it fall upon the head of the child, killing it upon the spot. Kais, seeing the fright displayed on the maiden's countenance, exclaimed, "I free thee in the name of God, and consider thee blameless." Behold what generosity and benevolence!

The following is related of Jaafer bin Suliman, one of those persons who were celebrated for their natural kindness and benevolence of disposition. One of his servants purloined a very valuable jewel from him, and sold it. Some time afterwards the jewel was seen in the hands of a merchant; and on being asked of whom he had obtained it, he replied that he had bought it of a certain individual for one thousand dinars. So they apprehended the merchant, and took him and the jewel before Jaafer bin Suliman; to whom the merchant stated that such a one had sold it to him. It happened that the person indicated was in the presence of Jaafer at the time; and suddenly his countenance changed through shame. Jaafer took the jewel in his hand, and addressing him, said, "At such a time I made you a present of this jewel; and you sold it, perhaps, on account of your necessities." Then giving the full value of the jewel to the merchant, he presented it again to the man, saying, "Receive it as a souvenir from me; and let them not cheat you another time when you sell it, but dispose of it at its just value." At the same time he added several other gifts on his part.

One of the great sultans, Behram Ghior, was a very brave, benevolent, and equitable sovereign. One day he mounted his horse with the intention of going to the chase. On his way a gazelle was started, which he pursued, chasing it to a considerable distance, until it disappeared from sight. When separated from all his attendants, his strength failed him; and dismounting from his horse, he seated himself under the shade of a large tree. Opposite him he perceived a shepherd, whom he called, and requested to hold his horse while he went aside for a moment. The shepherd, finding himself alone and unobserved, took out his knife and began cutting off the jewelled chains of Behram Ghior's bridle. Behram Ghior happened to see the shepherd; and rather than put him to the blush, he turned away his head, and walked in another direction. The shepherd, after cutting off the chain, put it in his bosom; and Behram Ghior, coming up soon after, mounted his horse and rode away. When he came to his people he told his equerry that a shepherd having done him some service, he had presented him with the chain of his bridle. "Do not, therefore, think it is lost," said he, "or charge any one with having taken it."

It is narrated in the book called Nizam es Selateen, that one day Nooshirvan the Just (the flowing water, the cream of the Chosroes kings of Persia) assembled all his attendants and people for the purpose of making a great feast, and numerous varieties of choice fruits were brought in on golden dishes. After eating and drinking till they all got drunk, they retired to a corner to converse, and Nooshirvan remained alone with one attendant. Nooshirvan also being drunk, he half closed his eyes in a doze, with a golden plate before him that weighed one thousand miscals. The attendant, deeming this a proper object of acquisition, was putting it in his bosom just as the eyes of Nooshirvan opened and met those of the thief. The attendant put his finger to his mouth, and saying, "*Fash makun*, let it not be known," concealed the vessel. When the officer charged with keeping the plate came to collect the vessels, and missed Nooshirvan's dish, he exclaimed, "Stir not from your places; I will search you all, until I find who has taken the dish." Nooshirvan, hearing this, became angry with the officer, and ordered him not to talk foolishly, "The person," said, "Who has the dish will never return it; and he who saw him take it would rather be reprimanded than expose him, since he would not wish to be considered an informer." He added, "I do not wish you to seek for him; let the meeting be broken up, and every one depart in peace." So the meeting dispersed; the Nadim (attendant) also returning to his dwelling. He melted the gold, and made out of it a most elegant khondjar. He also bought him a fine suit of clothes, and in all their newness returned again before Nooshirvan. The latter, on beholding his attendant, called him to his side, and in a low voice asked him whether all his new and elegant apparel was out of that dish. The attendant replied, "It is from my sovereign's favor, may it be everlasting; and may his life and empire endure to eternity." Nooshirvan was greatly pleased with his reply, and bestowed upon him yet more presents and gratifications.

CHAPTER TWENTY-SECOND.

On remarkable coincidences, strange things, and wonderful creatures.

The Sheik Abd Allah, author of the work entitled *Tohfeh el Elbab,* relates as follows. In the year 500 of the Hedjreh, I saw a man belonging to the tribe of the Ads in the Bulgar country, whose height was more than twenty-eight cubits. He had a handsome figure and agreeable features, and was very remarkable for his strength: for instance, he would overtake a horse going at full speed, seize it with one of his hands as if it were an apple, snatch it up under his arm, and return it to the ground again. He could pluck up a palm or an oak tree by its roots, and with one blow could break a sword in pieces. This man had a sister remarkable for her beauty, whom he gave to a man in marriage; but the first time they embraced each other she squeezed him so tightly as to break his back, and caused his death. After which event every one was afraid to release her from her widowhood. This author adds, "I saw both of these individuals; and there was no other like them in all the country of Bulgar. They were both unrivalled for their beauty; but there was not a bath in their country into which they could enter. They were, indeed, wonderful creatures; but Allah is omnipotent!"

The Imam Shafaee, may Allah sanctify his tomb, says: Once, as I was journeying to a country in the vicinity of Yamin, I met a man who from his waist upwards had two bodies, each with two arms, whilst the remainder of his members were perfect. From his waist downwards he was like other men, and he ate and drank like any other person. These two individuals would at times offend each other, quarrel, and become friends again. Some years afterwards I happened to have occasion to visit that same place, where I found that one of these men had died; that they had tied very tightly the ligament which confined the two bodies together at the waist; but that when they had divided this part so as to separate the living one from the dead, the former also fell ill and died.

In the history of Kazveenee it is related as follows: I was once in a vessel bound on a voyage; but meeting with a great storm, we were cast away on an island, where we had to remain several days. During our stay there, one moonlight night we heard laughter and playing like that of men, but were unable to understand the language. Some of the sailors ran in the direction from which the sounds proceeded, and caught two of the persons who made them. They were so beautiful, that one never could be satisfied with looking at them. They were mermaids. Each of them had black hair hanging down to their ankles; and great Allah! but such beauty as theirs was never seen before. One of the sailors kept one of them for three or four days, and then let her go; but another kept his four or five years, living in free intimacy with her. She bore him three sons, each as fair and beautiful as the Perees.

Four or five years afterwards, this sailor, having occasion to make another voyage in the same direction, took his wife with him. One day when the vessel was sailing very fast, she threw herself into the sea; and her husband would have followed her had his comrades not prevented him. Some time after this occurred, as they were returning by the same place, they beheld the mermaid in the sea, approaching the vessel, and holding in her hand a box. Having delivered it to her husband, she, by signs, commended her children to his care, and then, after swimming for some time by the side of the ship, disappeared in the sea. The sailor on opening the box found, besides several jewels, two royal pearls of great size. These, on arriving in port, he sold for a large sum; which made a considerable capital for him, so that he became a wealthy merchant. There are other instances besides this in which fishermen in those parts have caught mermaids, and found them most affectionate and grateful.

In the time of Nasir ed Dowlet some presents were sent him

on the part of the Armenian patriarch, among which was a young lad who had all the members of two persons united to a single body. Nasir ed Dowlet sent him to his physicians, to see whether they could separate him. These persons replied that if both usually ate at one mouth it would be impracticable; and in fact, on questioning the lad, it turned out as had been surmised. He lived to a good old age.

It is related in the history of Ibin Zulak that once a man was voyaging among the islands of Andalusia, when he fell in with a woman at the Isles of the Sea, whose beauty is described by those who saw her as being that of an angel come upon earth. She lived with this man some seven or eight years, and bore him three or four children, all very handsome.

One day whilst making a voyage at sea, accompanied by her, she took up a child which she was yet suckling, and approaching the waist of the vessel, seemed greatly agitated; she finally threw herself into the sea, and dived to the bottom. Soon afterwards she re-appeared, having a large box in her hand; approaching the vessel, she delivered it to her husband, and then again dived down into the sea. The box was found to be filled to the brim with pearls, by the sale of which the man became very rich. Blessed Allah! there is no end to his power; I put faith in him, and am preserved by him.

In the work called "Tariki Guzideh," by Jelal ed Deen Turk, is the following narrative of what occurred in the time of Aboo Said:

I saw a calf with four eyes and two feet; also a man with a beard like that of an ordinary person, but his reins were hairy like those of a bear, and his language could not be understood, although he comprehended all that was said to him. He was kept constantly confined by a chain.

It is related by the author of the same history that once a woman appeared in the city of Gazveen, whose head was like that of any other woman; but her reins were hairy, like those of a bear, her hands and feet were precisely like the paws of a bear, and she had no teeth. The inhabitants of that place said that a bear having carried off her mother, this monster was the fruit of their union.

* * * * * * *

CHAPTER TWENTY-THIRD.

Of those who are skilled and perfected in the sciences of astrology and soothsaying.

Ibin Kethir in his history, quoting Ibin Sekit, relates and tells that, among the sages of Arabia and the poets and masters of politeness, Ommieh ibin Abi es Salat was celebrated throughout the world. Once, when the excellent and most noble Prophet, may God be propitious to him and bless him, was in the company of some of his worthy friends, they asked him, saying, "Would you like to hear some of the poetry of Ommieh ibin Abi es Salat?" He replying, "Yes," they read some poems. He cried, "Encore," asking for more; and as he stood and swayed his body to and fro with delight, his cloak fell from his blessed shoulders. His friends around him seized it, and tearing it into pieces divided it amongst them as relics. He was the poet of poets among the Arabs, but, though often in the company of the Prophet, did not embrace the blessed religion of Islam. His death was a curious one.

One day he took a cup in his hand; and as he was about to drink its contents, he heard the voice of a crow proceeding from a corner of the room in which he was with some friends. He replied to the crow, "*Vafeek et turab*, to the earth with you." Again the crow spoke; and again he answered as before. Those present now asked him, "O learned soothsayer, what have you understood from the voice of the crow?" "It said," replied Ommieh, "Know that in the same hour in which you drink of the cup in your hand, you will die;" to which I answered, "To the earth with you." The second time it said, "If you want proofs of what I say, I will fly from here and perch upon the dunghill opposite us, feed there on something, and die of a bone sticking in my throat; you will then drink of the cup in your hand, and die immediately."

As he said this, the crow flew and lit on the dunghill; where, after scratching two or three times, it fell down and expired. Ommieh now exclaimed, "Behold the crow's words have been verified; I will therefore also drink of the cup in my hand, and see what will ensue." The moment he drank it he fell down and delivered up his soul.

What sagacity and wonderful knowledge!

In the nine hundred and ninetieth year of the Hedjreh, and during the reign of Sultan Murad bin Selim Khan, Molana Taki ed Deen, of Damascus, the inventor of the astronomical tables, had a brother who attained to the government of a Sandjak, in the province of Diar-Bekir. He had the rank of a Meeri Liva, and was even more perfect in astronomical tables than his brother.

One day being unwell, all his friends called to inquire after his health. In the course of conversation the Meer directed one of his attendants to bring him his astrolabe. Taking it in his hand, he examined it attentively; then addressing his friends, he said, "To-morrow I shall bid you all farewell; do not forget me in your prayers. My life is about to close, and I have but two days more to live." He then freed all his slaves, made his will, and commenced reading the great Koran. He made his peace with every one, divided his property among his children; and after repentance and asking divine pardon, on the second day he expired, and delivered up the precious jewel of his soul to the house of fatality.

It is related in the medical history called Kitab el Embafee, that Mahmood bin Salih, vizir of the sultan of Aleppo, excited the sultan against Mutezee, by telling him that the latter deserved to be put to death, and that moreover it was demanded by the laws. So the sultan ordered his people to bind Mutezee; and no less than thirty or forty persons set out for that purpose. These individuals put up at a house which happened to be that of Mutezee; and the latter, mistaking them for ordinary guests, was getting ready a dinner for them, when his brother informed him that they had come to make him a prisoner. "What," continued he, "is to be done? if we let them take you, it will be a disgrace to us, and yet we have not sufficient force to oppose them. Let me know your opinion on the subject." Mutezee replied, "Be not troubled;

let them repose to night, and we will see what will turn up on the morrow." So he arose at midnight, and said his prayers; and his brother coming in, he said to him, "Tell my pupil Salamee to come to me." Salamee came; and Mutezee directed him to go out and observe the position of the planet Mars; for though Mutezee was one of the most distinguished men of his time, he was blind. Salamee went out as he was bid, and informed Mutezee of the place of the planet. Mutezee bade him next take a balance, bind it with a cord, and tie one end of the latter tightly to his foot. Salamee did as he was bid; and Mutezee commenced repeating to himself the Azaïm, or those verses of the Koran which serve as a charm, among which were the following:

"O Eternal of speedy diseases, O Maker of all creation, O Constructor of all constructions, give me thy glory which ceases not, and thine asylum whose meats thy guests can never consume."

He added a few more words to the preceding, and then cut the cord bound to his foot. Suddenly an alarming noise was heard. Some people entered hastily from without, and announced that the house in which the guests were had fallen down and crushing all those who were under it.

Morning came, and an hour or two afterwards a messenger arrived from Aleppo, with strict orders to do no harm to Mutezee, and not even to remove him; for the vizir Mahmood bin Salih, who had wished to do the venerable man harm, having gone into a bath, it had caved in upon him, and killed him on the spot. His son, the successor to the vizir, being one of his (Mutezee's) best friends, sent to salute him and beg his good prayers in his behalf.

In the reign of the deceased and pardoned conqueror, the Sultan Selim Khan, there was a famous soothsayer named Remmal

Hyder (the lion soothsayer). For discovering the occult things of the world, and exposing all that was hidden and secret, he was unique, and the wonder of that period. Sultan Selim, who was constantly endeavoring to make him commit errors, one day mounted his horse and paid a visit to the mosk of Ayoob Ensaree (may the Creator sanctify his tomb!) attended by Remmal. On the way the sultan, addressing Hyder, inquired, "What gate shall we go out at? Test your geomancy, and tell us. See what it shows you." Hyder drew some magical signs upon a paper, and wrote, "By an unusual and strong passage, which will be broken open for that purpose." And then folding up the paper, he handed it to the colonel whose duty it was to accompany the sultan. The latter, after proceeding a little further, turned his horse's head directly against the wall of the tower, and ordered an opening to be made there. Immediately a passage was made with picks and spades, and through the aperture the sultan chose to pass.

Immediately afterwards, the sultan calling the colonel near him, asked for the paper written by Hyder, and to his astonishment read, "By an unusual and strong passage, which will be broken open for that purpose." The sultan was much pleased, and praised Hyder's talent, and bestowed upon him several costly gifts.

People yet pass through the opening made at the tower. It lies on the way to Ayoob, and is called Egri Capoo, or the Crooked Gate.

Naïm bin Abd Allah narrates this as coming from Ziad bin Mesood. He says, A learned man (*ulema*) told me as follows: "I and an intelligent merchant, a resident of Alexandria, once set out together on a pilgrimage to Mecca. I, being somewhat acqainted with geomancy, was desirous of perfecting myself in that science. One day, accompanied by the merchant, I went into the

Holy Caaba of Mecca. We performed our ablutions at the well of Zemzem; and, after making a few genuflections, seated ourselves, and commenced a conversation. Now my comrade had five hundred pieces of gold about him in a roll; these he took out of his pocket, and placed under the border of his robe. After a little time had elapsed we arose and, forgetting the roll, left the Caaba. Soon afterwards, the gold coming to his recollection, we returned in search of it, but found no traces of it. As we were talking about it, an inhabitant of Mecca, an intelligent person, addressing me, said, "There is a man here well skilled in the art of geomancy, who, if you have recourse to him, will doubtless find out what you have lost, and perhaps even procure it for you." Having a considerable knowledge of the science myself, and a great passion for it, I accompanied the merchant to the geomancer. I found the plan (*niet*); and giving the instrument (*kura*) into his hands, he looked at it, and said to me, "Is not this project yours?" To which I replied, "Yes; I made it for another." The soothsayer then observed it again attentively, and said, "You have lost a roll of gold; but be not grieved, it can be found." Then addressing me, he continued, "The money has fallen into the hands of your son." I answered, "I am a stranger, and have certainly no one here related to me." The soothsayer became angry with me, and said, "My art has never belied any one; do you speak the truth? The individual who has taken the money came from the east. It is strange; but he must have some relationship with you. What place are you from?" I replied, "I am from Bagdad, and it is now thirty years since I left that city." "Have you no son there?" he asked. I answered, "When I departed I left a wife in the family way, from whom I have never been able to obtain any news whatever, nor do I know whether she yet lives." "Go," said the soothsayer; "the person who has found the money must assuredly be your son. Cry out, and he will appear; and you will have the happiness of seeing your own child in him."

Full of astonishment as we were, I went with the merchant to the court of the Caaba, where I cried out aloud, "Has any Mussulman found a roll of money? if so, let it be returned to its owner, and a reward will be given to the finder." Suddenly a handsome young man approached us and said, "I found one on this spot;" and forthwith drawing out the roll, he placed it before us. I asked him from what country he was; and he replied, that he was from Bagdad. I asked him from what quarter and house, and found that he was from my own house. I next asked him what was his father's name. He answered, "I know his name, but am ignorant of his appearance; for whilst I was yet in my mother's womb he went on a journey, since which nearly thirty years have elapsed." He also gave me news of his mother, and I was assured that he was my own son. I embraced and kissed him, and he acknowledged me as his father.

My companion the merchant was greatly rejoiced with me at the discovery of my son; and taking out of the roll one hundred pieces of gold, he presented them to him, and gave me also fifty pieces. I returned with the merchant to the soothsayer, to whom he also gave several pieces of gold. The soothsayer was much gratified with the proof which the affair furnished of the truth of his art, and thanked God. I, being a zealous devotee of the same science, begged that the soothsayer would allow me to enter his service; which favor he granting me, I remained three or four years with him, perfecting myself in it.

CHAPTER TWENTY-FOURTH.

It is surprisingly strange, how, by following in the path of the Divine will, destiny will lead you, without any intention or design on your part, to the proper and suitable place.

The Emir Azz ed Deen says: It is related by Daood Ezdee that the Melek et Takir, one of the Tcherkes sultans, had a strong desire for the acquirement of knowledge. He sought for such persons as, like himself, held the belles-lettres in respect, and showed countenance and protection to their followers. He also was acquainted with the science of moral philosophy. During his reign his confidential secretary was one Ahmed bin Saidee, an Aleppine, whom he took with him to Egypt.

One day when the sultan was engaged in conversation with the chief judge, Ahmed bin Saidee entered to kiss his hand and ask his orders; after which the sultan thoughtfully recited at random the two following verses:

"Ahmed bin el Hassan el Hazee gave me much information about travellers; we have since then heard of his verses with our own ears."

Cadi Tadj ed Deen, on hearing the verses, exclaimed, "Barik Allah! whose are they? do you know?" The sultan replied, "I do not know whose they are; they only happened to come to my recollection." The cadi exclaimed, "They are the verses of your secretary, Ahmed bin Saidee, who just now kissed your hand." What was remarkable in the circumstance was, that the writer should happen to be present at the moment.

The Cadi Shems ed Deen ibin Helkam relates the following: Several literary men of that period, travelling together, arrived at a village near Bagdad called Sermenray, where they saw the palace of the Shereef Radee, then going to ruin, its beauty vanished, and its foundations alone remaining. One of them, on beholding the wreck of so goodly an edifice, expressed his astonishment by reciting the following verses:

> "We stood on the place of their ruins, where nothing remained but the foundations of their walls. I wept until blood fell from my eyes; where so many men once dwelt, now you find but the end. My eyes since then are ruined; for the sight of such faded grandeur has made a waste of my heart."

Whilst repeating them, one of the company inquired whose they were; to which he replied that he did not know. The inquirer exclaimed, to the astonishment of all present, "They are the verses of the owner of the palace, Shereef Radee."

A REMARKABLE COINCIDENCE.

The author of the work entitled Durret el Ghawas, "the Pearl of the Diver," relates, that Abeed el Jerhemee was three hundred years old when he became ennobled by the true faith of Islam. One day being in the company of Muavieh in Bagdad, the caliph, in the course of conversation, said to him, "Pray Sheik, tell us what is the most curious thing you have met with in the course of your long life." The Sheik replied, "Once, in the beginning of my travels, I met with a tribe of people of which a handsome individual had just died, and his friends were conveying his remains to the tomb. Being afraid of their numbers, I joined the procession, and they began to bury the deceased. I was astonished on observing that some of those present laughed while others wept, when the following verses came to my recollection:

"There is jealousy amongst the tribes of men, when one is rich and one is poor; the guest however knows not that the former is not inherited, but obtained by theft."

One of the people of the place, on hearing them, asked me whether I knew who wrote the verses I had cited; and, on my replying that I did not, he said, to my astonishment, "Then learn that they were written by the person at whose funeral you are assisting." What a remarkable coincidence, that I should happen to be at his burial!

CHAPTER TWENTY-FIFTH.

On the misfortune which perfidy brings upon those who are guilty of it; and an explication of the verse which says, "Whatever you are comes from yourself; good is from good, evil from evil."

In the 160th year of the Hedjreh, Mehdee, one of the Abbaside caliphs appointed Isa bin Moosa to be the heir apparent or successor to the caliphat; though subsequently he changed his mind and appointed his own son Hadee, and sent him to govern Khorassan. On his arrival at that place, he governed it until symptoms of insurrection arose among its inhabitants. Certain perfidious hypocrites asserted to the caliph that one Ibrahim bin Zekvan was the cause of the troubles. The caliph, being enraged against him, sent several individuals to Hadee, whom he ordered to deliver Ibrahim up to them, that they might bring him before him. Hadee made a pretext for not sending him, and wrote a reply to the caliph's demand; which however proved ineffectual, for he persisted in having him sent. So, seeing the pertinacity of the caliph, he finally sent him.

When Ibrahim went into the presence of the caliph, the latter made some inquiries of him, and then ordered his execution. Ibrahim, innocent and helpless, on arriving at the place of execution, begged permission of the executioner to renew his ablutions and say a prayer of two *rakats*. In the meantime Mehdee withdrew into his palace; and suddenly a great noise proceeded from the Seray, as if the whole world was in affliction. Whilst all present were waiting to know what had occurred, the Aga of the harem appeared and gave news of the sudden death of Mehdee; the cause of which was, that one of the female slaves of the harem, being jealous of another, put an emerald into his drink, and gave it to him. The emerald was poisonous, and immediately caused the death of Mehdee, to the grief of all present, and the deliverance of the innocent Ibrahim.

Herthmah bin Ayin, a distinguished individual among the Emirs of the Benee Abbas relates this story:

Once a man came to me on the part of the caliph of the time, Hadee bin Mehdee, to say that he wished to see me. I arose and went to him. It was night; and as soon as he saw me he exclaimed, "I have called you, and desire that you show no opposition to any thing which I order you to do, but perform it." I replied, "O Emir of the faithful, how many heads have I that I should dare to disobey you?" So he continued, "My wish is this. How much have I suffered from Yahiya bin Halid! he has turned the people from me, and disposed them in favor of my brother Haroon er Rasheed. Go, therefore, without delay, to the prison in which Yahiya and his sons are confined; cut off their heads, as also those of all the descendants of Abi Talib whom you may find, and bring them to me. Take some soldiers with you; go to Cufah; and take out of it all the descendants of Abi Talib, and reduce the town to ashes."

Herthmah adds: When I heard this, I really expired with emotion. I begged him, saying, "O Emir el Moomeneen, this is an affair of great importance, which I am unable to accomplish; and by the souls of your ancestors I beg you to release me from it." I bowed my face to the earth to implore his forbearance; but becoming greatly angered, he exclaimed, "I swear, by the souls of my forefathers, that if you neglect to do what I have commanded you, I will inflict upon you the severest punishment, dishonor you, and cut you in pieces as small as your ears." He then in a great rage arose and entered his harem. I thought, that in his fury against me, he might order my own execution; and in my heart I formed the vow, that if I should escape from this abyss I would collect all my property and go to some other clime, where no one would know my history.

Whilst I was thus reflecting, a servant came and said the caliph wanted me. Believing that I should soon be a corpse, I repeated the creed of faith and went towards the harem, whence I heard a female voice exclaiming, "Come, O Herthmah! I am Hyzran; arise, come, and see what a misfortune has overtaken me." I entered the house, and found Hyzran concealed behind the curtain. Addressing me he said, "Hadee, who was inclined to violence and oppression, has now been visited by dark misfortune, and conveyed to the valley of corruption. The Preserver from all evils has delivered him from his own evil designs." He added, "Behold his present condition;" and raising the curtain, I beheld Hadee added to the list of the departed. Hyzran afterwards said, "When Hadee returned from without, I threw myself at his feet, embraced them, and begged of him to give me one drop of Haroon's blood. He shook me off, trembled, and in a great passion asked for water, which he had scarcely drunk, when he expired. God decrees all things. Now hasten to the prison, release Yahiya, take him with you, and tell him what has just occurred; so that the public may be disposed to elect Haroon to succeed him."

I departed in haste, and released Yahiya. I then went to

Haroon and saluted him. Astonished at beholding me, he exclaimed, "O Herthmah what is the cause of your visit?" So I related it to him from beginning to end.

He returned thankful praises to God, and at the same moment learnt that there had been a blessed and lucky birth in his harem. In consideration of the fortunate circumstance under which the boy was born, he was greatly rejoiced, and forthwith called him Mamoon. The Arabs call that night Lailah Hashmieh, or the night in which one Hashemite caliph mounted the saddle of the hearse and rode to the clime of non-existence; another ascended the caliphite throne; and a third, appearing from behind the veil of nothingness, entered the palace of the world. The page of existence is like unto the painter's canvass, from which objects can be effaced and others drawn on it at pleasure.

STROPHE.

"It still remains, no time removes the stain,
Whatever the canvass has received remains;
All that God has traced upon the page of this earth
Can be seen in an instant of time."

During the reign of Valeed bin Abd el Melek, one of the Ommiade sultans, Tarik bin Ziad, a very brave man, was appointed to the chief command of the army, and sent to conquer the coasts of Andalusia in the county of the west. This general, accompanied by his valorous troops, subdued Andalusia, and became possessed of so much wealth that it was more than Nisab. They obtained as much wealth as was collected in the time of the prophet Suliman. In one place were found one hundred and seventy khosrevan (royal) crowns, set with rubies, diamonds, emeralds, and other precious stones, until it is said that each crown was worth as much as the tribute (*heradj*) of Room.

They entered a wonderfully wrought palace, fifty cubits in height; from bottom to top it was incrusted with silver, and its furniture was so richly embellished that man is incapable of describing it. They found also the dining-table of Suliman, son of David, on whom be peace. It was made of a green emerald, and its vessels of pure gold; its feet were of white jasper, and it was set with false pearls. They also found a book, in which all kinds of stones, and plants, and metals were explained; in it also the sciences of chemistry and magic, that relating to preservation from fire, and the science of astronomy, were profoundly treated. The same book discussed the subject of rubies and jewels, and also the rules of poisons and antidotes. It contained likewise drawings of the earth's form, and of its seas, islands, and mountains. Among other useful things which they found, there was an elixir so powerful that were a single drachm of pure gold adulterated so as to form several thousands, it would render the whole pure again. They also found a mirror which showed the world, made for the Prophet Suliman, of different medicinal compounds, in which you could see, at one moment, all the climes of the universe. In the vestibule of the edifice was an apartment where they found, on one of its sofas, a camel-load of rubies of Behreman, and other jewels; all of which the general-in-chief, Tarik bin Ziad collected together, and sent to the caliph of that period, Veleed bin Abd el Melek, who, his historians unite in saying, became so wealthy that no sovereign has ever equalled him.

A CONFERENCE BETWEEN HASHAMAND AN AGED MAN, HIS GUEST—A STRANGE OCCURRENCE.

It is written in the history of Ektemi Cufah, that Hasham bin Abd el Melek was famous among the Benee Ommieh for his villanous aspect, and the disagreeableness of his conduct. It happened one day that his attention was attracted to a great cloud of dust which made its appearance on the high road. He turned his steps in that direction, accompanied by one of his attendants named Refia, and remarked a caravan on its way from Damascus to Cufah. Hasham's eye falling upon an aged person in the caravan, he inquired of him whence he came, from what tribe he was, and whither he was going. The old man replied, "I am from Cufah; but what does it interest you to know to what tribe I belong?" Hasham replied, "The reason is this; you are from an intelligent tribe." The old man answered, "I am from the tribe of Hakkem, and am related to the tribe of Dakeh." Hasham exclaimed, "*El hamdu lillah!* praise be to God! one should be thankful not to be connected with that bad tribe." The old man replied, "As you know whether a tribe is good or bad, pray tell us what is your own family." Hasham answered, "Our origin is the Koraish." The old man replied, "The tribe of the Koraish are innumerable; among its people are high and low, wise and ignorant. From which portion of its people, pray, are you?" Hasham answered, "I am from the celebrated Benee Ommieh." The old man, now smiling, ironically exclaimed, "Merhaba! Merhaba! well met, well met! O brother Ommiade; it is well that you let us know your tribe. Greatness of origin and noleness of descent are united in your person; the blueness of your eyes, the unequalled features of your physiognomy, the eloquence of your tongue, and the gentleness of your expressions, render you more than man." Then changing his tone, he added, "We have a right to rebuke you, who are the most abased of creation; you belong to that tribe of which it is stated, in the book of the all-knowing Sovereign, that you are descended from the accursed tree pointed out in the verse. 'The wicked became pious, not the faithful.' Your males are wicked and sinful, your females are of evil condition and of unchaste propensities. One of your great men, Uffan, raised the standard of opposition against the Prophet of God, on whom be peace and blessings. You pride yourselves on Sohar ibin Harb. In the days of his ignorance he was but a farrier; and on turning Mussulman, he became a hypocrite, tyrant, and deceiver. Akbeh bin Abi Mueed was refused by 'the faithful news-giver' (Mohammed) the claim of belonging to the Koraish, whilst you give him that descent. His filthy, drunken, and evil-minded son Valeed, when performing the morning *namaz,* made four *rikats* (instead of three); and in his drunkenness asked whether he should not make some more. You have made a filthy fellow like him governor over the faithful Hakkem ibin el As; and although his son Mervan was repulsed by the Prophet, you took him up and showed him respect and regard. Is not one of the chaste females of your tribe, Hammalet ul Hatab placed on the same footing with Aboo Laheb?* Another too, named Hind, gave rich objects to Vahshee for his sinful deeds, to induce him to murder the chief of martyrs, Hamza, on whom be peace;† and after he was killed she tore him in pieces with her teeth.

VERSE.

'Have you not heard the story of the son of Hind, what she did to the relation of the Prophet; to whose family she showed much evil, and sucked the life-blood of the Prophet's uncle?'

What more, fellow, shall I teach you?" exclaimed the good old man, and then continued on his way.

Hasham remained silent, and finally turning to his page, said, "Have you seen what this old man has done to us?" "His temerity," answered the page, "and my own astonishment have driven everything he said out of my mind." "It is well for you," exclaimed Hasham; "but if any thing has remained, keep it to yourself, or I will kill you."

When Hasham had returned to his people, he sent messengers

* See chapter of the Koran, called Aboo Laleb.

† Uncle of the Prophet. See Ockley's History of the Saracens, p. 37.

in every direction to find the old man ; but the latter was lost like a spirit, or like a Jinn. No trace of him remained behind—in short he had fled from the abyss of danger to the skirts of safety.

AN ANECDOTE.

It is notorious that Abdul Melik bin Mervan, of the Ommiades, dreamed that he made water four times on the Holy Caaba. Having told this dream the next morning to Said bin Meseeb, (on whom be the mercy of Allah !) the latter interpreted it as follows: "Four individuals from your tribe will hereafter govern that very respected and holy place." And, in fact, Valeed, and Suliman, and Yezid, and Hasham, who are at the head of the list of the tyrannical, became the administrators and governors of the affairs of the Islamites, and continued in iniquity. It is not astonishing that their government soiled the purity which should pervade offices.

CHAPTER TWENTY-SIXTH.

On the subject of great eaters.

It is related by Veheb bin Jezzir, that there was once a celebrated glutton named Meiseret el Abresh. One of his friends asked him if he ever astonished any one by his great eating. Meiseret replied, "One day I arose at daylight, and there was no food prepared in the market. It was the season of fresh dates ; so I ate a hundred loaves of bread with a *mekook* of these dates." The *mekook* is a Syrian measure equivalent to twelve Stambool *kilehs* or bushels. "And did it not hurt you?" I asked. "It only swelled my belly," replied he.

One day Meiseret el Abresh mounted a large ass which he owned, and journeying onward he came to an Arab village on the road. Its inhabitants on seeing him went out to meet him, and invited him to a feast. Dismounting from his ass, and tying it up, he entered their tent. At night they killed his ass, cooked it, and served it up before him. He ate the whole of it alone, and went to sleep. On rising next morning he asked for his ass; and they told him he had eaten it the night previous for his supper. They then presented him with a camel, on which he mounted and departed.

It is related by Mutamir bin Suliman, that one Hellal Maznee was a famous glutton. Some one once addressing him, said, "People say you are a great eater; now, pray tell us the truth." Maznee replied, "Vallah! yesterday I had a goodly fat young camel of four years old, which I killed for food. They stuffed its liver with spices, and made it into a hash. My wife and self sat down to this and ate the whole of it. At night as we sat together I attempted to kiss her, but found I could not make our lips meet. Whereupon which she laughed and exclaimed, 'Do not forget, O husband, that a camel lies between us.'"

ANECDOTE.

Suliman bin Abd el Melik, one of the Ommiade caliphs, was a very great eater. Esmaee,* the quintessence of the excellent, relates: One day the caliph and Omar bin Abd el Aziz went together to the town of Taifeh,† to pay a visit to a farm owned there by Omri bin Asim. After riding about for some time, we dismounted from our horses; and the caliph, addressing the cook of the farm, asked him, "O Shemerdil, have you any thing ready for our dinner?" Shemerdil replied, "My Sovereign, I have a fat goat, fifteen geese, and twenty fowls each fatter than a goose; and they are all ready." He forthwith ordered them to be brought in; so the table was prepared, and they commenced eating. The caliph invited Omar bin Abdul Aziz to join him, but the latter declined on the plea of fasting; so he ate all himself. The meats being removed, the dessert was served, consisting of one hundred pomegranates, four hundred figs, and much other fruit; all of which he ate. Then after a little conversation, he walked about, and approached the kitchen, where, meeting with the head cook, he inquired of him what he had to eat. This person replied, "There are thirty-three pots boiling." Opening each, he took out three ladlefulls, and swallowed them; after which he walked away. At the table set for the attendants he ate again.

Historians relate much relative to this sultan's gormandizing characteristics; but the most remarkable of all is, that he daily ate to the amount of one hundred Damascus *ruttels*, a *ruttel* being equivalent to seven hundred dirhems. He at length died of a

* Esmaee, the Author of the Arabic novel of *Antar*, was a *Nadim*, or boon companion, of the Caliph Haroon er Rasheed.—A. T.

† *Taifeh* is a small town near Mecca; from which place, my teacher tells me, the finest grapes of Constantinople, called *tchavash*, were originally brought.—A. T.

surfeit caused by eating too much fruit. May God have mercy upon him!

It is related that among the greatest eaters known was an acquaintance of a monk. Once passing by the convent he was invited in by the monk, who asked him if he would not take something to eat. The monk told him there were boiled lentils in the kitchen, and said, "Will you eat some if they are brought in?" "Bring some," was his reply. So the monk placed before him ten loaves of bread, and then went to the kitchen to bring him a vessel of soup. Perceiving on his return that the bread was consumed, he put down the soup, saying that he would go now for bread, and brought him ten loaves more. On returning he observed that the soup was done; so putting down the bread, he took up the empty dish, and refilled it from the kitchen; but by the time he got back, the bread was gone. In this manner the monk brought in ten loaves of bread at ten different times, and, finding the soup consumed, returned for more; until finally the glutton was satisfied. After a little conversation, the man mounted his ass, and bade the monk adieu. When the monk inquired of him where he was going, he replied, "I am going to the opposite village to consult a physician much praised for his skill." "What do you want with a physician?" asked the monk. The fellow answered, "My stomach has been out of order for some days past, and my appetite much weakened in consequence. I purpose asking him for a restorative." The monk answered, "Pray grant me a favor." "What is it?" asked the man? "It is," said he, "that after you have corrected your stomach, you will not pass this way again."

CHAPTER TWENTY-SEVENTH.

On the subject of those who are censured for their great avarice.

Of all the caliphs Mansoor Devankee was most celebrated for avarice. One of his own servants, named Rebia, relates as follows: We once set out on a pilgrimage to Mecca; and when on our way, the famous Selem Hadee, following after the caliph's *taht revan* (palankeen), began in a loud voice to recite some verses. The caliph much pleased, struck the bottom of the *taht revan* with his foot and called to me. I approached; and when I asked for his orders, he exclaimed. "The sultan is much pleased with Selem Hadee, and gives him half a dirhem; let him continue reciting." At the same time he directed his accountant to register the sum in the book of expenses. When Selem Hadee saw the half dirhem, he exclaimed, "O glory of the family of Abbas, O Emir el Mumaneen, when I went on a pilgrimage with Hasham of the Benee Ommieh, I recited some verses near his *mahfeh* (litter), and he bestowed upon me thirty thousand dirhems." To this Mansoor remarked, "O Rebia, Hasham wronged the treasury of his people; it would therefore be but right for me to take from Selem what was given him, and restore it to the treasury." It was not till after an hour's dispute with Selem that I prevailed upon Mansoor to abandon the idea of compelling him to return the money he had received from Hasham; and then only on condition that every day and night during the pilgrimage he should recite verses in front of Mansoor's mahfeh.

Mansoor was a most pious and just man; but parsimony is most censurable in sovereigns. They require to be always gracious and benevolent to the world, and ever keep open the door of liberality and generosity.

THE STORY OF ABOOL CASIM TAMBOOREE.

It is related that there once resided in Bagdad a very wealthy man named Abool Casim, who was noted for his avarice and parsimony. So strong was his ruling passion, that he could not even be prevailed upon to throw away his old shoes; but whenever it became urgently necessary, he would have them stitched at a cobbler's stall, and continue to wear them for four or five years. At length they became so heavy and large, that it was proverbial in that city to say that a thing was "as clumsy as Abool Casim's shoes."

One day as this man was walking in the bazaars of Bagdad, a friend of his, a broker, informed him that a merchant from Aleppo was just arrived, and had brought some bottles for sale. "Come," added he, "I will get them for you at a low price; and after keeping them a month or so, you can sell them again for three times as much as you gave, and so make a handsome profit." The matter was soon arranged between them. Abool Casim bought the bottles for sixty dinars; and after employing several porters to carry them to his house, he passed on. He had also another friend, an auctioneer, whom he likewise happened to meet, and who told him that a merchant from the town of Yezd had some rose-water for sale. "Come," said he, "I will get it for you now at a low rate, and dispose of it for you at some other time for double the amount." So Abool Casim was prevailed upon to buy the rose-water also; and on reaching home he filled his bottles with the water, and placed them on a shelf in one of his apartments.

The day following Abool Casim went to the bath. As he was undressing himself, one of his friends going out saw his old shoes, and jokingly said, "O Casim, do let me change your shoes; for these have become very clumsy." Abool Casim merely replied, "Inshallah, if God wishes;" and continuing to undress himself, he went into the bath. Just then the cadi, or judge of the city, came to the bath, and undressed himself near to Abool Casim. Some time afterwards Abool Casim came out of the inner room of the bath, and, when he had dressed himself, looked for his shoes. Not finding them, but seeing a new pair in their place, he thought his friend had made the change that he desired; so putting them on, he returned to his house. When the cadi came out of the bath, and had put on his clothes, he asked for his shoes; but lo! they could no where be found. Seeing, close by, the old ones of Abool Casim, he naturally concluded that that person had purloined his. So the cadi was greatly incensed; and ordering Abool Casim to be brought before him, he accused him of stealing shoes out of baths, imprisoned him two or three days, and fined him.

Abool Casim, on his release, said to himself, "These shoes have dishonored me, and I have been severely punished for their sake." So with revengeful feelings he threw them into the Tigris. Two days afterwards some fishermen, on drawing their seines in the river, found a pair of old shoes in them, which they immediately recognized as those of Abool Casim. One of them remarked that perhaps he had fallen into the river. He took the shoes in his hand and carried them to Abool Casim's house; but finding its door closed, he threw them in at a window which was open. Unfortunately the shoes fell on the shelf where the bottles of rose-water were ranged; so that it was thrown down, the bottles broken, and all the rose-water spilt.

When Casim returned to his house he opened the door and beheld the loss he had sustained. He tore his hair and beard with grief, wept aloud, and charged the shoes with being his ruin. "To be free from further misfortune from them, I will bury them" said he "in a corner of my house, and then all will end." So the same night he arose and commenced digging a hole in a corner of his dwelling. His neighbors, hearing the noise, thought he was undermining their house; and rising in affright, they complained to the governor of the city, who sent and apprehended Casim and threw him into prison; from which he was released only on the payment of a fine.

After this Casim returned to his house, overwhelmed with grief; and taking his old shoes, he threw them into the sluice of a neighboring caravansary. In the course of a few days, the sluice being stopped, it overran its banks; and workmen having been called to clean it out, lo! Casim's shoes were found to be the cause of the inconvenience. So the governor again threw him into prison, and fined him to a large amount.

Abool Casim, now perfectly in despair, took his old shoes, and after washing them clean laid them on the terrace of his house, with the intention, after they were well dried, of burning them, and so putting an end to all shame and misfortune on their account. But it happened that while the shoes were drying a neighbor's dog passing over the terrace saw them, and, mistaking them for dried meat, took one in his mouth, sprang from one terrace to the other, and in doing so let it fall. The neighbor's wife was enceinte; and as she happened to be sitting at the foot of the wall the shoe fell upon her, and in her alarm she was prematurely brought to bed. Her husband, in great anger, complained to the governor; and Abool Casim was once more thrown into prison, and made to pay a fine.

Abool Casim now tore his hair and beard with grief; and accusing the shoes of being the cause of all his misfortunes, he took them in his hand, and going before the Cadi of Bagdad, related to him all that had befallen him. "I beg you," added he, "to receive my declaration; and I hope all these Mussulmans will bear witness that I now break off all further connexion between me and these shoes, and have no longer any thing to do with them. I also ask a certificate showing that I am free from them, and they from me; so that if, henceforth, there are any punishments or fines to be incurred, questions to be asked, or answers to be given, they may take them all upon themselves." The cadi, much amused with what he heard, gave the desired certificate, and added a present to Abool Casim.

Behold in this tale to what misfortunes the avaricious subject themselves!

CHAPTER TWENTY-EIGHTH.

Concerning those who fall in love and are captivated by the tender passion.

The following is told by the sultan of traditioners, Abool Feredj ibin el Joozee.

I heard my master, the Sheik Abool Hassan, relate, that a person of his acquaintance, a learned man, became enamored of a beautiful Nazarene (Christian) woman, and fell a captive to the chains of love. His affection for the object of his passion impaired his strength, and the pain of love rendered him ill. This love-sick man possessed a true friend and constant companion, who endeavored to procure a relief for his disorder. As he was become very weak, his friend mounted him on an ass, and conducted him to an infirmary, where he left him in charge of the physician. But the poor man's illness only increasing, he called his true friend to his bed-side, and informed him of the cause of his complaint, saying, " It is now some time since I fell a captive to the love-locks of such a Christian woman ; and since then I have been unable to obtain an interview with her. The hour of my *edjid* (fatal moment) is now near, and the interview cannot take place except at the great day. It has not been our destiny to be happy together in this world; my grief and affection have increased, and we can only be united in the other." He then closed his eyes and expired, and his friend prepared his body for interment. " Some days after the funeral," says he, "I went to the Christian woman, to tell her what had happened. I found her very ill and afflicted; and when I informed her of her lover's death, the excellent creature sighed, and wept, and exclaimed, 'It was not our lot to come together in this world, and our union is deferred until it can take place in the other. Be witness that I now forsake this futile religion, and accept that of Mohammed, on whom be peace.' She then recited the *kelami shehadit,* or confession of faith, embraced the Islam religion, and immediately expired in a state of fidelity." The relater adds, "Never in my life have I met with a stranger thing than this." *

NARRATIVE OF FAITHFUL AND LOVING PERSONS WHO HAVE FALLEN BY THE SWORD-POINT OF LOVE.

It is narrated in the history of Aina, that once in a social assembly of persons of education, the conversation turned upon the subject of love, and each one related a story. Among those who listened to the different tales was an aged man, who, being requested by those present to tell what he had seen and heard, related as follows:

I once had a daughter unequalled for her beauty. Moreover there resided in our quarter of the city a merchant's son, in whose society she had grown up, and to whose love-locks she fell a captive. She concealed her passion within her heart, and hid it from us. Our neighbor, the merchant's son, was also deeply enamored of a very worthy youth, the slave of a person residing near us.

STROPHE.

"Although a slave, he was fairer than his master."

Now this last mentioned youth made love to my daughter, and was a captive to the chains of her ringlets. One day there was a large assembly in which I and the youth who made love to my daughter happened to be, as well as the merchant's son who was in love with the lover of my daughter. Suddenly the youth repeated to himself in a low voice the following verses:

* It is no doubt from such religious belief as this that, in the interior of Asia Minor, Christians frequently are compelled, as it were, to marry Mussulmans. Some adopt the Islam faith, whilst others do not.

ARABIC COUPLET.

"The sign of those who are tormented by love's passion, is tears; above all, of that lover who finds none to sympathize with him."

When the merchant's son heard these words, he exclaimed, "*Ahsentu ya saidee!* I admire you, O my lord! do you give me permission to die in the path of love?" The youth replied, "Yes, if you are true to your love, and your condition is confòrmable to your words." Scarcely had he ended saying this, when the merchant's son fell backwards exclaiming, "*Ya Mahboob el ashikeen!* O thou Friend of true lovers!" and expired. All those present were shocked, and rising, they took their leave. I did so likewise, and went to my own house, when I related the occurrence to my wife. My daughter, unknown to us, was listening to my words, and we observed that her complexion changed. She asked her mother whether the son of such a one was really dead; and being replied to in the affirmative, she shrieked out and expired. "What shall we do? All knowledge is with Allah," we said; and having prepared her for interment, we were on our way to the cemetery when we met the funeral procession of the young man who had been beloved of my daughter, and had expired first. We carried them together to their graves. Now the youth who had recited the verses, and was in love with my daughter, on hearing the news of her decease, shrieked out and expired. His master prepared the body for interment, and we witnessed its burial also. All three were interred side by side. Thus wère these two lovers and a mistress, in the same day, both in life and in their tombs. May God have mercy on them all!

CHAPTER TWENTY-NINTH.

Some stories of an amusing nature.

It is related that once an Arab named Moosa, whilst travelling, came to a chapel in which the people were assembled for prayers. The Arab, who had a purse of money in his pocket, followed them in and took a place behind the Imam. Prayers commencing, the Imam exclaimed, reciting the verse of the Koran, "And he asked what is in thy right hand, O Moses (Moosa)?"

The Arab, pulling the purse from his bosom, exclaimed, "You are a sorcerer—there can be no doubt of it;" and fled.

It is related that an Arab of the desert had once stolen the saddle-cover (*ghashieh*) of another person, and put it in his bosom. It being prayer-time the people assembled in a chapel, whither the Arab also went. The Imam accidentally commenced reciting the chapter of the Koran, entitled El Gashieh (the day which envelopes): "Hath the news of the all-enveloping (El Gashieh) day of judgment reached thee?" The Imam then continuing, had just added, "The faces of some on that day shall be cast down;"* when the Arab drew out the saddle-cover, and begged him to take it and let his face alone.

It is related that an Arab named Moosa, one day entering a

* Koran, chapter 88.

chapel, heard the Imam recite the verses, "O Moses, verily the magistrates are deliberating concerning thee, to put thee to death. Depart therefore; I certainly advise thee well."* The Arab hastily finished his prayer, and as he left the chapel heard the Imam's voice continuing, "What is in thy right hand, O Moses?" "Ho! Imam, this stick is mine. Come after me, and know that with it I will dig your grave at the chapel door."

CHAPTER THIRTIETH.

On the subject of placing our confidence in God, who has said, "Put thy faith in that life which dies not; and when thou art in want, ask of Him; if thou need aid, ask it also of Him. Know that all people, if united, could do thee nothing, nor benefit thee at all, except in as much as He has written it; and that should all people unite to do thee wrong, they can not harm thee, except when God has written it." Thus has the Prophet stated.

It is related that in the time of Haroon er Rasheed there was a great famine and dearness of provisions. Many persons died of hunger. Haroon er Rasheed and all the people repented of their evil acts, implored divine pardon, and refrained from the use of forbidden things. He had all the instruments of sin broken, and forbade all kinds of plays and amusements.

One day during this period, observing an Arab dancing and clapping his hands, he ordered him to be brought before him and said, "How is it, that whilst the people are in so much distress and affliction, you dance and play?" The Arab replied, "Elham-

* Koran, chapter 28.

du lillah! God be praised! My lord has a magazine filled with grain; he leaves no one hungry or in want, but provides for my support; and in my delight I dance." The caliph wept and replied, "Put confidence in your own Lord, and be not grieved; for he is the Creator of his people, and it is He who provides for them out of his endless bounties when unable to help themselves. He is security for the necessities of his people;—never will he leave them hungry or in need of others. This famine is, no doubt, caused by our want of confidence." So saying, he returned to the path of reliance on God's mercies.

It is related that once there was a great famine in Bagdad; so that most of the inhabitants left the city, and went every one to a different place. Among them was a poor but learned man, the neighbor of a wealthy person, named Ibin Abdallah. This man, with the hope of doing something for his family, wished also to depart. But his wife said to him, "If you leave us here alone at such a time, what will be our lot? who will look after us, or provide for us?" The man replied, "I have a bond against Ibin Abdallah for money lent him; after I am gone, present it, and he will every day give you provisions." He wrote these lines on a paper, and gave it to his wife: "My wife said to me, 'When I am left in this place, who will aid me?' I replied, 'Allah and Abdallah;'" after which he departed. His wife and children took the paper and presented it to Ibin Abdallah, who read it, and appointed a man to supply them with food daily; and, until the husband returned, he continued to bestow his generosity upon them.

THE STORY OF THE PIOUS AND UPRIGHT HATIM ASAM.

It is related in the history called "Mirat ez Zeman," that Hatim Asam was once reduced to extreme poverty. He was, however, a pious and zealous servant of God. One day one of his friends set out on a pilgrimage to Mecca. This inspired Hatim Asam with the desire of doing the same. So returning to his wife and children, he said to them, "Will you give your father permission to go to Mecca this year, that he may acquit himself of that divine ordinance, and offer up prayers for you?" His eldest son replied, "You have not a farthing, and are not acquainted with any one who will defray your expenses; neither have you any thing to leave to your family." But he also had a young daughter, who, addressing her mother, said, "God will provide for us: our father is also an humble servant of Him; why should you therefore object to his going? Leave him alone; let him depart to accomplish his wishes, and pray for us." All the other children exclaimed, "True! it is just; let him go." So early in the morning Hatim Asam bade them farewell, and set out on foot for Mecca.

That day all the neighbors collected around Hatim Asam's house. They asked, "Why did you let him go, and leave you all in this needy condition, without any one to aid you." Hatim's oldest son replied, "I endeavored to prevent him; but this little girl was the cause of his going." They all blamed the girl; and she, turning her face towards the Judge of all wants, prayed: "O God, thou hast promised to my people to bestow thy excellence on them. Thou will not harm them, nor place them in danger; do not now, therefore, make me ashamed among them;" and she rubbed her face against the earth in humble devotion.

Now it happened that, at the same hour, the Emir of the faithful went forth to the chase. The day was very hot; and the heat making him excessively thirsty, he cried out, "Let us hasten back to the city, where I can procure a drop of water." Just then they came to Hatim Asam's door; and, on knocking at it, this same little girl approached, and, inquiring who knocked, heard the reply, "Help, help! open the door. The Emir of the faithful is here, and asks a cup of water from you." Hatim's wife, turning her face towards heaven, exclaimed, "Thanks be to God! Last night Hatim's poor children went to bed hungry; to-day the Emir el Mumaneen comes to his door to crave a cup of water." The little girl handed the caliph a draught of water in a clean cup, which he drank; and receiving fresh vigor from it, he inquired whose house it was. His vizir replied, "It belongs to a pious man named Hatim Asam. I have heard that he has put on the *ibram*,* and gone on the holy pilgrimage, and that his wife and children last night went supperless to bed." The caliph replied, "We have also come to be an addition to the number of his family, having been a burden to them, and having drunk of their water. It is not generous to leave them unrequited." So, unbuckling a golden belt from his waist, he threw it on the sill of Hatim's door; at the same time exclaiming, "Let those who love me show regard to Hatim's family." All his followers immediately unfastened their belts, threw them on the door-sill, and departed. The vizir told the family that it was the caliph's bounty. "Wait an hour," said he, "and I will bring you the value of the belts." In fact, soon afterwards he returned and redeemed them with a hundred thousand pieces of gold, which he put into a bag and presented to Hatim's wife. When Hatim's little girl saw the splendid sight, she wept; and on being asked the cause of her tears, she replied, "Because last night I lay down a hungered; and to-day, the look of an humble being like ourselves has conferred upon us so much wealth. Now, therefore never let those who are under the favorable regard of the King of kings beg of any other. Our poverty is from the smallness of our patience; and my confidence in him is the cause that he has bestowed so much bounty on Hatim's family."

* Penitential cloaks, in which pilgrims dress during their visit to Mecca.

But let us return to Hatim, who, having journeyed one station with the caravan, stopped at a *konak* (hotel), where the Emir el Hadj (the chief of the pilgrim caravan) fell ill of a complaint for which no remedy could be found. The Emir ordered those about him to make search in the caravan for some pious person to pray for him, and have him brought before him; saying, that he would ask, in person, his assistance for his recovery. Some one replied, that Hatim Asam was in the caravan among the pilgrims. "Hasten," replied he, "and look for him." So, search being made for the pious man, he was brought before the Emir, at whose feet he knelt and saluted him with good wishes (prayers); and in the same hour that he did so the Emir recovered. He had a tent pitched for Hatim beside his own; and collecting all the poor around him, he, the same night was about recommencing his journey, when the reflection entered the mind of Hatim, "O God and the Prophet! Hatim has received your favor—what may be the condition of his wife and children?" Whereupon he heard a voice crying out, "O Hatim, whoever arranges his affairs peaceably with us will be treated peaceably by us;" which assured him that his wife and children had received divine favor. Hatim returned grateful thanks; and with heartfelt joy and contentment he performed his pilgrimage. On returning home, his wife and children came out to meet him. Hatim kissed his youngest daughter and wept. He exclaimed, "Know that God regards not your great men,—but he views with favor those who know the most; therefore what is most needful to you is knowledge. Whoever confides in God will find mercy from him."

The Sheik Jemal ed Deen bin Abdallah, of Damascus, relates the following:

Once, in company with a number of choice friends, I made a visit to Mount Lebanon; and, as it was much frequented by holy and devout persons, we hoped to fall in with some of them. We ascended the mountain; where, after walking about a great deal, I became fatigued. Coming to a stream, I seated myself beside it, and told my companions that I would wait for them there. So they continued on; and I, after going through my ablution, performed several *rikats* (genuflections in prayer). I then arose; and whilst wandering about, I heard a voice. On proceeding in the direction from which it came, I entered a cave, in which I walked for a considerable time. At the end of it I perceived an old man of a frightful figure, engaged in reading the Koran. He was however blind of both eyes. I saluted the alarming, though holy person. I asked him whether he was a human being or a jinn, adding that I myself was a man. He was greatly surprised, and replied, "It is now more than thirty years since I have seen any of my brethren of humanity." I approached him, kissed his hand, and seating myself beside him, saw three tombs near him. After reposing myself a little, I arose, made my noon-day prayers, and then occupied myself with my own affairs whilst the holy man was engaged in his devotions. When the *ikindee* (the third hour of daily prayer) was come, he performed his *namaz*. Raising his hand he commenced his prayers, saying, "O God have mercy upon the people of Mohammed; rejoice the people of Mohammed!" He remarked to me, "Every one who day and night repeats this prayer will receive the degree of an *abdal* (Santon), and be of Him who taught me, as it is written, 'He (God) who taught man what he did not know.' Go, look into the cell opposite you; and whatever you find there, eat." I went into the cell, and saw lying on a black stone several clusters of fresh grapes, fresh figs, and other fruits; and being surprised, I asked how they came there. "Have a little patience," was his reply, "and you will soon see." Shortly afterwards I saw a beautiful bird, with white wings, a green breast, and a yellow neck, and altogether adorned with plumage of various colors. It held in its mouth a cluster of grapes, and in its two claws it brought two figs. It entered the cell, where it put the fruit down. In this manner it returned twice, each time bringing in fruit, and departed. The Sheik said to me, "Do you now see, O Abdallah?" I replied, "Yes." He continued, "It is now more than fifty years since I first entered the cave. This bird, by divine command, serves me in the manner you have witnessed; and I with a pure heart put confidence in the Creator of all things: for it is written, 'He who fears God will receive from him the supply of all his wants, when he least expects it.' Up to the present time this bird has come to me ten times a day; but now, in honor of you, it will come twenty times,—for which God be praised!"

This holy man had on a *caftan* (cloak) quite new, and so transparent that I never, in my life, had seen anything like it. I inquired of him, "Where did you obtain this cloak; does it never wear old?" The holy man replied, "This bird, every Ramazan, brings me ten pieces from the back of a tree; out of which I make a cloak, and wrap the remainder round my head." Near the holy man was a stone, on which the bird would pour a little water; this the Sheik rubbed over his head, and the bird would take every hair out of his head, cleaner than if cut with a razor.

One morning, as I was conversing with the Sheik, seven persons entered from without; their eyes were divided lengthwise, and their feet were formed like the hoofs of a goat. The Sheik said to me, "These persons are Islam jinns; every day they come to me and take a lesson." Approaching him, they read the chapter T. H.,* which the Sheik commented on; and after saluting him, they departed. He now asked me how I found the cave, and who showed it to me. I told him how I had left Damascus with my companions; and how, they having separated from me, I was

* The 20th chapter of the Koran.

left alone, and, whilst wandering about, by Divine providence fell upon the entrance to the cave, on coming into which I had the honor to meet him. "God be thanked!" said the Sheik; "were it not for your companions, I would keep you all night; but they must be troubled by your absence, so now go and deliver them from anxiety." Kissing his hand I arose, and the Sheik accompanied me to the entrance of the cave, where an enormous and frightful lion met us. The Sheik spoke a few words to it, and then bade me mount its back. "Fear not," said he; "he will carry you to your residence, and save you from all trouble." I kissed his hand again, and invoked his good prayers in my behalf. Whereupon he said, "If, hereafter, you should make the holy pilgrimage, do not neglect to look at the side of the Zemzem gate for a man of such and such an appearance. Kiss his hand, and you will obtain all your desires; for he is a holy man, whose prayers are acceptable. Give him my salaams; and should he inquire whose they are, tell him they are from Ibraheem Kermanee." On ending these words he left me.

I mounted on the lion, which carried me into Damascus and then returned. I there entered the mosk of the Benee Ommieh, where when my friends saw me, they were greatly rejoiced. I related to them all that had happened to me, and returned with them to the mountain; but, notwithstanding all our researches, we were unable to find the entrance to the cave. My friend observed to me that it was a divine gift, which would not be found when sought after. Finally we entered Damascus.

Each year I went to Mecca; but it was only at the eighteenth pilgrimage that I found the holy man, when I kissed his hand, and informed him that Ibraheem Kermanee saluted him. "Peace be on you and on him!" he exclaimed, "when did you see the Sheik?" So I related to him the circumstances, and invoked his good prayers for me. He informed me that what had occurred to me was a divine favor, or I never could have seen the Sheik; for when he entered the cave and took up his secret abode there, he prayed,

"O God conceal me from thy servants, and only permit me to meet with any one by thy holy will;" and his prayers were accepted. "I have recently buried him," continued he. On my asking, "How did you know of his decease?" he replied, "A voice went from the East to the West, saying, 'O faithful one! O man of God! be ready to assist at the funeral of Ibraheem Kermanee.' All the men of God assembled there, prepared the body for interment, and buried it beside those tombs which you saw."

It is related that there was once a holy man, a man of great piety, who, by Divine favor was, wherever he went, accompanied by a small cloud of Paradise*; and his prayers were always accepted by God. By Divine providence, a weakness coming upon him, his limbs became shortened, and the cloud which usually accompanied him left him. The holy man (hermit) was much grieved. He arose at midnight and wept; and whilst praying to God, he heard a voice, saying, "The acceptance of your prayers and the success of your hopes are dependent on the prayers of the sovereign of such a country." The hermit departed to the king of the country mentioned, and sought an interview with his door-keepers, so as to make known his circumstances to the king. The door-keepers gave him this reply, "Our sovereign holds a divan once a week, and no one once sees his face at any other time." So the hermit passed a week in offering up devotions in the corner of a chapel; and when the king held his divan, he represented his condition to him. The king directed his people to have the hermit brought to him in his palace. After this he arose and entered his palace, where he sent for his vizir.

The hermit relates, "We went into an immense and splendidly furnished palace; and through it passed into a miserable apart-

* In Arabic *zilli zaleel*, shadow of Paradise,—one of the attractions held out by Mohammed to the sun-burnt Arabs of the desert.

ment, whose four walls were about to crumble down. Here we saw the same person who had held the divan; he had laid aside his silk robes, put on an old monk's frock, and was seated on nothing but an old mat. Near him was a moon-faced female slave, who was his wife; and a little boy passed in and out to them. When he saw me, he showed me very great regard and honor; and I knew that he was of the true sovereignty, one of the sultans of this world and of eternity. Addressing his wife (*khatoon*) he asked, "Do you know who this great man is?" She replied, "Yes; he is the master of the cloud." From this I saw that his wife was also one of God's people. The king, turning round, said, "God knows that I have no enjoyment from my sovereignty. My forefathers came and departed just as you see me; and now my time has come. I did not wish to accept the throne, and requested the people to choose for their king whomsoever they wished, it being my intention to withdraw into retirement; but I reflected that such and such things might happen,—that a tyrant might be placed over a division of God's people, and an injury be done to their laws, for which I would have to answer in the other world. So, in fine, I concluded that I would, once a week, hold a divan in person, to devote myself to the welfare of God's people, and spend the other days in prayer to the Creator. My chief vizir oversees the affairs of the Mussulmans with justice; for which God be thanked! though no other vizir or public servant knows anything about my conduct. This poor creature is my uncle's daughter and my wife; she is always with me, and is faithful to me at all times. You to-night are our guest; and to-morrow, God willing, you may depart rejoicing." He then took two baskets of palm-leaf, and gave them to a boy who attended upon him, directing him to go and dispose of them, and bring him some beans, sweet cake (*halwa*), and bread. The boy went and brought the things which were asked for, and we ate and slept. At midnight they arose, and remained praying until the morning. After finishing the morning prayer they lifted up their hands and prayed, 'O Allah, thy servant begs thee to return him his cloud—that one which thou gavest to him as a guide; return it, O God.' The wife responded, 'Amen;' and I saw the cloud descend again from heaven. He rubbed his hand against it, and exclaimed, 'God be praised! Your prayer has been accepted; joy to you!' So I arose; and embracing him, I kissed his hand, took leave of him, and returned to my own country. I always mention them in my five daily prayers; and whatever I pray for, or ask, is accorded to me. For which God be praised!"

Sehil bin Abd Allah Testeree, one of the most pious of men, relates the following:

"When I was three years old, my uncle, the Sheik Mohammed bin Suvar, used to arise and pray in the night; and I would also arise with him. My uncle states that I was born in the holy month of Ramazan. The Almighty would generally send a sleep upon me during the days of that month, and I would continue sleeping and nursing from my mother's breast until the sunset call to prayer. One of God's acts of grace to me was this: Once when I was passing through a desert field, I looked for water to perform the ablutions of the noon-day prayer, and finding none, my heart was grieved. Suddenly I perceived a bear bringing a basin of water, which it put before me. I refrained from using it for my ablutions; and whilst wondering whether it was pure or not, the bear spoke and said, 'O Sehil, we are a tribe cut off from the people, and rely upon love.' Suddenly I heard a voice from an unknown direction saying, 'Sehil asked water for his ablutions, but found none.' They then gave me this jar saying, 'Take it and depart.' When the jar was put before me I saw two angels pouring water into it, and I could hear their voices very well. Whilst yet astonished, and reflecting on what I had seen, I observed that the jar remained, but those who brought it had disappeared. I was greatly grieved, and conversed for some time with the bear. I performed my ablutions with the water, but when I was about to drink, a voice came to me from my *hatif* (guardian angel), saying, that it was not time to drink of that water. So I set the jar down; whereupon it moved, and continuing to roll, it disappeared from my sight."

The Almighty gave Sehil power over the wild beasts and birds. They would come and go at his call. He would buy meat in the market, and feed them one or two days at a time in his house; when the people would go to gaze at him and them. May God bless his secrets, and bless us with his bounty!

Aboo Hamza Soofee, the most eminent of the great Sheiks, relates: In the commencement of my travels, and in the times of religious wars and abstinence, I travelled every year one thousand furlongs. One year, as I made the holy pilgrimage, I fell into a well in the desert, so deep that a rope of one hundred fathoms *(koladj)* would not reach its bottom. Whilst there, I saw two persons come to close up the mouth of the well; for which purpose they brought some trees, and commenced filling it. I wished to cry out from the well; but a voice came from my *hatif*, commending me to put up a prayer of confidence and to ask aid of others. I therefore remained silent, and the two persons fastened the mouth of the well and went away. I continued there all night. The next day I observed that something had thrust its feet through into the well and was making a sign to me. I climbed up to the feet, and catching hold of them, was drawn above ground; when I beheld in my deliverer an enormous and frightful animal, such as I never had seen before. A voice at that moment came to me, saying, "O Aboo Hamza, we have delivered thee from ruin by means of thine associate." I prostrated myself to the ground, and praised God for his mercies. The servant of God, who puts firm trust in Him, will always be sure to receive aid from Him.

Sehil bin Allah relates: In the beginning of my travels I went to the abode of the tribe of Ad, and entered a large town of sculptured stones, where I saw a Sheik of extraordinary size engaged in prayer, with his face directed towards the Caaba. I remarked a *jebbeh*, or cloak, on the Sheik's back, the purity and cleanliness of which surpassed all I had seen in my life. When I saluted him, he returned my salutation, and said, "Know, O Sehil, that this cloak is tainted with the odor of old sins, and that it is one remaining from the time of Jesus. I once saw Mohammed Mustapha* with it on, was honored with his regard and believed in him." I asked him, "Pray what do men call you?" To which he replied, "The Surat which says, 'It hath been revealed unto me, that a company of Jinns attentively heard,' &c.† was sent down from heaven on my account!"

The most eminent of the great sheiks, Abd Allah bin Mohammed el Balkhee, relates: I once lived among the ruins of the illustrious city of Mecca. No one knew by what means I supported myself. One day, early in the morning, whilst seated in the holy temple in the place of Ibraheem, on whom be peace, the Sheik Mohammed bin Abd Allah el Basree came in, followed by four persons. After making a turn round the temple, they went off in

* The Prophet.

† The seventy-second Surat of the Koran, entitled "The Jinns."

the direction of the gate called Bab Benee Sheibeh. I, thinking it was a propitious time, followed after them. One of them turned and ordered me away; but the Sheik Mohammed, addressing him, said, "Do not offend him." So, that, counting myself, we were six persons; and the Sheik Mohammed addressing us said, "Follow each other in my steps, so as to make but the tracks of one person; and do not leave me." The Sheik preceded us, and we walked on as he had just commenced. The ground under our feet seemed to fold up like paper; and we continued on in this way until we arrived at the Seddi Yajooj, where we recited the evening prayer, and then proceeded.

As we went along we met a venerable and holy man, whom the Sheik embraced, and then held a friendly conversation with. The Sheik, with very great civility and calmness went towards him, and bade him sit down; and whilst they were amicably conversing together I beheld some men like birds fly towards and assemble around the venerable man. They talked about moral philosophy, and made some of those persons tremble like the shaking of an earthquake, whilst others cried out *Allah* with so much vehemence that I thought the earth and sky would crumble together. Some persons came up as quick as lightning and passed away. This continued until morning, when they performed the matin prayer, always following the venerable person. They then separated, and we went a short way on, until we reached the other side of mount Caf, where is a fine country, whose earth is whiter than snow, and with very many lights, but not resembling those of this world. Whilst going over this ground we met with wonderful and curious creatures. Their forms were like those of man; but their faces can be compared to nothing, and were more shining than the sun. Our eyes were dazzled, and our Sheik seemed like a drunken camel; he threw his head from right to left, until his thoughts left him.

We went on until the matin prayer, when we arrived at a place where there was a large town. All its walls were of gold and silver, and it was surrounded by trees interlaced in each other's branches. On every side rivers ran like torrents. We ate fruits of the most delicious kind, and drank water like that of the *Abi Zellal*. I never tasted any thing so exquisite as that fruit, and its flavor remains in my mouth to this day. It had the appearance of an apple; and the Sheik directed us to take one or two apiece. We each pulled off three. A person who had told me to go away could not reach his hand to the fruit; and it was remarked, that this was the result of his incivility, and the prohibition which he wished to put upon me. The Sheik now told him to put forth his hand; whereupon it reached the fruit, and he took one. Then, turning round, the Sheik inquired, "Do you know this city?" To which, they having replied in the negative, he added, "It is called the City of the Saints, into which none other than they can enter." After remaining a little longer we set out and continued on our way; and reaching Mecca at noon, we repeated the prayers of that hour. The Sheik then turned to me, and said, "Promise me never, during my life, to divulge our adventure to any one." As he departed, he added that he would again return to meet me. May Allah profit us with their blessings!

ANECDOTE.

The sultan of learned doctors, Yafee, says that one of the most devout and pure of men related to him as follows: I was seated in the mausoleum of the Prophet, when I observed three pious men enter by the portal called the Bab es Salam, who prayed over the head of the tomb and departed. A benevolent individual near me informed me that these persons were "men of God." "Arise," said he, "lose not the opportunity, but follow after them." So I did as he recommended, and was following them, when one turned round and looked closely into my face. This alarmed me so that I was near fainting; nevertheless I continued in their footsteps. They left the chapel, and I did the same. One of them, now turning round, again looked in my face and said, "Depart and go after thy gains; thou canst not accompany us." The chief of them added, "It is proper that the Most High should leave his exalted place for one still higher."

They again continuing on, I followed. I distinctly saw the earth and mountains folding up under our feet like a carpet; and I heard a voice coming up from under the earth with a roaring sound. The treasures of the earth, one by one, were exposed to my view, and then again disappeared. We reached a valley in which they recited their prayers under its trees, and where we met with seventy glorious and pious individuals. Arising the next morning, and proceeding on our way, we came to a city, which had a castle whiter than snow, built of stone. From each of its walls flowed a stream of great size, the source of which was within the city. They ran out by openings latticed with pure gold. We entered by these same openings, and beheld several banks, and balconies, and palaces, all covered with arches of gold resting on columns of silver. The gravel beneath the water consisted of the most precious jewels; the ground was covered with many kinds of flowers, and different fruits; and on the trees, birds of many species were singing. The fruits were so delicious that a man would not be satisfied with eating a whole *rutel* (a pound of twenty ounces).

We remained forty days in that city, enjoying the pleasures of devotion, and then departing by the way through which we had entered, that is, by the water-passage. We had not proceeded far, when my companions asked me where they should take me to. I replied, that I hoped they would conduct me to Mecca. The chief of them then told me, that the city which we had just visited was the "City of the Saints," that the Most High had appropriated it especially to them, and that no one else could enter it. "It is not always found in the same place," added he; "it is alternately in Yemin, in Sham, in Room, and in Adjem; for it makes the circuit of the four quarters of the globe. None but those who have reached the degree of holiness of the forty, can enter it."

After going a little further we saw another city, which he told me was the city of Yemin. Soon afterwards, reaching the city of Mecca, we entered the Holy House (Caaba), where they took leave of me and departed. I had put a few of the apples of that city in my bosom; and on them I subsisted four or five months, eating nothing else. They are, when compared with the power of the Lord of the two worlds, but as a drop of water taken from the sea.

ANECDOTE.

Abd er Rahman el Bestany relates, that it is said by one of the learned and miraculous persons with whom he met, "The surface of the earth contains one thousand cities, which I have visited; the smallest and most insignificant of them is 'Zatal Imad made a garden unequalled in the universe.'* When Abd Allah entered the city called 'Medineti Nidjash,' he found in the road to it the tomb of Gush bin Shedad bin Ad; and near its head he saw a table made of yellow wood, supported on four legs of cypress. On the sides of the table was written, 'A thousand kings eat off the table which you have seen, and made merry, all of whom were blind of their right eye; and among them, God only knows how many were perfect.'

PERSIAN VERSES.

'Jem drank his cup, and many thousand Rustems have passed over us. The same social system remains,—the world is still the same.'"

* Koran.

If my heart was not oppressed with grief, I would have added many more things here.

STRANGE OCCURRENCE.

It is related, that once in Bagdad, "the place of Paradise," the Sheik Abdallah Andalusee (of Andalusia, in Spain), who was one of the greatest of Sheiks and the most pious of men, as well as a very upright person every way worthy of confidence, determined to spend a year in travel. For this purpose he left that city, followed by no less than ten thousand disciples, among whom were Jeneed Bagdadee and Sheik Shebly. By the permission of the Sheik they all returned except the Sheik Shebly and forty other persons, who remained in his service.

On their way they came to one of the infidel towns; where the Sheik having asked for water for his ablutions, no sign of any could be seen. At one end of the town they perceived a church, which was well built and furnished with bells, and where numerous priests, deacons, and monks, all assembled together for the purpose of making their devotions according to their religion. In front of this church was a large well, from which a number of women were drawing water; among whom was a most beautiful girl, dressed in silk, with many valuable and jewelled crosses suspended around her neck. Those who beheld this fair creature exclaimed, "What a beautiful woman!" When the Sheik Abdallah saw her, he became a prey to the snare of love, and asked whose daughter she was. He was told that she was the daughter of the king of the country; on which he inquired, why she was then engaged as he saw her. They told him, that her father had placed her there for the purpose of being educated in abstinence, so that when she was given in marriage she might know her husband's worth and be respectful towards him. In fine, the beauty of this girl made such an impression on the Sheik, that he became quite beside himself, and remained three days in that place without once speaking to any one.

Sheik Sumballee states that he went to him and said, "My sultan, your disciples and all your fakirs are in despair at your affliction; and it is now three days since you have eaten or drunk any thing, or spoken a word to any one." To this the Sheik replied with a sigh; but at length arising, he called his disciples around him, and said, "I am indeed in a bad state, and have no power over myself; that beautiful creature has imprisoned my heart in such a way, that none but the All-Just can free me. I am wholly unable to separate myself one step from this place. What was to come upon me has come. Forget me not in your prayers, and depart in peace." All his fakirs (disciples devoted to meditation and austerity) lamented and wailed over him; and Shebly speaking, said, "O Sheik, do not dishonor us in the midst of these infidels. Your orders are obeyed from the east to the west, and all look to you for protection; how can we leave you among the infidels?" To which he answered, "I knew all this; but thus has the pen of fate decreed. I have fallen into the sea of nothingness; the knot of command is loosened, and my ability to direct is rolled up." Then falling down upon his face, he wept so violently, that even the infidels, the trees, and the stones wept with him. Afterwards he arose, and again commanded all his friends to depart and leave him to himself. "Destiny and fate have reached me," said he; "therefore forget me not in your prayers." We all in tears exclaimed, "O Lord of the two worlds, be kind to him!" and then left him. On our return to Bagdad, more than forty thousand persons, composed of the magistrates and the people, came out to meet us. On expressing their surprise at not seeing the Sheik, we explained what had occurred to him; when such a sound of grief came from the crowd, that it seemed a signal of the judgment-day. Many individuals were nearly killed with sorrow, and raising their hands in prayer, exclaimed, "O thou Guider of the erring, we ask of thee the Sheik who is confided to thee." Then turning round they departed.

Sheik Shebly relates: Grief deprived me of strength, and one year afterwards, desirous of learning what had become of the Sheik, I started from Bagdad for the town where we had left him. On inquiring of the people of the place about him, they answered, that he was herding swine at the foot of the opposite mountain. I asked the cause of his being there; and they replied, "He asked for the king's daughter, and it was agreed that he should tend the king's swine one year in place of a dowry (*mihr*)." Shebly adds, that on hearing this, a torrent of tears fell from his eyes; and approaching the mountain, he saw the Sheik clothed in the dress of a monk, with a hat on his head and a cord round his waist, and leaning upon a staff. On seeing me he inclined his head, and tears of blood fell from his eyes upon the ground. I saluted him; and when he had replied, I said to him, "What a condition you have got into, O Sheik!—is it just that an Imam of your celebrity, the author of so many commentaries and traditions, should change his honors to so great debasement." Turning round he answered, "O brother, I have no longer any command over myself, and am become as a slave who obeys whatever his master orders him to do; from being the most famed of all, I am become so dependent upon others, that if my master pitilessly debases me and rejects me, he alone has the power to command. O friend, flee from such injurious things!" Then turning his face towards heaven, he added, "My God, my lord (Mohammed), my master, I did not think this of thee." At the same time weeping, he said, "O Shebly, pray for me." Whereupon I commenced praying, "O Allah, thou art He to whom we look for help; Thou art the Helper, we confide in thee; free us from this sorrow, for none can do it but thee." On ending this prayer, the Sheik added, "Amen," and then rubbed his face upon the earth, weeping and wailing in the most piteous manner. Alarmed at his cries, the swine made a sudden strange noise like that of the last day; then collecting around him, they also rubbed their faces on the earth. So speaking to the Sheik, I begged him to occupy his mind in thinking of commentaries and traditions,—of something of special selection. But he replied, "I have forgotten them all; nothing now remains in my memory but two Ayats (verses) of the Koran: one is, 'And whomsoever God shall render despicable, there shall be none to honor;' * and the other, 'He that hath exchanged faith for infidelity hath already erred from the straight way.' † The tradition is as follows, 'Put to death him who changes his religion.' ‡ This is all that has remained within me." "Blessed be God," exclaimed I; "this is what is needed." At the same time I asked him whether he would not accompany us to Bagdad. He replied, "From being the shepherd of the hearts of so many pure and pious men, I have become a keeper of swine; how then can I go there?" He added however, "Go, collect my friends together, and wait for me at such a place; for the world is again my own."

So I returned to Bagdad, and gave the joyful news to all his friends. Three days afterwards we set out from that city; and as we were looking out for the Sheik at the appointed place, we saw him repeating with a frightfully loud voice, the Kelimehi Tevhid, or profession of God's unity, along the banks of a large river. The sight of him gave us all infinite pleasure. He approached us, and crying out to me, said, "O Shebly, give me one of your garments." I did so; and when we had dressed him in it he renewed his ablution, recited his Namaz (prayers), and returned thanks and praises to God. We also all exclaimed, "We thank thee, O God, that he is returned to us, and that thou hast restored us to him." On our inquiring after his health, and what had

* Koran 22:19. † Koran 2:102.

‡ This tradition has been violated by the present Sultan Abdul Mejid, who forbade in 1843 the execution of such as return to Christianity from Islamism.—A. T.

happened to him after our departure, he said, "After you left me I rubbed my forehead upon the ground in humility, and prayed to God to pardon the sins of his servant, and the All-merciful God was good to me." We now continued on to Bagdad; and on the day of our arrival there all the pious persons of the city, males, females, and children, came out to meet us. Seventy different communities came out to receive and greet him; and they conducted the Sheik to his own dwelling. That same day some one or two hundred infidels embraced the faith.

A month afterwards I was seated one day with the Sheik in a private cabinet, when some one knocked at the door. On opening it, we beheld a woman dressed wholly in black, who replied to our interrogations, by saying, that she was the handmaid of the Sheik who had visited the Nazarene village. On bringing her to the Sheik, his countenance changed color, and he trembled like the leaves of autumn; he wept and asked who had sent her. She replied as follows. "After your departure I had no rest or comfort, but lay overwhelmed in grief and tears. In my sleep I heard the terrible voice of some one saying, 'If you leave this infidelity and idolatry, and embrace the true faith, I will cause you to reach the side of the Sheik, and all your desires to be attained.' On my consenting, he recited the Kelimai Shahadet or profession of faith, and bade me wink my eyes. I did so; and on opening them again I found myself in the outskirts of a city. Then placing himself at my side he brought me into the city, to a door at which he knocked, saying, 'Pray give my compliments to the Sheik, and tell him that his brother Hadee sends him many salams.'" "Welcome!" exclaimed the Sheik, on hearing this; and receiving the maiden into his house, he rendered her so devout, so assiduous in her fasts, and so prayerful, that she became the object of the reverence and demands for prayers of all the most celebrated and pious women of that country.

Some time after this she fell ill, and asked for the Sheik. We found her reduced to a spider's web by her austerity and devotional exercises. The Sheik inquired how she was, and wept. Whereupon shé exclaimed, "Weep not, O Sheik; for we will soon be resuscitated together. I will be your companion in the abode of the All-gracious in Eden." On uttering these words she gave up her soul, and we buried her with marks of respect and regard. One night I saw the Sheik in a dream; he was seated on an elevated throne, ornamented with jewels, with that pure girl by his side. Seventy Hoorees waited upon them; and she and the Sheik walked hand in hand in the inner court of the exalted place, rocking to and fro as they went. May God have mercy on them all!

CHAPTER THIRTY-ONE.

On the subject of those kings who have possessed fortunate ways, gracious manners, and a harmonious deportment.

Ibraheem bin Mehdee, one of the descendants of the caliphs, was a youth of noble attainments. He was the Nadim, or boon companion, of one or two caliphs. He says: Jaafer Beramikee, the vizir of Haroon er Rasheed, was one day sitting in his private apartments with his own Nadims, and invited me to be of their company. Then calling his door-keeper, he ordered him to let no one enter, not even Abd el Melik bin Salek (the caliph's uncle) himself. A bountiful repast was then spread before us, and we ate and drank to our great delight. The door-keeper however neglected to inforce the orders which he had received; and lo! we saw the uncle of the caliph, Abd el Melik bin Salek, enter the apartment in which we sat. Jaafer was much confused, and we all immediately jumped up to show the respect due to the visiter;

who, observing the confusion of Jaafer went directly to a seat and sat down. He inquired after Jaafer's health, and begged that his entrance might not put a stop to the amusements in hand. He then laid aside his turban and cloak, and took part in the repast. Salek was, however, a very abstemious man, and never even sat down with the caliph during the meals of the latter. At length every one became again at his ease and we renewed our mirth. When the cup came round to the old gentleman, he drank it off without hesitation, begging us to excuse him for the act. Jaafer smiled, then took his hand and kissed it, and inquired what he could do for him. Abd el Melik replied that he would call upon him some other time to talk about his business. But Jaafer persisted in asking what he desired, and declared that he would not eat another mouthful until he was informed. Abd el Melik then answered, that he asked for three things; one of which was, that, as the caliph was displeased with him, he desired to be restored to his favor. Jaafer replied that the caliph not only was pleased with him, but felt greatly obliged to him. "Moreover," said the caliph's uncle, "I owe ten thousand pieces of gold, and ask it to be paid for me;" to which Jaafer answered that the caliph had ordered a debt of his amounting to that sum to be paid out of his treasury, and added, "I beg you also to accept of another similar amount from me for your own expenses." Abd el Melik next said, that he wished his son to be united in marriage, on terms of equality, to the daughter of the caliph; and Jaafer replied that the caliph had commanded his daughter to be united in wedlock to his son, adding also the government of Egypt as a gift to the latter.

Abd el Melik now took his leave, and on his way thought that Jaafer had promised these things whilst under the excitement of wine. "Let us see," said he, "to-morrow, what he will do." In the mean time Jaafer continued his amusement with his Nadims, who were surprised at his conduct towards the uncle of the caliph; "For," thought they, "though he may give away offices and money, how can he, without permission, give away the caliph's daughter in marriage? True, never were such favors given before to any vizir; but to-morrow will show the result."

The meeting broke up, and on the following morning Jaafer waited upon the caliph, who asked him whether it was just for him to make merry in private without him. Jaafer replied that he had thought himself perfectly private; but though he had directed no one to be admitted, lo! Abd el Melik appeared and saluted him with "Peace be upon you." "I was so confused," added he, "that I answered him, 'Allah be on you!' then arising, I showed him the proper evidences of respect." "Is this true?" asked the caliph, "or do you not make a mistake?" "It is the truth," answered Jaafer, "and he acted towards me in the most generous and affable manner possible." "How?" exclaimed the caliph; "pray tell me what he did." "Seeing our confusion and disorder," replied Jaafer, "he forthwith threw off his cloak and turban, took a seat amongst us, and drank off a cup of wine, asking me at the same time to pardon the act. I kissed his hand, and inquired what were his orders. 'No,' said he, 'I will come to-morrow and talk with you about that.' But I insisting, he added, 'In the first place the Commander of the faithful is displeased with me;' but I assured him that you were not offended with him. 'I owe,' continued he, 'ten thousand dinars, which I desire the caliph to pay for me.' I then told him that you had commanded ten thousand dinars to be paid for him out of your own treasury, begging him, at the same time, to accept of the same sum from me. 'Next,' said he, 'I have to beg that my son be married to the caliph's daughter;' to which I replied by telling him that you had not only determined to give your daughter to his son, but would give him also the government of Egypt with her." The caliph exclaimed, "Good! I accept all you have done, and confirm your promises."

Jaafer now threw himself at the feet of the caliph, and proceeded on to his bureau of affairs, where, in the presence of all the nobles and chief men of the court, he sent twenty thousand dinars to Abd el Melik, and invited him to come to see him at his divan. Abd el Melik consequently presented himself with his son, and found there a large concourse of people assembled, and the caliph on his throne surrounded by all his court. On his saluting the caliph, the latter arose to his feet, and made his uncle sit down on the edge of the throne along side of him. He next ordered the marriage of his daughter to be registered, and bestowed several dresses of honor in succession upon him and his son. He also commanded the latter to be girded with (the sword of) the government of Egypt. All the officers of the caliph accompanied Abd el Melik to his dwelling, and each asked of the other which of these three benevolent persons was the most gracious. Ibraheem Mehdee adds, that all allotted the title of superiority to Abd el Melik, who was of a very austere and pious character; some thought that Jaafer's temerity and benevolence was greatest; and others praised the caliph's great goodness and amiableness of character.

This occurrence shows the degree of authority which the caliph bestowed upon Jaafer Beramikee, and the favor which he displayed towards him; and yet subsequently he cut off his head, and showed his anger even against his servants and followers, verifying the Persian adage, which says, "Near the sovereign the fire burns hotest."

AN ANECDOTE.

It is related in some histories, that a wealthy and influential man of the Benee Ommieh was once calumniated, out of envy, to the Abbaside Caliph, Haroon er Rasheed, by the Governor of Damascus. It was said that he lived with great pomp and luxury; and that, as a measure of precaution, his removal would benefit the country. The caliph, a most intelligent and wise sovereign, had a confidential person in his service, named Menar, likewise very wealthy; him he called, and ordered to set out immediately for Sham (Damascus), to inquire into the circumstances of the case, and bring the man bound before him. He also commanded him to report whatever the individual might say to him.

Menar mounted his camel, and in eight days reached Damascus; having found the house, he dismounted at it, and learned that the person for whom he searched was in his bath. The latter, however, sent his sons and servants out to meet Menar, and conducted him into the dining-room of the house. Then, after performing his *namaz*, he came out to see his guest. A repast was brought in, and a bounteous meal was spread before them. After its conclusion, he returned thanks to his Creator, and prayed for the caliph; he next renewed his expressions of welcome to his guest, and asked what was his business.

Menar relates: "I gave him the order which I had received respecting him. He kissed it and put it upon his head, (as a mark of respect,) and, after opening it, read its contents. Then, calling together all his people, in the course of a few minutes nearly one thousand men were assembled, which made me suspect that he intended to offer resistance. Turning to these, he said, 'May my bread be lawful to all of you, and may you be freed from all duty towards me, if you act contrary to my orders.' 'God forbid,' exclaimed they, all at once; 'we are submissive to your commands.' 'Then, let every one occupy himself, each with his own business; bring me quickly a *melifeh* (litter).' This being done, he said to them and his sons, 'I am going to the caliph; attend all of you, as usual, to your own concerns until I return.' Then, entering the melifeh, he left Damascus and proceeded towards Bagdad. On the way he came along side of me, and, at the sight of every village that we entered, he would exclaim, 'Menar, this is mine; this vineyard is mine, it produces me so much revenue.' The greater part of the country round about Damascus belonged to him, and people were envious of his wealth.

After continuing on for some distance, he said to me, 'Menar, where is your note-book?' This I handed to him, and he fastened it to his belt. Soon after coming near a large town, 'This also is mine,' said he; on which I exclaimed, 'My good friend, we are getting far away from your family, you journey in fetters, and who knows what may befall you; why, therefore, do you tell me so much about your property?' Turning towards me, he replied, 'O Menar, I have made a mistake; I thought that, being in the service of the caliph, you were a man of wisdom and intelligence, whilst you are an ignorant fellow. You tell me that we do not know what may happen to me, or how my affairs may turn out. The lot of you, of me, of the Emir of the faithful, and of all men, is in the hands of the Most High; he commands and directs all things, and nothing occurs but by his destination. Should the world and all it contains be brought together, and be given over to you, it and they would not be able to do the smallest thing of themselves, or without the destiny of God. Be it good, or be it evil, it will happen; put your confidence in Allah, O Menar. I have committed no fault against the caliph which I should guard against. The caliph is a just and mild prince, who does nothing against the Holy Law; but, were he the cruel and tyrannical man that you say, your reflections might become verified. God be praised that he is free from the traits of character which you seem to apprehend. He will certainly investigate the charge against me, and separate the truth from the false; in which case I have no cause for grief; in fine—but I will say nothing more to you on the subject.'

"With the conclusion of these words he commenced reading the great Koran, and continued doing so until we reached Bagdad. I there preceded him into the presence of the caliph, and related to him all the conversation which we had held from Damascus to Bagdad. The caliph lent an attentive ear to my words, and said, 'This man must be a person of fidelity, and his conduct has been upright. I believe that what has been represented against him is false. Go, produce him, and be careful not to bring him in chains.' On entering the apartment he kissed the caliph's hand, who showed him much favor and regard, saying to him, 'I have given you much trouble in this matter.' He then bestowed several cloaks of honor upon him. He answered the caliph, saying, that 'It had been no trouble, but an honor to him; and his commands had been a distinction of which he was proud, for which God be praised.' The caliph, in reply, said to the man, 'Henceforward I shall expect to hear from you about that country; I have full confidence in you, let me see you exert yourself.' Then putting a royal firman into his hands, he commanded him in all cases to use it. Turning to me, he said, 'Menar, go, accompany our friend back to his residence, where let him meet his family again.' He also presented him with several horses and mules. On our arrival at Damascus it was like a festival; for all the people of the city came out to meet him, offering up prayers and blessings on the caliph."

What a religious caliph, and just sovereign, who attends to the investigation of his affairs, and acts conformably to the Holy Law!

AN ANECDOTE.

It is narrated by that quintessence of historians, Hokla, that there was once a benevolent merchant who owned a slave whom he had reared from his earliest youth, and in whose hands he confided all his property and wealth. He was likewise the keeper of his goods, and received all the proceeds of the sale of his merchandise. This merchant had a son who had scarcely attained the age of puberty. By divine wisdom the merchant left this perishable world; and the son, and the slave aforesaid, fell into a dispute about the inheritance. They carried their quarrel before the cadi, and each stood up in court against the other. The dispute increased, and the cadi was unable to decide it. Now the governor (*hakim*) of that country, who was a most intelligent and equitable person, whenever the cadi was unable to judge a case, had it referred to himself. So the suit of these two youths was made known to him; and he held a divan, in which they appeared to state their difference. The elder of the two invited the other to point out his father's tomb, if he knew it; to which he answered, "I was a guest at such a place when my father died; and on hearing it I came to his grave, which was pointed out to me." The governor then asked the youth who disputed the other's legitimacy, whether he knew where his father's tomb was, when the same replied that he did; "for," said he, "I interred him there myself." "Go then," added the governor, "and bring me a decayed bone of your father." The lad departed, found the grave, and returned with a bone for the Hakim, who sent for a phlebotomist to take blood from the youth who had been the slave of the deceased. The blood was allowed to flow over the bone, and it spirted to the right and left of it, without one drop remaining on it. Afterwards blood was taken from the son who had really been the fruit of the reins of the deceased, and the whole of it was absorbed by the bone. The governor now exclaimed, "See, this is the real and true son of the deceased merchant, and he has a right to the inheritance." So he decided that all the property should be delivered up to him; which was done, and the slave was punished. Behold what intelligence!

AN ANECDOTE ABOUT A WOMAN WHO SPOKE BY THE KORAN.

Abd Allah bin Mebarik, a well instructed and talented person, relates the following:

I once set out on a pilgrimage to visit the *Beit Ullah* (or

Caaba) at Mecca, and one day lagged behind the caravan to perform my devotions. After saying my *namaz* I remounted my camel; and on the way I fell in with a woman travelling on foot, wearing a black shawl on her shoulders, with another like a cap over her head. From her slow walking, I knew that she had been left by her animal; and approaching her, I said, "*Es salam alaikum,* O woman of Allah." She answered, "*Ve alaika salam,* O Abdallah, for peace is spoken by the God of mercy." "God have mercy on you; why, pray, are you walking here on the high road all alone?" She answered,* "None can show the straight way to him whom he misleads." From this I knew that she had lost her way, and therefore inquired of her whence she came and whither she was going. She replied, "God be praised, who makes his servants walk in the night time, from the Mesjed el Haram (Caaba) to the Mesjed el Akza (Temple of Jerusalem)." From which answer I understood that she was on her way from Mecca to Jerusalem. I next asked her how long she had been in that place. "Three consecutive nights," said she. "Have you no provisions?" I asked. She replied, "He who gives me to eat and drink." "With what do you make your ablutions in this place?" I inquired. She answered, "Whenever you can find no water, use good clean earth." I said, "Will you not eat something from my stock of provisions?" Upon which she immediately exclaimed, "Wait until the night." I remarked to her that the month in which we then were, was not one of fasting. "God recompenses him who performs a good deed for his sake." I mentioned then that no one is compelled to fast on a journey; and she replied, "But if you prefer it, it is good." Much surprised at her answers, I asked her why she did not reply in the manner that I did (and not from the Koran); when she said, "Nothing is ever spoken which He does not know." I next asked her from which tribe she was; and she answered; "Ask it not; God alone, who hears and sees all things, and knows what is in the hearts of his

* All this woman's replies are passages from the Koran.—A. T.

people, can make such inquiries." "Pardon me," said I; "forgive my faults." She exclaimed, "Be it so; but God alone can pardon." "Can I not put you on my camel and conduct you to your *cafileh* (caravan)?" I asked. She answered, "Whatever you do with a good design He knows." So putting her on my camel, which I made to kneel down for that purpose, I said, "Pray, be comfortable." To which she replied. "Tell the faithful to turn away their eyes." I looked aside, begging her to take a seat; but at the moment when she was about to do so, the animal rose, and her dress catching on the saddle, it was torn. She immediately exclaimed; "No harm comes upon you but what comes of your own hands." "Wait," said I; "let me put the noose on the camel." As I did so, she observed, "And we have explained that to Suliman," and mounted the animal. She then added, "Praise be to Him who has made them (the camels) submissive to us, who conquered them for us; and we will return to him." I now took the animal's noose in my hand, and pulled it quickly after me, animating it with my voice; when she exclaimed, "Walk slowly and lower your voice." I walked on slowly, humming some verses that came to my recollection; but displeased at this she said, "Read on as much of the Koran as you know." "God be thanked," added I, "for the good I have heard from you;" to which she answered, "The wise only utter useful things."

After proceeding in this manner for some time, I inquired of her whether she had a husband in the caravan, and she answered, "Oh, those who believe ask not after those things which you change for the worse." I said nothing more until we had reached the cafileh, when I inquired whom she had in the latter, and she answered, "Goods and sons are the ornament of the life of this world." From this I perceived that she had sons there, and asked her about them; when she said, "They incline towards the signs of the stars," which words taught me that they were leaders of the escort. So on approaching the tents, I remarked to her that we had reached the same, and asked whom I should call for. She replied, "God called Ibrahim his friend, spake with Moses, and (said to) John, this book is with power." I therefore immediately called out for Ibrahim, Moses and John; when three young and handsome men came forward to meet her, and take her off the camel. Addressing them, she said, "Send one of you with a note to the city, and let him see what food is best to be bought here." So one of them departed, and returned with a dish of food. They conducted me to their tent, placed it before me, and the mother remarked, "Eat and drink, and much good may it do you for what you have done in times past."*

But I told the sons that I would not partake of their food until I learnt something about their mother; when they answered, "It is now forty years since she has spoken either with us or any others, words of a worldly nature; and as if she feared to say something wrong, her whole conversation with us is from the Book of God." "Blessed be He, who is the author of all good and excellence," exclaimed I; "her prayers do a benefit in either world (this and the other)."

May the Most High have mercy on all and every one of the faithful of both sexes!

AN ANECDOTE.

Hind binti Numan was one of the most eloquent of women. She was also the envy of the world for the great perfection of her beauty and intelligence, and was descended from the most noble of the Arab tribes. One day she was mentioned in the presence of Hedjadj: her beauty, eloquence and superior intelligence were praised; and it was remarked, that she was the most eminently fair and best mannered woman of the age. Hedjadj became

* Koran, 69 : 24.

deeply enamored of her from these commendations, and asked her of her father in marriage, sending several persons to him for that purpose. He went to an immense expense for her; and besides the established dowry, he acknowledged (as a promise) that he owed her also two hundred thousand dirhems. After espousing her, he remained some time with Numan; and, on his being appointed Valee or Governor of Bagdad, carried her there with him.

Some time after this, he one day entered his harem (private female apartments), and heard the voice of Numan in the yard. Walking slowly and softly to where she was, he saw Hind with a mirror in her hand, in which she gazed upon her own beauteous face and recited the following verse:

"What is Hind but an Arab's filly?
"She is a horse's foal with a mule for her partner.
"If my colt takes after me, it will be a horse;
"But if after him, it will prove a mule."

Hedjadj listened, then turned back, and, without letting Hind know what he had done, determined to divorce her. He sent for Abdallah bin Tahir, and ordered him to act as his proxy, to inform Hind in the proper terms of his determination. He also sent her the two hundred thousand dirhems which he had imposed on himself. Abdallah departed and performed his errand; when Hind, arising from her seat, exclaimed, "Well met, O Ibin Tahir. I swear that we praised God, but never associated with that person." She ordered Abdallah to keep the two hundred thousand dirhems in return for the good news which he had brought her; "for," added she, "you have freed me from that unclean dog." From that moment she became separated from him.

Some time after this the matter was spoken of before the Ommiade caliph Abd el Melik bin Murvan, and the story of Hedjadj's separation from Hind binti Numan was narrated; whereupon some one remarked, that really so beautiful a creature as she ought not to have been united to that sanguinary man.

The caliph became enamored of her from what he heard, and despatched one of the higher officers of his court to ask her in marriage. He sent her numerous splendid presents, and wrote her a letter, in which he made his request. The caliph's proxy went to Damascus, where he offered Hind the letter and the presents of the caliph. On reading the former, she raised it to her head (in respect); then taking a pen in her hand, she addressed the caliph a letter, saying, "May the life and honor of the Caliph of the faithful be everlasting! The reply of your handmaiden Hind is, that the once pure vase, which you consider worthy of your service, has been defiled by the use made of it by that unclean dog's mouth; nevertheless she awaits your majesty's commands." The caliph, on the receipt of this letter, read its contents and was much amused. He praised Hind's delicacy and elegance, and wrote on the margin of the letter the following maxim: "When a dog laps from your cup or dish, wash it out seven times, then rub it with earth, and you may use it;" and returned it to her.

Hind was much pleased and accepted his offer, with this condition however, that Hedjadj should accompany her from the place of Numan's (her father's) residence, to the caliph's palace in Damascus, and hold the bridle of the camel which carried the *mahfeh* in which she rode; and that on the day of her entrance into the city he should dismount from his horse, and with head and feet bare conduct her camel to the palace of the caliph. The latter on reading the condition laughed with great mirth, and was very anxious to have an interview with her. He sent orders to Hedjadj to do as she might command, and bring her to him with as much speed as practicable. On the receipt of the caliph's orders, Hedjadj got every thing ready and set out from Irak for Damascus; and on his arival at Maareh (where Numan resided) he dismounted from his horse and took the reins of Hind's camel in his hand. All the principal people of the city (Damascus) went out to meet her. She got into a richly ornamented *hevdedj*, the camel of which was quite enveloped in costly paraphernalia.

Hind thus rode along, surrounded by her maidens, and led by Hedjadj. She ordered one of her women to raise the fringe of the cover of her hevdedj: which being done, Hedjadj was greatly ashamed and pained; whilst she and her maidens amused themselves and were very mirthful. Passing from Maareh they entered Damascus; and that same day Hedjadj led her camel with bared head and feet. On the way Hind took a piece of gold out of her purse and let it fall; on which calling to one of her attendants, "Tell that *hammal* (porter)," said she, "that a dirhem has been dropped, and let him find it." Hedjadj sought for the piece of gold, and finding it, handed it to the woman, saying, "It is not a dirhem, but a dinar;" whereupon Hind exclaimed, "We lost a dirhem (copper piece), and in its place have found, thanks be to God, a piece of gold." Hedjadj, hearing this remark, was greatly ashamed; and in this way they continued on to the palace of the Commander of the faithful, who showed Hind marks of great regard, and went in person to meet her. When the camel knelt down, he himself lifted her out of the hevdedj, and accompanied her into the harem, where he was much pleased with her society, and conceived a warm affection for her. He always treated her with respect, and for some time enjoyed her society.

ANECDOTE.

It is narrated that the noble and high born Kereem el Melik was one of the most pious and eloquent of men of his age. One day, whilst passing through a garden, he observed a fair creature, as beauteous as the forehead of Venus, amusing herself in gazing from a balcony. Falling excessively in love with her, he sent her a souvenir of some elegant articles, through the hands of her confidential handmaiden; at the same time he wrote her a missive in verse and prose, begging her acceptance of them, and soliciting an interview. The lady was a very knowing and sensible person. She accepted of the present; to which she replied by means of symbols, that is by sending him a pastille of ambergris containing a piece of red gold. Kereem el Melik received the present, but did not understand what it meant, and was consequently greatly troubled. He had, however, a son, unequalled for his comprehension and sharpness of intellect, who, seeing his father's trouble, inquired the cause of it. The father then showed him the pastille with its contents, at which the son laughed heartily. His father asked him why he laughed; and the cunning boy replied by saying, that her object in sending the things was very evident, reciting at the same time the following lines:

ARABIC VERSES.

"I present you with the amber, pure gold from the mine concealed in its centre, hiding the reins.
"The meaning of the gold and the amber together, is that the former is hidden in darkness."

Kereem el Melik praised very much the delicacy, intelligence, and purity of the beautiful female, and was greatly pleased with the brightness and wit of his son.

ANECDOTE.

It is related, that in the reign of Bibers, Sultan of Egypt, there was at Cairo (Misri Cahireh) a woman remarkable for her beauty and for her thefts; in short, so much was she superior in personal attractions and in the intelligence of her mind, that no man had ever seen her equal, and no woman had brought forth such another. She was also most expert as an intriguant, and cunning in the science of judging others. She could pass a thread through her evil eye; and, as if she possessed the power of a magnet, could attract others, as smoothly as a hair passes through oil.

One day this beautiful creature attired herself in the most costly gold-embroidered garment, and attended by seven or eight female slaves went to a vapour bath (*hammam*). Towards evening she sent her slaves home, while she herself remained in a corner of the bath until the hour for retiring to rest. After that time the governor of the city saw a woman at the head of the street, and inquired who she was. The woman answered, that she was the wife of one of the principal men of the place; that her dwelling was in the outskirts of the city; that a friend had invited her to the bath, and having obtained leave of her husband, she went there; that after leaving the bath, she felt inclined to make a short turn in the bazaars, and having sent her servants away, she had walked about for some time, until her strength gave out. Unable even to reach the dwelling of any one, she feared her husband, and begged the governor to place her under the care of some trusty person, until, in the course of a night's time, she would be able to satisfy her husband.

Now the chief judge (cadi) resided near the spot; and the governor of the city, on his way to the woman's house, knocked at his door, and, after relating all about the female whom he had fallen in with, asked him to receive her under his roof for the night. The cadi consenting, he had her placed in his own private cabinet, where all the public effects were deposited for safe keeping. He showed the woman evidences of respect, had her bed prepared for her, and then left her alone. After seeking repose for a short time, the woman arose, opened the boxes contained in the room where she was, and took out as much of their contents as she could carry away, amounting in value to some twenty thousand pieces of gold. She next took her own drawers and chemise, and a cloak which was embroidered with gold and pearls; and digging a hole in the cadi's yard, she put them into it.

Early in the morning, whilst every body yet slept, she opened the door, and departed. Afterwards when all had arisen, they sought for the woman; but in her place there was nothing but the wind blowing by. Entering the cabinet, they perceived that all the boxes had been opened, and that the articles confided by the Mussulmans to the care of the judge were gone. The cadi tore his beard and hair, and sent immediately for the governor of the city, whom he accused of having introduced an accursed woman, a thief, into his house, by means of a ruse; and said that, using her for the purpose, he had stolen goods belonging to the Mussulmans of the city and to himself, to the amount of twenty thousand pieces of gold. "Either find that woman," exclaimed the cadi, "and bring her to me, or go with me before the sultan, and be tried for the crime which you have committed." The head of the police threw himself at the cadi's feet, and begged that he would grant him a few days' time in which to make search for her; "after which," said he, "if I have been unsuccessful, I will refund the value of the stolen goods."

He then went through the whole city, corner after corner. One day, having heard the voice of a woman proceeding from the cupola of a house, he looked in to see whose it might be; when a female slave calling to him said, her mistress wished to see him. The governor immediately got off his horse; and on opening the cupola, he observed a large quantity of valuable objects. After conversing for some time with the lady, she told him not to be grieved; for, having shown her so much generosity and goodness, it was not just for her to afflict him. "I have no need of wealth," added she; and opening the boxes about her, she showed him that they were filled with purses of money. "See," said she, "this treasure. Promise to arrange this matter with me; and if, after that, you will marry me, all this wealth and these rich clothes shall be yours, which enjoy to your perfect contentment,—for I truly wish this—I swear it." The beautiful creature added, "Go immediately to the cadi's house, tell him that I have sought him every where; and if he is alive I will find him, and his own house shall certainly be also examined." The man, overcome by the wealth thus shown him, did as he was bid; and having reported the woman's words to the cadi, the latter exclaimed, "Ah! infidel, so you give me the appearance of a thief! Perhaps you will next endeavor to deprive me of life; but my character will not allow of this. Come, however, and search." Now the woman had also told the man where she had hidden her clothes. They went there; and after looking in several places, they finally dug near the sink and brought forth a pair of drawers, a chemise soiled with blood, and a cloak wrought with pearls and jewels. On this the man exclaimed to the cadi, "So, wretch! you are both murderer and false accuser; but I will bring you to trial in the presence of the sultan." The cadi was amazed, and exclaiming "There is no power but what comes from God," threw himself at the feet of the governor. "I did it," cried he; "nothing now remains but my character: do not therefore, I implore you let it be ruined." In fine, his entreaties overcame the governor. They kissed and made friends, and declared that neither had any right to prosecute the other. The governor of the city was greatly rejoiced. "Let the past be past," said he, "and what has happened be forgotten; but come, let us find out how this beautiful female has been able to acquire so much riches and costly objects. I will marry her, and for a few days enjoy the gifts of heaven."

So they went to the place where she resided and knocked at her door. No one answered. One of the neighbors put his head out of a window, and cried out that the house was empty, and that no one dwelt there. "Do not, therefore," said he, "be knocking there uselessly." The governor answered, "On such a day persons did occupy it; for I saw them." To this the fellow replied, "You are right. The house had been a long while empty; but four or five days ago a female came and occupied it for a short time.

Since then, however, she has removed again, and I do not know where she has gone. None of us know what kind of a person she was; and it is now three days since she left here. See, this is the key which she asked us to deliver to the owner of the house." The governor opened the door, and did not find in it as much even as an old straw mat; so he turned back like a dog who has been hit in the reins, and stood filled with astonishment.

Besides the roguery of this woman, she must, like the Prophet Suliman, have possessed command over the air, to be able, in so short a time, to remove so large a quantity of effects; for none other than that prophet could do such things. The cunning rogue appeared for a moment to exculpate the governor, and that in a dishonest way; after which she disappeared, and never was heard of again.

CHAPTER THIRTY-TWO.

On the laws of beneficence and bounty.

God the Most High has said, "If you are thankful, I will increase my gifts; but if you are ungrateful, my punishments are great." (Koran.) Wise men have remarked, that "respect for benefits bestowed by benefactors, is an obligation upon the sons of Adam; and that it is the most important of all duties."

PERSIAN VERSE.

"Never forget the benefits which others have bestowed upon you,—bear them always in mind."

There are those who, whilst all mankind are confused and astonished, at the day of judgment will hear a voice crying out, "O ye praisers, arise, and assemble in the shadow of the standard of the celestial Paradise." The select will ask of the best of prophets, on whom be blessings from the Lord of the universe and on all other prophets, and learn that praisers are those individuals who are sensible of the obligations conferred on them by the bounties of the All-Just, and act accordingly."

Sefian Thooree, on whom be peace, one day as he went along the high road saw a youth who had caught and held captive a poor nightingale in a cage. The unhappy bird, from the extent of its grief, threw itself from side to side, until it was near death. Its cries reached the ear of Sefian Thooree, who jocosely addressed the youth, saying, "If you release this poor bird from the confinement of its cage, you will receive great benefits in this world, and also attain those of eternity." The youth released the bird; and as long as Sefian Thooree lived, the bird offered up prayers for his welfare. At length death came upon him, and he expired. That nightingale went and lit upon his coffin, where it wept and lamented him. On his interment it remained amongst those who were around his tomb, and would not leave it. Some time later it also expired, and was buried at his feet.

See the gratitude even of a bird, which never forgot the benefits bestowed on it! Man could not do better.

It is related that in the country of Babel there was once a just and talented sovereign, of benevolent sentiments, who had a handsome son, scarcely arrived at the age of puberty. In the course of divine providence, that sovereign died; and when on his deathbed, he summoned the vizirs, ministers, and other chief men of his kingdom into his presence, and made known to them his last will. It was, that his brother, the uncle of his son, should carry on the affairs of the state until the latter became of age; after which he was to take possession of the government, and no one was to interfere with him. "All of you be obedient to him," said he. Then turning to his brother, he continued, "And do you conform to this arrangement: and should Satan tempt you, or you be led to the commission of any improper act, resist and refrain from it; and do not neglect the command (from the Koran), 'Certainly God has commanded thee to execute what has been confided to thee by its owner.'"

Now when the sovereign had expired, his brother, according to his last testament, directed the government until the prince came of age, when the chief men of the state were determined that the will of their deceased lord should take immediate effect. They therefore made this demand of the uncle; but his throat having tasted of power, he was averse to leaving it, and spent his days and nights in imagining some device by which to rid himself of his nephew.

One day he and his courtiers mounted their horses and set out on a hunting expedition. The prince also was with them; and riding near his uncle, they proceeded on together. Finding a moment when they were separated from the rest of the court, the uncle, with his own hands, tore out his nephew's eyes, placed him near an oak-tree, and left him there. The mutilated prince sought about in the forest for a place of retreat and safety. He came to a tree; and having by great effort succeeded in climbing into it, he sat down on one of its branches. Now through the overrulings of divine Providence, the shade of that tree was the place of abode of the king of the Perees (*Anglice* Fairies). Every night they all usually assembled there, and spent the time in amusement. When they met in the evening, they, as was their wont, talked over the events of the day. One of them said, "I have a most strange piece of news to tell." "What is it?" said the others. He added, "To-day the brother of the sovereign of

Babel has inflicted a great cruelty upon the prince of that country: he has plucked out his eyes, and rendered him completely blind. The prince is now seated on a branch of this tree." The king of the Perees, observed, "If the prince only knew the qualities of that tree, he would attain the object of his desires." "What are its qualities?" inquired the other Perees. The king replied, "If he pulls off two of its leaves, and rubs them over his eyes, their sight will be perfectly restored, so that he will be able to see even better than before."

The unhappy prince heard these words, and thanked the Author of all good; then breaking off two of the leaves of the tree, he rubbed them over his eyes, when they immediately opened, and he once more looked upon the world. He next plucked a quantity of the leaves and put them in his bosom, and then prepared to descend from the tree. When about to do so, the king of the Perees, exclaimed, "There is a snake in the tree opposite to us, whose fate is the same as that of the brother of the (deceased) sovereign of Babel; both are made upon the same grade and move upon the same point: so that if the snake is killed, the uncle of the prince will at the same moment expire." The prince listened to this conversation, and returned thanks to God. He next found the snake and killed it; whereupon his uncle immediately fell down dead.

The unfortunate prince now proceeded directly to the city; and the inhabitants, filled with joy, went out to meet him. With a heart full of happiness, he took possession of his throne, where he ruled with much felicity. The uncle, who had disregarded the rights of benevolence, lost the throne on which he might yet have sat happily, and entered the earth of shame (fell ignominiously).

PERSIAN VERSE.

"Every one is recompensed according to his deeds: he receives good for good, and evil for evil."

AN ANECDOTE.

Sheik Abd ul Muta relates, that once a venerable man was observed at the Haram (sacred Caaba) of Mecca, repeating, "O Thou who drawest me towards thee," and then walking about to and fro. When asked what these words meant, he replied, One night I was occupied near the holy Mosk of Mecca in making the prescribed turns around it, when something struck my foot. Looking down I observed that it was a purse, which, on examination, proved to contain a thousand dinars. My evil nature tempted me to do what was wrong, and my covetousness told me that it was a handsome and lucky windfal, and that I ought to keep it to myself, and assuage my wants by its means. The principles of Holy Law, however, coming to the aid of equity, I determined to render its possession legal.

VERSE IN PERSIAN.

"Eat what is lawful, such as game from the market; and do not, like the vulture, prey on carrion."

"It is not just," said I to myself, "for me to keep the property of a Mussulman; what answer could I give about it, to-morrow, in the other world?" So I waited awhile to see if the owner would make his appearance, when I would restore him his property. The cafileh of the pilgrims suddenly coming by, I ended my turns round the Caaba, and left with it.

The next year, however, I heard a cryer proclaim, "Whoever has found my purse, I will give him thirty sherifs" (a gold coin). Considering the blessing of that much legitimate money as better than the holy House itself, I gave him the purse, and received in return the thirty sherifs. Then going to a slave-merchant's shop, I purchased a little Arab boy, whose figure was somewhat that of a human being. I nourished him as if he were my own child, until the arrival of the Habeshees (Ethiopians), with whom the boy conversed in their own tongue. They remained a few days and then departed, when I asked the boy what they had desired with him. He answered, "I am the son of the sultan of the West (Magreb, from which is derived Morocco). The king of Habesh made war with my father; who being defeated, they took me a prisoner. These people have come on my father's part to procure me; he gave them a thousand pieces of gold with which to purchase me, and sent them off in search of his son. I have experienced kindness from you, and therefore disclose this secret to you; do not give me for less than that sum."

On the following day, they again returing, I sold the boy to them for fifty thousand dinars; with which sum I purchased stuffs of Irak, and set out with the cafileh for Bagdad. Shortly after my arrival there, a broker one day came and informed me that a hapless merchant had died, leaving a very handsome daughter. "Come," said he: "I will get her for you." So I asked for the maiden, and was united to her. I was surprised to observe that the *jehaz* (or dowry which she brought with her) was composed of nine purses of gold money, placed on nine dishes; and that on eight of them, one thousand was written, whilst on the ninth there was only nine hundred and seventy dinars written. I asked why there was this difference of thirty pieces between the last purse and the others. The maiden replied, "My father once lost this purse of money in Mecca; and the subsequent year, having gone there again on a pilgrimage, he caused a crier to proclaim that he would give thirty pieces of gold to whoever had found it. A good man came and put the purse into his hands, just as when he lost it; whereupon my father presented him with thirty gold pieces out of it; and this is the cause of the contents being less than those of the others." "Holy Allah!" I exclaimed; "all these goods of mine are the fruits blessed to me of the thirty dinars which I accepted as a legal gift. May God have mercy upon your father! the pious feeling which caused me to abstain from what is forbidden has drawn upon me this grace."

PERSIAN VERSE.

"To act with uprightness, is to conform to the will of God.
"I have never seen any one who did evil, and whose path was straight."

BLESSINGS WHICH HAVE ATTENDED JUSTICE IN SULTANS, EMIRS, AND HAKIMS.

ANECDOTE.

The Prophet, on whom be peace, has said: "The sultan is the shadow of God upon the earth, and the oppressed seek refuge under it."

PERSIAN VERSE.

"Justice brings perfection upon the country:
"Equity ever does good by its deeds."

It is related that once Behram Ghior mounted his horse with the intention of going to the chase; and that when he arrived at the place where game was known to exist, a heavy rain began to fall. Like the eye of the weeping lover, the world became submerged with water; each individual sought a place of shelter, and even Behram, foregoing his chase, went directly to the hut of a villager, and demanded his hospitality. The person not knowing who his visiter was, and also being unable to show that respect and attention which is due to sovereigns, Behram Ghior was displeased, but yet did not show it.

At eventide the peasant's cattle returned from their pasture towards his cottage, when the shepherds remarked that they had not obtained as much milk from the cows this day as on other days, nor as much as they had anticipated. "The pasture," said they, "is the same as formerly; what then can possibly be the cause?"

Now the peasant had a pretty and very intelligent daughter, who said to her father, "The *ulema* (learned) have written, that the cause of such occurrences as that now observed by us, is, the sovereign's having changed the good intentions he entertained towards his people. The displeasure and ill-will of kings has an effect upon fallow fields and the dugs of milch animals; from which circumstance it has been said:

PERSIAN VERSE.

'Sorrow in the minds of sovereigns
'Brings ruin on the hearts of the world.'"

The father replied, "You are right, my daughter; it is necessary for us to leave this country and seek a home in some other place." The daughter to this answered, "It is extremely difficult to do that; it therefore seems to me better for us to serve well our guest, who is a man of authority, and be careful not to neglect any token of respect and consideration towards him. The result will depend upon the commands of God." So the peasant, early in the morning, brought out food and drink worthy of the sultan, and placed them before Behram; who ate and drank, and, becoming good humored, called the peasant before him.

PERSIAN VERSE.

"Come let us sit down and enjoy ourselves;
"Let me, at least for one day, be a Kaikobad."

After a moment's conversation with the peasant, Behram lost all sense of shame, and addressing him, asked, "Have you no pretty-faced daughter, whose beauty I can contemplate and chase away my melancholy?" The peasant on hearing this arose, and going into his harem, he led his daughter, fair and modest, into the presence of Behram; who, on seeing the handsome girl, immediately became enamored and love-bound by the band of her ringlets, and was soon quite beside himself. Yet in the presence of the father he behaved with decency towards her, and immediately conceived the idea of being generous to the girl's parent, of marrying her in the presence of the chief men of the country, and compensating the father for the loss of the girl's services. They ate and drank together, and early the next morning the peasant's shepherds said to their master, "God be praised! the cows have given a greater quantity of milk than they have ever done before." The peasant was greatly astonished at this, and his daughter told him that it was the blessing resulting from the chaste conduct of their guest. Behram overheard this remark; and on the following day, when he had ascended his throne, he assembled all the ministers and chief officers of his court, and in their presence appointed the peasant, whose hospitality he had enjoyed, to be chief over all the country where he resided. He also espoused his daughter, and had her conducted to his *seray* (palace), where he afterwards spent many years with her most happily. She bore him several handsome children, and they lived together in perfect unity.

Now, from this tale it is seen how the justice and uprightness of kings and governors, and their pure intentions, are the occasion of life, blessing, and prosperity to their subjects; and that, on the other hand, the happiness and contentment of the subjects is the cause of the prolonged life and reign, as well as the increase of the glory and majesty of kings.

AN ANECDOTE.

Once upon a time an Arab of eloquence, a poet whose writings are esteemed, was travelling alone over a desert, when an enemy who had long fruitlessly sought an opportunity to effect his pitiless designs, fell in with him; and the poet, knowing the impossibility of escaping with his life, addressed his enemy by name, and said to him: "I know that you seek my life; but I request that you will go to my house, knock at the door, and say to my daughters,

'Keep watch, O daughters of the tribe; for surely your father—'" The enemy was an ignorant fellow; and after replying, "On my head be it," he put the poet, without mercy, to death, and then went directly to his house. On his knocking at the door, the poet's daughters presented themselves, and he exclaimed as above. Immediately the girls seized hold of the Arab's garments, and, crying out to the Mussulmans that the man was the murderer of their father, had him conducted before the governor; when the latter asking the daughters how they knew he was the murderer, they replied, "Our father by telling this man to go to his daughters and say, 'Keep watch, O daughters of the tribe; for surely your father—' meant that they were to supply the following words, 'is killed. Seize on him who repeats these lines.'"* As soon as the governor had struck the Arab a few times, he acknowledged his crime, and he was forthwith put to death in obedience to the law of talion.

ARABIC VERSE.

"Put faith in the merciful God in all his commands; none ever found harm who confided in him. Confide in God, and be patient under his judgments; and thus attain to what you desire of Him."

It is related that when Abd Allah bin Amir was appointed governor of Irak he had two old faithful friends, one of whom was an Ansaree, and the other a Thekefee. One day the latter remarked to the former, "Pray join me in a visit to our friend Abd Allah bin Amir, I am confident we will be greatly the better of his bounty." The former replied, "The Lord of the universe gives or refuses all things. He that gave Abd Allah the place which he occupies is merciful and gracious; and He who gives us hope in the favor

* From the celebrated Arabian poet Mutanebee.—A. T

of the governor is able to assist us. He is also able to send to us here the gifts which we may hope to obtain by visiting Abd Allah. I will therefore place my faith in Him who made you, and me, and Abd Allah out of nothing."

So the Thekefee joined a caravan and set out alone for Abd Allah bin Amir, who on seeing him showed him much regard and attention. When he inquired after the Ansaree, the Thekefee replied, "Of a truth he was afraid of the trouble of a journey, and offered reasons as an excuse for not accompanying me; he however prays for your prosperity." So Abd Allah bin Amir presented the Thekefee with ten thousand dirhems and a female slave, and kept him a few days with him; after which, he having asked permission to return to his wife and children, Bin Amir added four thousand dinars more. At the same time he gave him eight thousand dinars and some clothes, and begged him to present them to his friend the Ansaree. He also wrote the latter a letter begging him not to forget him in his prayers at the holy hours of supplication, and assuring him of his sincere friendship for him. The prayers of the Ansaree and the faith which he placed in God were of more use to him than the trouble which the Thekefee took to make the journey to Abd Allah, and brought him one or two thousand dinars more than his friend obtained.

Be not therefore doubtful of the value of faith in God, who provides for all, and whose gifts are bestowed upon all his creatures without distinction.

It is narrated that the Prophet Suliman, on whom be peace! once addressing an owl, asked it why it kept aloof from man, who is the most noble of all creatures. The bird replied, "O prophet, I would have lived with man; but I have observed a certain degree of untruth in him which prevents me, and has caused me to believe that it is better for me to keep apart from him, and reside alone." "Pray," continued Suliman, "tell me what you observed?" To which the owl replied:

"There was once a pious person—a man of truth—who had a wife as pious as himself. These two were always together, and used to offer up their prayers to the All-Just at one time. There was a tree growing near that pious man's dwelling in which I had taken up my abode; and I was continually envious of the affection and good will that these two individuals evinced towards each other. One day during their conversation, the woman said to the pious man, 'Should I be called upon to die before you, would you forget me?' To this the good man replied, 'We have our refuge in Allah! Should such a sad occurrence take place, I would bury you under that tree, and, retiring within our house, never again cross its threshold.' The woman also promised that should he die first, she would never again look in the face of any human being, but inter him under the same tree, and watch over his grave until death released her.

"By divine will it happened that the man died first; and the woman, according to her promise, buried him under the tree, put on mourning, and spent her time in devotional exercises. One day some one knocked at her door, and she demanded who it was. 'Open, for God's sake,' was the reply; 'I only crave a drink of water.' The woman handed the person what he asked; and the fellow, who was one of the city guards, drank it, and then said to the woman, 'I am surprised, O woman, at your grief; pray what is the cause of it?' 'My faithful friend,' she replied, 'has expired; and I am mourning for his loss.' The guard, on hearing this, wept and sighed, and said, 'We are just alike; for my wife died only a week or two ago. What can we hope for in this life, with any certainty of obtaining it, but death; and if we weep a thousand times, what will it profit us? See, we are two persons afflicted by the command of God. Come, let us live together and pass our days in remembrance of those who are departed.' By this language the fellow brought the woman over to him; and he married her. She dressed herself and girded herself up, and, quite forgetting her late husband, made merry with the new one.

"Some days after this the guard entered the house in great trouble, and told the woman it had become necessary for him to leave the city. On her asking after the cause, the guard replied, that the governor of the city had hung a Christian subject, and ordered his body to be left suspended to the gibbet for forty days. 'Whilst I was with you,' continued he, 'and in consequence of my negligence, some persons have stolen away the body; so that should its absence be perceived I shall certainly be hung up in its stead.' 'Is there no remedy?' asked the woman. 'There is no other,' replied the guard, 'than to put another body in the place of the stolen one.' The woman immediately remembered the remains of her deceased husband; and proposed, as they were still fresh, to hang them up in place of the body which had been stolen. The guard having consented, she took a spade in her hand and dug the body up out of the grave. But on seeing it, the guard exclaimed that it would be known; 'for,' said he, 'when we hung the other person we put a hot bowl on his head, on account of which his hair and head all fell off.' On hearing this, the woman immediately heated a bowl as hot as fire, and clapped it on the head of the unfortunate pious defunct, which soon made his hair and head to disappear. Then carrying the body to the gibbet, they hung it up.

"Some days later, the fellow and his wife had a quarrel, in which they spoke to each other in most injurious terms. The guard told her that if she had been capable of fidelity, it would have been shown to her late husband. After the altercation had been prolonged for some time the fellow drew a khandjar, with which he stabbed his wife and killed her. The neighbors came in, and found the woman dead; so apprehending the fellow, they bound him closely, and led him before the governor. I was present," added the owl, "at this occurrence, and involuntarily fled away. This is the reason why I choose rather to remain in solitude."

The prophet Suliman, on whom be peace! on hearing this tale, profited by the example which it offered, and was greatly surprised at it. Indeed it is a strange thing to hope for fidelity from the female sex. That "women are unfaithful," cannot universally be said: and yet we need not be astonished at the women of our times; for what says the poet?

"The dog is faithful, but woman not."

A traveller who had journeyed over land and seas, and who was a person of much knowledge, relates: Once, in the course of my travels I visited a place in Roomely, a town called Karilly, where I was the guest of a military man who possessed an estate in that country. He treated me with many marks of regard and consideration; and I remained for some time an inmate of his hospitable house. This person had four or five sons, who were even more generous than himself, and of very agreeable and pleasant manners. Their father had both of his ears and his nose cut off; and one night, whilst we were making merry, I looked up in his face wondering how so excellent a person as he should have become so disfigured: perceiving which, he thus addressed me, "I think, guest, that you are wondering what is the cause of the condition of my ears and nose." I answered that I should truly be greatly obliged to know the cause. "Pray," said I, "was it done in some holy war! I presume it was." "I will tell you," replied he: "I once had a cousin, the daughter of my father's brother, to whom, in my youth, I made love; and, finally, her father having given her to me, we became very happy together. We owned a farm near the sea-shore, which was the most delightful part of the city. We moved thither; and, whilst amusing ourselves and making merry, infidels attacked our city, and took me, my wife, and some Mussulmans prisoners, and carried us off to their own country. An iron was attached to my leg, and my wife was separated from me without my knowing where they had taken her. I remained for a whole year at work in irons, at the expiration of which time they put confidence in me, and took them off, and I was permitted to walk about at my ease. I inquired after my wife, and was informed that the commander of such a castle having asked for a handsome female slave, they gave my wife to him, and that she now resided in affluence. Inspired by warmth of affection for my wife, I wandered about until I reached the castle which had been indicated as that containing her. I entered a vineyard situated immediately opposite the entrance to a large palace, where I mixed myself up amongst a number of prisoners at work there, and joined them in their labors.

"One day there was a great festival, and they commenced making merry. My wife also made her appearance, and sat down in the midst of the company. The day ended in this way, and night set in. The candles were lighted; and all those who did not reside there took their leave, and the commander was left alone with his own people. I do not know whether my wife was informed of my presence, or whether she recognised me; but I was caught and bound fast to a marble pillar, and they then recommenced eating and drinking. As I stood thus confined, the man arising from his seat approached and caressed her before my eyes, and asked her if it was true that that person (meaning me) had been her husband. She owned that I had. 'So then,' said he, 'you love him more than me?' She answered to this in the negative. He said, 'If you truly love me more than him, seize and cut off his ears.' She at once arose, and, without any pity, cut off my ears with a knife; then resuming her seat, they continued eating and drinking. Soon afterwards, the commander again addressing her, said, 'If you love me more than that man, arise and cut off his nose.' So getting up from her seat, she cut off my nose likewise; and, after continuing for some time longer eating and drinking, they went to bed together, whilst I remained tied to the marble column.

"Not long after this, I suddenly felt my arms released by a woman, who came up behind me for that purpose. Then, leading me away from that spot into a place of retirement, she put healing salve upon my wounds. She inquired who had treated me in this manner; and I told her, with many thanks for her benevolence. The woman exclaimed, 'The person who has so ill-used you is my husband; but since the arrival here of this woman, he has never looked upon my face, nor come near me. All his wealth and money is, however, in my charge; can you not serve the infidel a good deed?' Inspired to exertion by her words, I asked her what I should do. 'Had I but some weapon,' I added; whereupon she arose and led me into the commander's store-room, where she told me to select whatever sword I might choose. So I picked out one which would suit my arm, and proceeded to the place where they lay asleep, drunk and entwined in each other's arms. With one blow of the sword, I cut them into four pieces. The woman who had bound my wounds gave me strength by saying, 'If you do not put them to death now, he will to-morrow morning leave neither you nor me alive.' To which she added, 'Do now whatever you will, then take me with you into Islam lands.'

"She filled seven or eight boxes of gold out of the money in the treasury, laid aside rich and costly garments, and then told me that the garden of the house ran down to the sea-shore, where there was a galley fastened close by it. She ran and fetched the key of the prisons, and, opening their doors, let out all the Mussulman captives confined there. She took ten of these latter to carry valuables from the treasury to the galley; and, after adding a small store of provisions, we embarked all the Mussulmans there on board of it. We ourselves then went on board, weighed the anchor, set sail, and that same night left the place of our sorrows. We continued under sail during all the following day; and, in fine, after sailing four days and four nights, the fifth day we beheld before us as it were a black bank of cloud, which, by God's grace, proved to be our own country.

"We landed at my own farm, and all the people of the city came out to see us; but supposing from our appearance that we were the infidels who sometimes visited the coast, they began to fly. However, recognising some of our friends, we called to them not to fear, for we had returned from captivity. On hearing my words they came back, and we cast anchor near the shore. 'Pray get us one or two wagons,' said I; and they were forthwith brought us. Into them I placed the costly effects and the woman whom I had brought with me. I gave every one of the captives who returned with me money to bear their expenses to their own homes. I next married the woman after the ordinance of God. She became blessed with the holy faith of Islamism; and these fine children by whom you perceive me surrounded were borne me by her.

"Praises be to the God of all benevolence! this is the history of what occurred to me," added the man. He would not let me leave him, but kept me as his guest for a long time. This is what he related of his travels; but the truth of the statements rests upon the narrator.

In the year 958 of the Hedjreh, a fellow in Cairo picked up a woman whom he took to his house. He put her inside of it, closed the door upon her, and, taking the key with him, returned to the bazaar to make purchases of some articles of which he stood in need. He then bought a piece of meat; and as he was about to give it to the keeper of a cooking establishment to have it roasted, he met with an individual to whom he owed a sum of money. This person, having apprehended him, had him taken before a cadi, when, the debt being proved, the latter put the fellow into prison. The woman thus remained alone in the house. Now the prisoner had an old friend, who, hearing of his confinement, went to see him. The friend found the man in chains, and, after saluting him, inquired the cause of his present situation. "My tale is a curious one," answered the prisoner. "This morning I went out to buy some provisions from the market; and, after purchasing a piece of meat, was about giving it to a cook to be roasted, when I fell in with a person to whom I am indebted. He had me carried off to the Mehkemeh for trial; and threw me, as you see, into prison. I have a favor to ask of you. Take this key, and go to my house; open the door, and tell the woman there what has occurred to me. Let her return to her own home; then close the door again, and bring me back the key."

The friend promised to execute what had been asked of him. He took the key, went to the house, and, on opening the door, beheld his own wife seated alone upon the sofa, arrayed in elegant attire. The woman was a cunning person; and, as soon as she recognised her husband, she exclaimed, "O man, you have found me in this predicament. If you accept of me, your reputation is good; but if you do not, I gladly release you from all ties of matrimony." Then, taking her anklets and bracelets off, she handed them to her husband, adding, "Be these also yours; and let us separate according to the known requisitions." The husband accepted of the things offered to him, and put them in his bosom. He then said to the woman, "Come, let us go before the cadi, and have a legal decision *(hujjet)* drawn up for our divorce; then return you to my house."

The man and his wife closed the door, and set out directly for the Mehkemeh of the judge. When they arrived there, the man exclaimed, "O Molana (sir), this woman is my wife. It is now three days since we agreed to be divorced from each other; let, therefore, a document be drawn up attesting our separation." The judge now, turning towards the woman, asked, "O woman, what have you to say in this matter?" She immediately replied, "He speaks falsely. To-day he took me to an improper place, and then took off my anklets and armlets; which he, at this moment, has in his bosom. If you do not credit my words, search him. And, as he has pronounced my divorce in your presence, let my dowry and clothes be restored to me." With these words she began to cry out for justice; and the judge, having searched in the man's bosom for the articles, produced them, and handed them over to the woman. At the same time, he commanded the man to give her her *mihri muedjil* (dowry of divorce).*

The husband was likewise sent to prison; and on entering it he was asked by his friend, who had been put there before him, what was the cause of his imprisonment. He replied, by exclaiming, "May your face be black! your ill conduct and bad luck have brought upon me all this misfortune." "Why," asked the fellow, "did you not go to my house? what have you done with the key?" "Wretch!" answered the man, "I did go to your house, as you requested; and on opening the door I found my own wife there, who, on seeing me, forgot her duty towards me, and, handing me her anklets and armlets, bade me also keep her dowry and divorce her. So I took them; and, putting them into my bosom, I went with her to the Mehkemeh to be divorced from her in form. When I there asked for a *hujjet* to be drawn up, the woman asserted that I had committed violence upon her, and had beat her and deprived her of her clothes; and she demanded that, as I had divorced her, I should give her her dowry

* By Islam law, a marriage is made with two dowries, one called *mihri muêdjil* and the other *mihri muâdjel*. One is given to her in effects, on the occasion of the wedding; and the other, always in money, is to be given her in case of being divorced. The latter often prevents divorces for trifling causes.—A. T.

of separation. This the cadi having required, he sent me here to prison until it should be complied with. Here," added the man, "is your key; and I have fallen a victim to the contagious ill luck which accompanies it."

STORY OF THE DISHONEST GOLDSMITH AND THE INGENIOUS PAINTER.

It is narrated by a person of veracity, that once in the land of Adjem (Persia), a master goldsmith and a painter of talent for a time formed an association together, and lived on terms of brotherly intimacy. After this, being disposed to travel, they entered into a covenant to remain faithful to each other, and not to go one step beyond their association,—that one should not act without the consent of the other, nor in any manner be treacherous to the other's interests.

Having made this agreement, they set out upon their journey. Their means being rather limited, on coming to a great convent, they put up there as guests. The monks of that convent, being pleased with them, showed them respect and tokens of esteem. They, particularly the painter, covered the walls of the convent with curious paintings; and the monks paid him much attention, and begged them to remain awhile with them. Having assented to this, they spent some time in the convent; and the monks placed so much confidence in them as to disclose to them the places containing the gold and silver idols of the convent. So one day they collected all these idols, and at night they made their escape with them. On reaching a city in a country of Islamites, they took up their abode there; when, according to their agreement, they put the gold and silver into a box, and spent only as much of it as their necessities required.

It so happened that the goldsmith married a person's daughter, and the expenses of the association were thus increased. In the course of time the wife bore her husband two children; and one day, when the other was absent, the goldsmith opened the box containing the treasures, and, stealing away one-half of the gold and silver, carried it to his own dwelling. On the painter's return he remarked that the box had been opened, and a portion of the contents taken out. When he questioned the goldsmith about it, the latter said that he had not touched it, and denied the theft.

Now the painter was a cunning fellow, and he immediately saw that the matter required good management. In the vicinity of their residence lived a huntsman, to whom he applied to procure him two bear cubs, for which he promised to pay him handsomely. The hunter consenting, he was soon furnished with the cubs, which the painter took and tamed. There was in that city also a carpenter; and, going to his shop, he bought of him the figure of a man made out of wood, and returned home. He then painted the figure, so that it was quite impossible to tell it from the goldsmith. This he put in a place by itself; and when the bear cubs were to be fed, he always had it done from the hand of the figure, until they became in time so accustomed to the sight of it as to treat it like their father or mother.

One day the painter invited the goldsmith to his house; and he accordingly came, bringing his two young sons with him. He treated them hospitably, and they passed the night there. On the following day he put the sons of the goldsmith in a secret part of his house; and when the father asked permission to take his leave he inquired for his sons. The painter replied, "An occurrence has happened which may serve as an example to others;—I am really ashamed to relate it to you." "What is it?" asked the goldsmith with surprise. The painter added, "Whilst your sons were at play, and running about, they both became suddenly metamorphosed into the form of two bear cubs; and the affliction which has befallen these two innocent children must have been sent on account of some great sin." The goldsmith became excessively grieved. "What does this mean," exclaimed he; "and why have you done this to my sons?" They quarrelled, and finally both went before the cadi of the place. The cadi and his associates were greatly surprised at the strangeness of the case. "What can this mean?" exclaimed they all. "Never has such a thing happened before since the coming of Mohammed. What are the evidences of this remarkable occurrence?" "I am quite as much astonished at it as yourselves," answered the painter; "but if you will allow me, I will bring the two metamorphosed children into your presence. The case will then be clear, and we will see whether or not they recognise their father."

The cadi and his company at once agreed to have the cubs brought before them. "Let us see," said they, "and judge for ourselves." The painter had cunningly kept the cubs hungry from the preceding night; and he now brought them from his house to the Mehkemeh of the judge, and placed them opposite the goldsmith. The cubs, as soon as they saw the latter, supposing him to be the same figure which the painter had made, rushed towards him, licked his feet, and began caressing him. The cadi and those with him were much affected at the sight, and exclaimed that if the cubs had not recognised their father in the goldsmith, they certainly would not act as they did. The goldsmith was bewildered between doubt and conviction; and so taking the two cubs with him, he returned to the house of the painter, where he begged pardon for his fault, and avowed it. He also returned the gold and silver effects which he had stolen from the box, and placed them all before the painter; at the same time he acknowledged his fault, and repented of what he had done. He likewise begged that the painter would pray to God to restore his sons to man's form again. The painter now led away the cubs, and putting them into the same house in which he had confined the goldsmith's children; he sat up all the following night apparently engaged in prayer. Early the next morning he went for the boys, and taking them by the hand, brought them to their father, exclaiming, " God be praised ! our prayers have been accepted ;" and delivered them up to their parent. The goldsmith was very much rejoiced, and offered many thanks to the painter, after which he carried his sons home.

Now news of this occurrence became spread about in the city, and it was told how the two sons of the goldsmith, after becoming metamorphosed, were again restored to human shape. Upon this the cadi had the painter cited before him, and required him to relate the truth about the matter. The painter informed him that such and such a compact had been made between himself and the goldsmith,—that the latter had acted so and so towards him, but that he was unable to prove the charge. " So I got up a ruse," said he, " to make him acknowledge the theft of the gold and silver, and succeeded by my skill in the art of painting." " *Barik Allah !*" exclaimed all those who heard the recital ; " a person's talents should be such as these." They added also many compliments and praises to the painter, on the ingenuity of his thoughts, and his success in laying so wise a plan.

CHAPTER THIRTY-THREE.

Narratives about those who have been rendered miserable by the permutations of Time, and those benevolent persons who, when filled with misfortune, have become the recipients of the divine favor of the Eternal God.

THE TALE OF THE HAMARVIEH AND THE UNFORTUNATE YOUTH.

Hamarvieh, the son of Ahmed bin Tooloon, was sovereign of Egypt. During his reign he was in the constant habit, every Friday and Monday, of getting into his *carafah* (barge) and paying visits to sacred places.

One day he visited one of these places (a holy man's tomb), and observed a young man of a handsome countenance seated near the tomb, weeping. Hamarvieh, touched by his tears, asked him from whose oppression he was suffering; and the young man replied that, oppression aside, his condition was a most unhappy one. "Do you know to whom this tomb belongs?" asked Hamarvieh. The youth answered, "It is now forty years since its occupant died." Hamarvieht hen added, "For more than twenty years I have been a visitant at the tomb, and have never met you here before; so that you must be agitated by some great affliction which induces you to come and weep here thus." The youth answered, "The occupant of this tomb was my father. He left me much wealth and possessions; all of which I have spent, until there is now nothing left except a handsome young female slave. Driven to the step by necessity, I have just given her to a broker to sell for me, and an agent of the sultan bought her. When I bade her farewell and returned to my home, the grief and wretchedness occasioned by parting from her nearly caused my death. The hand of separation tore the collar of my patience, and my will has taken the reins of direction, and tranquillity fled from my hand. Filled with this grief, I have come to my father's tomb to weep over my condition."

Hamarvieh was deeply touched at the tale of the young man. "Be no longer troubled," said he, "for you have attained the object of your desires. Behold! I am the sultan; my deputy bought your female slave for me. He purchased a suitable house, furnished and got it ready, and presented me with the whole. I accepted of them, and should have gone to see the girl; but as it is, may the Most High bless your slave to you. I give you, besides her, the house and all that it contains. So, go immediately, and this night let your desires be attained; forget me not in your devotions—and this is all I ask of you."

The unhappy young man, like one who has at last met with his destiny, set out forthwith for the house presented him by the sultan. He became perfectly happy in the company of his slave; and, as long as he lived, never ceased praying for the long life and prosperity of the noble and generous sultan.

It is related that once a very generous and wealthy man was reduced by the vicissitudes of the times to great poverty. He had left him, however, a female slave of incomparable beauty, whom he loved, and who loved him passionately. He, one day, addressing this young woman, said, "I have no hope of being freed from my poverty but by death. Yet I have thought that I may secure your prosperity by disposing of you to some generous individual; and if you are only happy and comfortable, I will be thankful to the All-Just for the blessings thus bestowed upon you." The slave answered, "It is better for me to be dead than to be separated from you; nevertheless, sell me for a good sum, which will deliver you from your indigence."

The slave was not only very beautiful, but she also possessed a talent for music. There was, at that time, a very benevolent man, named Ibin Mamer; and to him the owner of the slave conducted her. She performed a piece of music in the presence of this person; and, as he was greatly pleased with her talents, he offered to give three hundred thousand pieces of silver for her. But her master answered that he had spent quite as much as that in having her taught. The purchaser said, "But you have in the mean time been enjoying the sight of her beauty; here, I will give you also satin enough for ten drawers, ten head of horses and mules, besides many other objects." So the owner consented to let him have the slave; and having received the sum agreed upon and the aforementioned articles, he delivered her to the purchaser.

The seller of the slave accompanied her to the dwelling of her new master; and when she was about to enter the harem of the latter, she seized hold of the door-post, and began to weep, and addressing her late master, she bade him be happy in the enjoyment of the money which he had received. "As for me," added she, "there is nothing now left but adversity and my own unhappy thoughts; for, as you are helpless and desperate, you cannot effect any thing yourself, nor procure any assistance from others. Nothing but patience is left you; and I therefore recommend it to you." The man, on hearing this, wept, and replied, that as it was impossible to soften the harshness of faithless Time, nothing but Death was between them. "Pardon me," said he, "I leave you with a heart filled with sad thoughts, and will offer up my prayers in your behalf. I will say, Salams and praises be unto thee, O God! I have no hope of ever more beholding this beloved creature; yet may Ibin Mamer, the generous and gracious, reach the object of his desires." Uttering these words, the man wept bitterly. At this sight the emir of noble sentiments (Ibin Mamer) also wept; and taking the slave by the hand, he asked Allah to bless them both. "Expend the amount which I have given you," said he, "in providing for your support; and when you are in the enjoyment of this life's pleasures, do not forget me in your prayers."

The man thus becoming again the owner of his slave, they both expressed many thanks to the emir for his noble generosity, and filled with gladness returned to their home, where they afterwards spent a life of happiness.

TALE OF THE VIZIR AND THE INCOMPARABLY BEAUTIFUL FEMALE SLAVE.

It is related that there was once a king who was very fond of the society of females, and possessed one of superior beauty, to whom he was greatly attached. Now this king had a vizir who always prevented him from giving himself up to love for women. The sovereign consequently resigned all converse with his female slaves, and would constantly pass his nights outside of his palace.

One day, when this sovereign went into his harem amongst its inmates, the latter surrounded him, exclaiming, "O our prince, why have you abandoned us? tell us our fault." The sovereign replied, "You have committed no fault; but my vizir prevents me from enjoying more of your society, and states divers pretences as his reasons for so doing." One of the female slaves exclaimed, "I have the favor to ask of my sovereign, that you present me to that vizir, and some day witness his intercourse with me." The sovereign consenting, he had the vizir called before him, and then informed him that he presented him with that female slave.

The vizir accepted the gift; and soon becoming violently enamored of the slave, he wished to make her his concubine.* But the slave, being cunning, would not allow it; and the passion of the vizir

* The word signifying female slave, *jarieh*, is Arabic, and the only one used among the Turks. All *jariehs* are not concubines, and their condition does *not* depend entirely upon the views of the master.—A. T.

growing stronger, it quite mastered him. In fine, he begged and entreated her, and she now sent word to the sovereign to come and be witness of what was going to happen between her and the vizir. She coquettishly exclaimed to her lover, "If the whole world was given to me I would not acquiesce in your desires, except you do what I wish." "Command me," answered the vizir, "and I will obey you." So the slave had an ass's saddle and bridle brought, and told the vizir to put it on his back, and the bridle in his mouth, and let her ride him; in which case she would consent to his wishes. The vizir having acceded to her demands, she made him go down upon his hands and knees, put the saddle on his back, and the bridle in his mouth; after which she mounted on his back, and, whilst riding him about the house, lo! the sovereign suddenly entered.

On seeing his vizir in this position, the sovereign exclaimed, "How is this? you prevented me from enjoying the society of women; yet how do I see you employed!" The vizir answered, "My sovereign, behold what I always feared might be your lot; and I endeavored to preserve you against it. I have fallen into the very same misfortune which I dreaded you might meet with." The sovereign smiled, and was much pleased with the ready answer of his vizir. He made him numerous presents; and he also gave to the female slave many tokens of his satisfaction, and recommended the vizir to show her more favor than to his other women for his sake.

AN ANECDOTE,

Which shows the truth of the tradition of the Prophet, "He who lives and conceals his passion, dies a martyr."

The following is related by that very distinguished person Jahiz. One day the caliph Mutevekkel Billah sent for me to instruct his son. When I entered his presence he looked at me attentively, and was not pleased with my appearance; and so, after receiving a roll of gold pieces from him, I withdrew. On my way I met with one of the most celebrated emirs of that time, named Mohammed Yesar, who called me to him, and took me in his company in a boat on the Tigris. The boat was richly furnished; and, whilst passing over the water we partook of the most delicate viands, and drank of the most delightful wines,—in fine, we made a very pleasant and merry excursion.

Now the emir owned a beautiful female slave, who sang sweetly. She was with us, and sat behind a screen. Taking her instrument in her hand, she played an air; and then commencing with her voice, she sang these verses:

"Where is the heart free from love, which has not its tears and sorrows. O you who are faithful, your love is sufficient for you; as for me, how shall I conceal my own? I am wretched and forlorn."

The tremulous and plaintive tones of her voice, as she sang, showed that she was unhappy. She pulled aside the curtain which separated her from us; and her appearance struck me with an effect equal to that made by a bright new moon emerging from behind the dark clouds of night. Indeed, I never had beheld so beautiful a woman before in my life. After gazing at us for a moment, she suddenly threw herself into the Tigris. We all arose in alarm. Close beside the emir stood a youth of a handsome exterior, whose occupation was to fan the former. As soon as this individual saw the slave throw herself into the water, he let the fan drop from his hand, and exclaimed, "With what eye shall I henceforth look upon the world?" and recited this verse:

"Who dies for love, dies in this manner;
"The only happiness of love is to be able thus to die."

So saying, he threw himself into the river after the slave. Filled with astonishment, we called for aid; and divers immediately coming to our assistance, they jumped into the Tigris. Diving very deeply, they some time afterwards arose again to the surface; when we beheld the two individuals of whom they had been in search, closely embracing each other, and both dead. Mohammed bin Yesar was much affected at the sight of the sad spectacle before him; and seeing that his feelings were quite overcoming him, I exclaimed, "O emir, be not thus grieved, but be patient. If you will permit me, I will tell you a most singular occurrence, of which this one reminds me, and which may offer you some consolation." "Speak, O Jahiz," he replied, "relate the tale, and relieve me of the sad thoughts which now oppress my mind."

So I said, "O emir, one of the Ommiade caliphs, Suliman bin Abd el Melik,* once purchased a most beautiful female slave, who possessed a very sweet voice for music. He soon became warmly enamored of her, and could not separate himself from her for a moment. Now whilst this slave was yet with her late master, she had a lover, a handsome youth; and one day when Suliman bin Abd el Melik was employed in examining the affairs of the Mussulmans, in a great divan (council), a young man handed him a petition, in which the caliph read, 'O Emir of the faithful, I have a favor to ask of your justice and generosity—it is that you command your female slave who sings so well to sing these verses in your presence. I, your humble servant, will then, by hearing them, have drunk two cups filled with my warmest desires, and will have had my share of this life.' The caliph, in surprise, asked whose petition it was, and who was the individual who had brought it. The person was called, and appeared in the form of a youth, who acknowledged that it was his. After some moments spent in reflection, the caliph told him to come to his palace of Zebr Jedee on the following day.

"The youth expressed many thanks,† and withdrew. The next

* The fifth Ommiade caliph.

† It is worthy of remark, that Orientals do not thank the person who bestows the favor, as is done by Occidentals; but offer a brief prayer to Allah for the benefit thus done them. The phrase expressing *thanks* is, however, always used in the translation.—A. T.

day the caliph went with a numerous suite to his palace above mentioned, situated in an elegant vineyard. I accompanied him. This palace was an elevated one that resembled that of the Khawrnak (of Bahram in Babylonia) in magnificence. Here the caliph was surrounded by his pages and courtiers; and soon the young man who had presented the petition made his appearance, very richly dressed. He was presented to the caliph; and, after kissing hands, stood before him. All the persons present were much touched at the beauty of the youth. The caliph now ordered the female slave, with her instrument, to be brought in; and she immediately made her appearance, dressed in rich and costly attire, and looking very timid and modest. Taking the instrument on which she usually performed, in her hand, she approached and seated herself opposite to the place where the youth was standing. A bottle of boiled wine and two Damascus goblets were now brought in, and placed before the young man; who, taking one of the cups in his hand, filled it with wine, and, turning to the slave, asked her to sing something,—on which she commenced:

> 'He who desires for love, must be generous; like Kab bin Mameh, who spent his soul. Whoso longs for riches, must not give away as much as a dove.'

On ending these lines, the youth drank off one of the cups, and asked her to sing something to the cup, when she continued:

> 'Man has ever complained against separation,—those who came before me, and those who follow, and the dead. But separation, such as has befallen me, none has ever seen.'

At the close the two spoke together in a confidential tone, and a servant handed the youth the other cup. Taking it in his hand, he offered a prayer to the caliph, saying, 'O Emir of the faithful, our hopes to-day have done violence to our minds. May the Most High render you happy both in this world and in the next.' Then turning to the slave, he exclaimed, 'This is our last pledge; pray sing something suitable to it.' So, tuning her instrument, she sang as follows:

'The longest and most insupportable of all days is that which separates lovers. O heart, why didst thou lend thyself to that cruel passion? Knowest thou not that it wrestles violently with lovers?'

On their termination the youth drank off the contents of the cup which he held in his hand, and after returning thanks arose. He bade farewell to all those present, and was in the act of withdrawing, when, approaching a window, he threw himself out of it, and, alighting on his head, was killed immediately.

"The caliph, on seeing this, was greatly distressed, and exclaimed, 'Wretched youth! what cruel haste he made to put an end to his life! Did he think that, after bringing my slave where he could thus sit and converse freely with her, I could ever take her back again into my harem? No, I swear by Allah, that my intention was to present her to him. But "we are God's, and to God we shall return."'* He ordered the superintendant of his palace to seek for some relations of the female slave and deliver her to them. 'Supply her,' said he, 'with whatever she may desire or need, and give her in marriage to some one.' The servant did as he was bid, and taking her by the hand said, 'Come let us go.' On reaching the head of the staircase she withdrew her hand from his, and, throwing herself down the stairs, fell upon her head and expired. The caliph, at this new disaster, was filled with amazement; he ordered the two bodies to be prepared for interment, and consigned them together to the same grave."

Mohammed bin Yesar, on hearing my recital of the foregoing tale, was a little relieved of the sad feelings which oppressed him.

* Koran, 2 : 151.

FIVE ANECDOTES.

ANECDOTE.

Fazeel bin Ayaz says, that if the Most High would accept of a prayer from him, his most humble servant, that prayer would be offered up in behalf of lovers; "for," adds he, "they are compelled and reduced to despair, and have no power over their own conduct."

Omar bin Abdul Azeez had a sister, who was a very pure, religious, and pious woman. One day she met in her house with Izeh, the celebrated mistress of Ketheer; and addressing the former, she asked the meaning of the verses which Ketheer had made about her, viz:

"The debts of all debtors were settled, and the money sufficed for them all.
She promised a kiss, and it has not been paid."

Izeh replied, "I had promised him a kiss, and had not fulfilled the same. He made allusion to it in these lines." The pious woman exclaimed on hearing this, "Cover your promise, and let the fault be mine." She immediately freed forty female slaves, as an atonement for the sin which the other had committed.

ANECDOTE.

It is related respecting Ketheer, the celebrated lover of Izeh, that he once sent a slave of his with some goods for sale to Damascus, who, on the way fell in with the village of his master's sweetheart. Izeh told a woman to go and purchase some garments for her from Ketheer's slave; "but," added she, "be careful not to tell him who they are for, nor even let him know that you were sent by me." The woman went, and procured some materials suitable for clothes for Izeh, as well as some others for the women of the village, paying for them all. One of the latter, however, did not pay for the stuffs purchased for her for some days; and when at length she brought the money, and was about to give it to Ketheer's slave, the latter cited very appropriately this hemistich:

"She paid all her debts, and also those of the debtors."

The woman who had gone on the part of Izeh, being quite surprised, exclaimed, "O fellow, why should I conceal from you, that all the things which I have taken of you are for Izeh, whose servant I am? and see, there is her house." The man replied, "And do you be witness that I am the slave of Ketheer. The servant and all he possesses belong to his master.* No money at all is necessary, and I will receive none." In fine, he returned the money to the woman, and withdrawing from that place went back to his master, to whom he related that he had sold all his goods to Izeh, but had refused payment for them. On which Ketheer exclaimed, "I call God to witness, that you did well; I free you from this moment, and shall consider all the rest of the goods as restored to me."

ANECDOTE.

It is narrated in the book of Mohammed bin Daood et Tay, that a youth belonging to the tribe of the Benee Azreh fell in love

* Mohammedan law.

with the daughter of some one. When the girl became aware of his affection, she chose to afflict him by refusing to meet him. The poor fellow concealed his passion from all others; and he became weak and thin from the strength of the love which he bore for that girl (*jarieh*).* He took to his bed, and was at the point of death. At last his relatives becoming acquainted with the cause of his illness, they pitied him, and carried news of his condition to the person whom he loved. The girl immediately went to the dwelling of her lover, whom she found reduced by the violence of love, and changed like leaves in autumn. On seeing this, she shed tears; and the unhappy youth opening his eyes also wept, and recited these lines:

"If she visits my coffin as it passes by, my hand will be stretched forth to implore her pity. If she visits my tomb and salutes me, my tears will flow ever in my grave."

His mistress on hearing these words from her lover was very much affected, and exclaimed, "I swear by Allah, that I did not know you were in this condition: my whole heart and soul are devoted to you." To this she added many kind remarks, and pressed her face affectionately against his. The poor lover opened his eyes; and after reciting a couplet suitable to his situation, he sighed once, and delivered up his soul. His mistress, who was a tender and affectionate girl, repeated the following lines:

"I no longer possess any means to meet you in life, therefore nothing remains for me but to die. We have no room even for hope, and God's command is for me to die."

And having sighed a few moments over his remains, she also expired. Their bodies were washed and interred in the same grave.

* Here this word is found used for a free woman.

ANECDOTE.

A person in the company of Halid bin Valed once related as follows: O Emir, there was an individual who had a very beautiful wife, and they were both warmly attached to each other. One day whilst conversing with his wife, this man looked fixedly in her face, and then burst into tears. The woman, much surprised, inquired the cause of his grief; and he replied, "Whilst thus in the enjoyment of your society, I suddenly reflected that death might separate us; that you would become the wife of another man; and that whilst you would be a source of comfort and joy to him, I would lie in the frightful and solitary tomb!" "God forbid," replied the woman, "that I should ever become the wife of another after you are gone." The man was rejoiced at this answer, and thanked his wife for her devotion.

Some time after this the wife's husband died; and faithful to her promise, she refused to marry again. This woman, however, had a father, who insisted so much upon her marrying again, that in the course of time she was, against her will, obliged to consent. The wedding took place, and during the night the woman saw her late husband in a dream, who coming to her house, took the ring of its door in his hand and recited the following verses:

> "All in this house are alive—I alone am with the dead. I have been exchanged for another, whom I know. The tomb still holds me. Whilst you have again become a bride, I remain in the cold tomb with the animals. Where now is that promise made in tears, that when I died you would go to no other husband?"

Suddenly she awoke, screamed out, and arose from her bed. She withdrew into an apartment alone, and told her parents that she would never sleep again with a man. "I never consented to this marriage," added she; "you compelled me to it against my will." In fine, as long as she lived she never would live with the husband her parents had given her to, nor with any other.

ANECDOTE.

There was once an inhabitant of Yamin, named Ibin Jeohery, a very wealthy man, who went to Bagdad. One day whilst walking along a retired street, his eye happened to light upon a beautiful female. A mutual affection was immediately conceived between them, and he promised the fair creature to go in search of her after dark. On entering her dwelling, however, he met with her father, who apprehended and conducted him before the Emir of Irak, Khalid bin Abdallah Kashree. "I caught him entering my house," said the father; "and he must be a thief." Khalid having questioned the man, he acknowledged that he was a thief; and the former immediately commanded one of his hands to be cut off. On hearing what had occurred, the fair creature addressed the following lines to the emir:

ARABIC.

"O Khalid, be not in haste; I am devoted to thee.
He who is bound by love's chains is never a thief.
He has avowed that he did not act with duplicity;
He preferred to lose his arm rather than expose his passion.
His heart and mine are burnt by his act!
Can you remove the passions of all lovers?
Who amongst you could thus devote his hand?
Thus acts the man who is urged by fidelity.
In fine, if you wish to be great, hold divine benevolence and generosity as one."

Khalid, on reading these verses, at once perceived the truth of the matter; and commanding Ibin Jeohery to be brought before him, he said, "I now know all about you; why did you acknowledge yourself a thief?" To which Ibin Jeohery replied in these lines:

ARABIC.

"O Khalid, I confess it; I no longer conceal my love.
I wish for nothing but the truth in my death;
If it is not forbidden—I regard it as being so.

If the world requires our separation, I will never consent.
Our secret is, God knows, that I love her;
For one glimpse I am proclaimed a thief.
If you are generous you will pardon that crime,
And thus do a good deed to one of God's creatures.
The end of all things is mercy;
It comes in fine to the lover and the mistress."

Khalid, much pleased with the conduct of Ibin Jeohery, assured him of his good feelings. He also commanded the father to give him the young woman in marriage; and as the father did not dare to refuse, a great wedding was made for them. Ibin Jeohery became known throughout all Bagdad by the name of Ashik, (the lover), and was much beloved by all its inhabitants for his conduct.

ANECDOTE.

It is related that one night during the caliphat of Aboo Bekr es Sadik,* on whom be peace, Aboo Bekr was walking in the streets of Medina, when he suddenly heard a low, plaintive cry, proceeding from a house close beside him. Approaching the door, the caliph heard a female weeping and reciting the following lines:

ARABIC VERSES.

"Thou hast made me a captive; I am lost in thy love;
Thy face is like the moon in her fifteenth night."

When he knocked at the door it opened; and the young woman coming out, Aboo Bekr asked her whether she was a free woman

* The first successor of the Prophet Mohammed.

or a slave. "I am the latter, O companion of the Prophet of Allah," she replied. "To whom have you given your heart?" next inquired the caliph. "By the respect which you bear for the tomb of the Prophet," said she, "leave me, I implore you, alone with my sorrow." But Aboo Bekr exclaimed, "It is quite impossible for me to depart until you have told me all about yourself." She immediately replied, by reciting these two lines:

ARABIC VERSES.

"Separation now disturbes my breast, and
I weep for love of Abool Casim."

From this the caliph at once knew what ailed the young woman. So continuing on to the chapel of the Prophet, he sat down, and sent a man for the owner of the girl. On this person's arrival he inquired about the young slave; and purchasing her of him at a handsome price, he sent her to Mohammed bin Casim bin Jaafer bin Talib, begging him to accept of her for his sake, and retain her in his service.

The noble generosity of the caliph may be seen in this occurrence. God be merciful to him!

ANECDOTE.

It is related that Siti Sekineh, the fair daughter of the Imam Husain,* on whom be peace, was unequalled for her learning, and became proverbial for her graciousness and generosity. One day a number of persons, distinguished for their talents and information, had assembled in her presence; when she corrected the errors

* One of the sons of the caliph Ali.

of the verses of the poets, and bestowed upon all numerous evidences of her favor. Amongst the poets were Ketheer, Izeh, Jemeel, Ahvas, Jerir, Nessib, and Ferzdek; all of whom came together to her residence. Siti Sekineh had prepared them an elegant repast; and each had some error in his verses, which she prettily corrected. Then turning to Ferzdek, she said, "Who is the chief of poets to-day?" Ferzdek replied, that he was. But Siti Sekineh denied it; she recited a verse and said, "See whose may these lines be." She then dismissed them. On the day following they assembled again, when the Siti met them and invited them in, and they seated themselves. At her side, this time, sat a handsome female slave, holding in her hand a fan, with which she cooled her mistress. When Ferzdek beheld the slave, affected by the sight of her shadow, he immediately became enamored of her (was captivated by the zone of her beauty). The poor fellow threw himself at the feet of Siti Sekineh, and exclaimed, "*Ya seidet en nisa*, O princess of women, I have strong claims against you; for I came expressly from Mecca to see and visit you, and have composed two verses explicative of my situation, which I beg leave to lay before you. You inquired who was the chief of poets; and when I replied that it was myself, you accused me of falsehood. Now you may ask for the verses of other individuals; for I am powerless, and my fear is that I may die before meeting with the accomplishment of my desires. In the name of the memory of your ancestors, I beg, that should I die, you may be so good as to put me in my coffin and inter me in the apartment of the female slave who is now in your service. This, O princess, is the last prayer of Ferzdek." So saying, he repeated two verses on the subject of love. The Siti, quite overcome by his language, laughed excessively, and exclaimed, "May God kill you for your tricks!" She then commanded the female slave to collect her wardrobe, and go and be a faithful servant to Ferzdek; which the woman having done, they two lived a long time afterwards happily together.

Yahiya bin Maaz Sinan, the author of the book called Mesariel Ushak (Lovers' Wrestles), relates as follows:

Once I was going from Mecca to Sena, and whilst still at the distance of five *merhalehs* (each eight hours) from that place, some of my companions ascended the mountain. "Come with us," said they to me; "let us all go up together, and make a visit to the tombs of Arvah and Afran." So I went with them, and on reaching the valley we beheld the tombs of this Sena and his mistress, placed side by side. Beside each grave grew a tree, which on reaching the height of a man inclined towards the other, and joined their branches together, as if two sighs (caused by separation) met and embraced each other. Over these two graves was a marble slab, on which the following verses were engraved:

ARABIC VERSES.

The two limbs of a tree grew up and entwined together;
But the vicissitudes of time threw them asunder.
These trees sprang up in the desert.
They will once more meet again in the other world;
They will be reunited whom the bowels of the earth have separated.
In life their hope was in union;
It took place in the grave, and will be perpetuated hereafter.

Leila Ahilieh, celebrated among the Arabs for her beauty, had been the mistress of Tevbet bin el Hameer. Leila one day mounted her litter (placed on the bank of a camel); and setting out in company with her husband, they continued on their way, until they reached the tomb of Tevbet. When they arrived there, her husband remarked, "O Leila, here is the grave of the liar whom they called Tevbet, and who wrote these verses:

ARABIC.

If Leila Ahilich salutes me,
Be there rocks and stones on my breast,
I will surely in joy return the salutation;
And a voice will proceed from my grave
Like that of a long absent friend to one who is beloved."

On repeating the lines, the husband added to Leila, "If you love the Most High, go to Tevbet's tomb and salute him." But she begged him to leave her alone, and refused to go. Her husband, however, insisted upon her doing so, adding that the unfortunate man who lay interred there had been made wretched through his passion for her. "Now if you have any regard for me," said he, "go up to his grave and salute him."

Leila, thus compelled, pressed her camel forward, until she came alongside of Tevbet's tomb, when she exclaimed, "*Salam alaik, ya Tevbet el Maanee,* I salute thee, O Tevbet the Maanyite." Now a bird had made its nest on the tomb of the deceased; and startled by Leila's voice, it rose up and flew away, frightening Leila's camel, so that it sprang aside and let her and the litter in which she sat fall to the ground, killing her on the spot. Her husband prepared her remains for interment and buried them beside those of Tevbet. The most remarkable part of this strange occurrence is that Tevbet should thus have performed, so long after his death, what he promised in his verses. It needs to be added, that this Leila Ahilieh is not she who was the mistress of Medjnoon, whose name was Leila Amir.*

It is related by Medain, that once Ibin Ziad was travelling with

* The love tale of Leila and Medjnoon is well known amongst the Persians and Turks as well as the Arabs. It is the most popular of all oriental tales, and is equivalent to the Romeo and Juliet of English literature.—A. T.

a number of persons on horseback, when they met a fellow having a very handsome female for his companion. Calling after this man, they approached him: he, suddenly fixing an arrow in his bow, seemed thinking whether or not he should let fly at them, when the bowstring snapped. At this they rushed upon him, and took the female from him. In one of her ears she had an ear-ring made of a most valuable pearl; and whilst they were endeavoring to get possession of it her master fled away. The woman now demanded of those who had seized her, what they saw in her ear-ring which made it such an object of their cupidity. "If you could get the large pearls which are in that man's turban," added she, "they are worth the entire poll-tax of Room, and would be to you a capital for life." Immediately letting the woman go, they all pursued after the man, and called out to him to give up to them the sums which were in his turban. Now, there was a bow-string in the man's turban which he had forgotten; and being thus reminded of it, he immediately took it out, and, fastening it to his bow, let fly an arrow at his pursuers. Being a skilful archer, he killed one of them on the spot; and the remainder turned and fled, leaving the woman once more at liberty. The man thus regained his slave, whom he warmly praised for her sagacity and fidelity.

STORY OF YAKOOB BIN DAVID, THE VIZIR OF THE CALIPH MEHDEE BILLAH.*

Yakoob bin David, the generous and excellent vizir of Mehdee, one of the Abbaside caliphs, tells the following story:

One day the Emir el Mumineen sent for me; and on going to him I found him making merry, seated in a beautiful garden like that of Paradise, and surrounded by his courtiers and by every thing

* The third caliph of the house of Abbas.—A. T.

of the most costly kind. He was served by a young female slave so exquisitely beautiful, that in all my life I never had seen any human being equal to her. As soon as he observed me, he exclaimed, "What do you say, O Yakoob bin David, to this jovial society?" To which I, offering him my compliments, replied, "May there never be any beauty and perfection like this; may your enjoyment be everlasting; and may the supporters of your majesty's greatness be perpetual." The caliph answered, "I bestow all the gayeties and appurtenances of this meeting, together with this female slave (*jarieh*), upon you. I also add to the gift the sum of a hundred thousand dinars, and command you to spend a few days in the most perfect gratification and enjoyment possible." Then turning his face, he added, "I have need of you in a matter in which you must be very zealous and attentive." In reply to this I kissed the caliph's feet, and remarked that I was his majesty's servant, whose duty it was to hear and obey his commands with all fidelity—commands which were always a source of honor to me.

The caliph now delivered over to me a dignified looking man, saying, "I wish you to put me at rest from all apprehension of this man's evil machinations; for if he lives, he will some day be a source of trouble and sorrow to me." I answered, begging him to believe that I would endeavor to relieve his mind from all apprehensions, by executing his orders respecting the man. The caliph then bade me swear to carry out the commands he had given me, —which I did.

I then took the man with me, and returned to my own palace, where I confined him in one of its apartments. I became so much enamored of the beautiful slave which the caliph had given me, that I had a suite of rooms prepared for her near my own divan, and was separated from her only by a curtain. Whenever I could be free from business I spent my time in her society, enjoying her conversation and intimacy. I passed a few days in this manner, and then ordered my prisoner to be brought before me

I inquired into his circumstances and history, and found that he was a most intelligent and well informed person, but had been calumniated to the Emir of the faithful by his enemies, who had accused him of having designs upon his majesty's throne. The caliph had been convinced by their accusations, and had therefore given his prisoner into my charge. The man threw himself at my feet, exclaiming, "O Yakoob, you are a man known for your intelligence and independence of opinion: be not a participator in the shedding of innocent blood; go not into the presence of God with the blood of a descendant of Alee upon you. If others choose to do it, let them." "I swear, by Allah," I replied, "and by the respect which I entertain for the Prophet's tomb, that you will meet with nothing but good from me." I then gave him some money for his expenses on the way, presented him with a horse, and bade him set out immediately, and conceal himself in some place unknown to me, where he should remain for awhile. The man did as I bade him, and departed.

Now, the jarieh which the caliph had presented me with, had heard all that passed between me and this man; and going at once to the caliph, she related it all to him. Immediately the caliph sent men; and, having again apprehended the person of the dignified figure, he put him once more in prison. He then ordered me to call on him; and, on my entering his presence, he inquired with an appearance of pleasure and gratification, "Well, Yakoob bin David, how have you performed the service which I confided to you?" "Long life to the Prince of the faithful," I replied, "his work is done." "Swear by my head that what you say is true," said the caliph; and I swore by his head that it was even so. "Go," said the caliph to those near him, "bring in that man." And lo! they led in the very person whom I had just released. "Is this the return which you make," exclaimed the caliph, "for the confidence and reliance which I placed on your fidelity? Is it right that you should thus treat me with deception and treachery?" I could make no possible reply, but stood for some time in silence. At length the caliph spoke. "Leave me, Ibin Yakoob," said he to me; and to those around him he added, "Take him and imprison him in the dark dungeon, called the 'Mutbik,' and enter into its registers that he is to be confined there for ever." Obeying the caliph's commands, they led me away from his presence, and let me down into a deep well, where I was provided with food and drink every three days. I was only informed of the five times a day for prayer, by some one striking on the trap-door of the well.

Here I remained for some length of time,—how long I did not know, the impurity of the place having deprived my eyes of their sight. At length, one day, the mouth of the dungeon opened, a basket was let down to me, and I heard some one cry out, "O Ibin David, be happy once more." I was then taken out of the prison and conducted to a bath, where, after being cleansed I was clothed and again led into the presence of the caliph. "*Salam alaik,* O Emir of the faithful," said I, saluting him. "What Emir of the faithful do you mean?" asked some one. "The Emir el Mehdee," said I. A voice from the hall then exclaimed, "God's mercy rest upon El Mehdee;" from which I knew that he was dead. I was bidden again to salute the caliph; and I said, "*Salam alaik, ya Ameer el mumineen.*" "What emir do you salute?" was again asked me. I replied, "The Emir el Hadee." The same voice once more spoke from the seat of honor, saying, "God's mercy rest upon El Hadee." So I again said, "Salams to the Emir el Mumineen Haroon er Rasheed;" and the same voice immediately responded, "And salams to thee, O Ibin David; and God's mercy and blessing be with thee." This person inquired of me how I was, and bade me pardon him for all I had suffered. I replied by saying that I pardoned El Mehdee, and thanked Haroon er Rasheed for delivering me from my prison; adding, "O Prince of the faithful, my eyes no longer see, nor my ears hear; and I am become an aged and infirm man." "Ask whatever you desire," said the caliph; "for I am grateful to you for many benefits and services which you rendered me." So

I asked to be permitted to go to Mecca, and spend the remainder of my days in the neighborhood of that sainted place, in prayers for the Commander of the faithful. Haroon er Rasheed forthwith granted my request, and commanded that all my wants should be provided for. I came, therefore, to Mecca, and am spending the remainder of my life in the service of all true believers.

The cause of all my misfortunes and sufferings was woman's deceit, which I did not preserve myself against; but, being blinded by the passion of love for the female slave given me by the caliph, did not conceal my secret from her. Becoming possessed of this latter, she divulged it to my ruin, and thus I was rendered miserable through my own fault. The moral of this story will be understood by persons of experience.

CONCERNING TRAITS OF AFFABILITY AND PIETY OF CHARACTER.

It is related that one of the military commanders of Mamoon, one of the Abbaside caliphs, Abdallah bin Tahir, was a very dignified and influential man. One day the caliph became enraged with him, and asked the opinion of the courtiers* around him as to what should be done to him. All advised his death; so the caliph ordered his confidential secretary to write a note summoning Abdallah bin Tahir to his presence, as he had some business with him. Now, the confidential clerk of the caliph was a great friend of Abdallah bin Tahir; wherefore, after writing the note, he added in a corner the words, "*Ya Moosa!* (O Moses!)" and sent it to the commander. On receiving it, Abdallah read its contents, and, in obedience to the order which it contained, was about to

* It is to be understood that the Oriental courtiers are not like those of the west. The term used is *nadims*, which signifies the private companions of the prince, who serve him and are dependent on his bounties.—A. T.

proceed to the caliph's palace; but, before doing so, he went into his harem, where he possessed a very beautiful as well as a most intelligent female slave, who moreover was a poetess. This young woman, for brightness of mind and for elegance, was quite incomparable. Seeing the note in his hand, she took it from him, read it; and, on perceiving the words, "*Ya Moosa,*" she screamed out, "For God's sake, O emir, do not go,—refrain from it; for the clerk who wrote this is your friend, and has given you notice to be upon your guard. The words, '*Ya Moosa,*' are the commencement of the line, 'O Moses, the people command thee to be killed.'"

Abdallah thanked God for the female's perspicacity; and having been able to show, in a reply which he wrote, some good excuses, he escaped the danger which threatened him.

AN ANECDOTE ABOUT BELKEES.

The wife of the Prophet Suliman—on whom be peace—was Belkees, and her tribe that of the *Jann.* Her story is so good an example to the world, and shows so much of the wisdom of the Creator of man, that it is deemed worthy of being cited here.

In ancient times the sovereign of the country of Saba was a person named Yeshrah. He was known as possessing a benevolent and peaceful character, and a mind full of talents and information. He ruled over his subjects in such a manner as rendered them tranquil and easy. One day, when this excellent prince was travelling, he came to an extensive plain where were two serpents resembling frightful dragons. One of these was white, the other black; they were entwined around each other in a desperate conflict, and the white one had received a wound in a very vital part of its body. The black serpent being thus victorious, the strength of the white one was exhausted; it could move no more, and the black one wreaked its vengeance upon the helpless animal. King Yeshrah, touched with pity, went to the assistance of the white snake, and aided it in its conquered state; he placed a diamond-pointed arrow in his bow, and, taking aim at the black snake, he let fly and instantly killed it. The white snake, now regaining its existence, crawled away until it became lost from the king's sight. King Yeshrah, much pleased, returned to his throne.

One day while this same king was seated alone, a youth of a handsome exterior persisted in being allowed to enter the presence of Yeshrah. The king, much surprised at the conduct of the youth, asked him how he dared be so bold as to approach his privacy uninvited; to which the youth replied, "Be not displeased with me, O king; the cause of my conduct is that I, who have been benefited by your goodness, belong to the family of the Jinns (*taïfeh jann*), and received my life from your benevolent hand on a certain occasion." The king, greatly surprised, bade the youth explain on what occasion; and the latter said, "I am the white serpent, which was engaged in a conflict on such a plain, and, when reduced to the point of destruction, was saved by you. You destroyed my enemy; and, to make a return for your kindness, I am come, according to the saying, 'Do good for good done to you,' to ask leave to enter your service." The king replied, "I have already many servants, and have no possible use for any more." "Can I not, then, procure you some precious metals for your treasury, or jewels of any kind?" asked the youth; but the king replied, "I already have these in abundance, and care but little for such things." "Let me know, then, what science or knowledge you have a taste for, and I will give you information about it." The king replied, "The foot of my throne is the abode of the learned, and I already possess a portion of all kinds of science." After a moment's reflection, the youth observed to the king, "O, sovereign of the world, I find that none of my offers have been acceptable to your majesty. Now I have a sister who is as beautiful as an angel (lit. a *Peree*); no eye of the world has ever witnessed her equal: and if you have a desire to marry her, it will be my duty to effect it." When the king heard the praises of the Peree-faced girl, he experienced, in the inmost part of his heart, a desire for her, and wished greatly to behold her charms.

The youth, much pleased at the evident inclination shown by the king for his sister, in an instant of time disappeared from sight, and like a spirit became, invisible. Immediately afterwards returning, he was accompanied by a Peree-faced girl, as splendid (as Khorsheed Phœbus)—a revolutioner of past times—a devastator of all human reason—a rosebud of silver lips—a double-chinned rose-form—a slender-shaped beauty gently moved by the wind, and each wave of whose curls was a snare for hearts. When this beautiful creature with the musk-scented locks came before the king's eyes, the reins of his self-control left his hands; he became greatly enamored of her charms, accepted of her for his wife, and immediately offered to espouse her. The Venus-like girl on her part expressed her willingness to be betrothed to the king, but however on one condition,—and on that would depend her union with him. "Let me hear what it is," said the king. The fair creature replied, "Every thing which I do, be it good or evil, you must consent to, nor must you think of changing it. In this manner no harm can come upon you from me; if you marry me, know that I am a Jinn, that my Junoon is a conquerer,* and I will vanish immediately from your sight, so that you can never behold me again."

The king, no longer master of himself, consented to her demand, and exclaiming, "On my head and eyes be it," expressed his compliance. They remained together a long time happily; and the lovely wife bore him a handsome son, as beautiful as an angel, much to the king's joy and satisfaction. One day when they were

* This account of the character of the female is not clearly understood. Junoon is a being superior to herself, who gives her strength to act—to disappear.—A. T.

enjoying each others society and conversation, a dog approached him; and his wife suddenly casting the child into its mouth, the dog fled away, and was lost from sight. The king was excessively displeased at what she had done, and became filled with sadness and melancholy; but concealing it, he continued to act up to the condition which he had agreed to. He renewed his intimacy with his wife; they were happy together, and she bore him an angelic daughter, which for beauty and perfection was splendid as a Hooree of Paradise. The king was now again greatly rejoiced, and was consoled by this daughter for the loss of his son. For some time he was made happy by this child; but once during the winter season, when the weather was most severe, as he and his wife were sitting around a brazier, she suddenly seized the child and cast it into the fire, where it was soon consumed by the burning coals. The king, not knowing the cause of this conduct, was excessively afflicted; he arose, and retiring by himself, gave vent to his grief in a flood of tears. The fire of separation consumed his liver;* but recovering from his pain, he again resumed a smiling countenance. Some time after this, by divine power, the king had another daughter born to him. The child possessed a pure aspect, and was so delicately beautiful, that, on account of its resembling the Hoorees of Paradise, it merited the name of *Belkees.* All watchful care was bestowed on its cradle; daily it increased in sweetness and beauty, and was a source of joy and gladness to the king.

Wondering whether it was his wife's design also to make way with this child, he begged her not to treat it as she had done the other two; "for," added he, "my heart is already become embittered with the loss of my offspring; do not, therefore, I beg you, add new grief to what it has already suffered." "By the compact which we made," she answered, "I was to admit of no infraction of its condition,—and you have no right even to ask me this ques-

* Among all Orientals the liver is supposed to be the seat of the affections.—A.T.

tion. However, I excuse you this time; but know that if it should ever occur again, our union will be changed to separation, our marriage tie will be loosed, and our joys and delights will be certainly turned into sorrow." The king on hearing this remained silent, and thus sought to excuse himself.

About this time a powerful enemy appeared against the king in person; and as no one else was capable of opposing him, the king set out to do it himself, taking the angel-faced woman with him. He entered a fortress, and his enemy surrounded it with his troops. The war becoming prolonged, the king's provisions began to diminish until there were but few remaining. He was occupied constantly with planning some means of relief, and had recourse to a vizir in whom he at all times placed confidence. The vizir had, however, joined himself to a party of discontented persons, and was disposed to deal treacherously towards his sovereign. The king, supposing him as faithful as formerly, took council with him as to what they should do on account of the shortness of the provisions. The vizir replied that the troops had not food sufficient for ten days, and sent a small quantity of biscuit to the king's tent. The queen was greatly pleased, and at night put the biscuit into the fire and consumed it. When this came to the knowledge of the king, it gave him great grief; and having no command over himself he exclaimed, "Ho! woman, are you my enemy that you should do such an act? or do you wish to be our ruin?" To which the woman replied, "I am not your enemy; but am, perhaps, your most faithful friend. Your infidel vizir, from enmity towards you, has joined with your opponents and poisoned the provisions, with the view of destroying both you and your soldiers. To prove my words, I have retained a small portion of the biscuit, with which you can make an experiment." The bread was given to an animal, which immediately fell down and expired.

The woman now added to the king, "Henceforth I can have no more intercourse with you; my worldly connexion with you now must cease. The son which I threw to the dog still lives, and has been brought up by a tender nurse in the form of a dog. The daughter which I exposed to the fire is also in perfect health; for the fire is its nurse. I must now bid you an eternal farewell—for our intercourse is at an end. When separated from me, do not be grieved, for I will send so many Jinn soldiers against your enemies, that the latter will be routed and ruined in a moment. Be happy, and keep with you my much loved daughter Belkees. She will succeed you upon the throne,—will become a great and illustrious queen, and receive great benefits. As for myself, I will not be neglectful of you, and have commended you to Allah." On finishing these latter words she disappeared from the king's sight for ever.

Some days after this, troops of Jinns came to the assistance of the king's army; and together they completely routed his enemy's forces, most of whom were killed. The victorious king returned as a conquerer to his throne; but he was afflicted by the loss of his wife. At length the "fatal moment" (*edjel*) arrived, and he died; his daughter Belkees succeeded him on the throne, and her history has been written in a detailed manner.

THREE ANECDOTES.

I.

It is related that once an individual named Baklan having revolted, Berak Khan, who was of the dynasty of Ektay bin Jengheez, assembled his forces and marched against him towards the country of Khoten. One of his soldiers on the way shot an arrow into a swallow's nest, and knocked it down. A pearl dropped out of this nest, and rolling along, fell into a well. On seeing this these Moguls followed it into the well, and discovered there a thousand purses of gold.

About the same time, a bey of these Moguls pitched his tent at the foot of a large tree, and he and his companions fastened their horses to its branches. During the night the horses quarrelled and split the tree into two parts; and in the morning the Mogulsfound inside and under the tree six thousand purses of gold.

II.

It is stated in the work called Medjemâ Nevadir, "Collection of Remarkable Occurrences," that during the reign of Sultan Melik Shah, there was a physician at Herat named Ismaeel Edeeb, who in knowledge was the unique philosopher of his time. One day on going into the bazar he saw a butcher devouring the entrails of each sheep which he killed, whilst yet warm; and not being pleased with his conduct, he remarked to a grocer in the neighborhood that the young butcher would soon have a bad illness come upon him. "But when he is taken ill," continued he, "come quickly, and let me know it."

Now, soon after this the young man died suddenly, and his relatives began to weep and lament his fate. The grocer went and informed the physician of what had occurred, but said it was too late to aid him, for he was already dead. The physician, however, went to see the body; and raising the veil from off his face he began to apply remedies for the butcher's disease, which was apoplexy. In three days the young man had recovered and greatly surprised the inhabitants of that place by his restoration to life.

III.

It is related in historical works that one of the celebrated men of Egypt had a stroke of apoplexy, and all the physicians of the place were called in at the death. The relatives and family of the deceased commenced preparations for the interment of the body. A physician named Katiyee happened to be present at the time. He looked upon the face of the corpse, and declared that the man was not dead. So preparing remedies for his restoration, he showed that he was a mighty man; for after applying some ten blows of a whip to the deceased, he felt his pulse and perceived a slight movement. Those around him declared that no one had ever known the pulse of a dead man to move. He, however, continued the application of the whip, until the deceased recovered his senses, arose, and began to ask for food. This person lived many years afterwards, and his history was a subject of astonishment to all who heard it.

CHAPTER THIRTY-FOURTH.

Story about the daughter of a powerful vizir, and what occurred to her lover.

In ancient times there was a fortunate sovereign, who in majesty and grandeur resembled Alexander. He had a vizir as wise as Jupiter (Mashtery), and who for knowledge and mental capacity was without his equal. The sovereign had a most beautiful daughter, fair as the setting sun; and all the world were her suitors. The vizir likewise had a daughter of angelic beauty, whose fairness shone like a bright moon in the sky of beauty; and those two girls rivalled each other in the sweetness of their charms. They were the ornaments of the world: they seemed to be two waving cypress-trees in the rose-garden of joy; and the buds of their eloquence were like two fresh opening roses. The whole world was like the fire-fly whirling around the torches of their sweetness and beauty.

The preference was given by the public to the daughter of the vizir; which excited the envy of the sovereign's daughter, until it induced the latter to complain of it to her father. She declared that either she or the vizir's daughter must rule alone, for together they could not exist. The sovereign, becoming desperate, sent for his vizir, and commanded him, if he had any regard for him, to sell his daughter, and, although it might be doing violence to his feelings, to thus remove her from him. The vizir on his part being helpless, in order to appease the anger of the king, did as he was bid, and doing violence to his heart, thought to marry her to some one. "But if I do this," said he to himself, "the king will be envious; and I shall bring upon myself his anger." At length he concluded to put his daughter into a box, close up its mouth, and deliver it to a broker in the bazar, with orders to sell it for forty thousand aktchas, proclaiming to the public that it contained a precious jewel,—that the person who took it would not repent it, and that he who did not take it would also repent it.

The broker did as he was bid; but every person in the bazar refused buying the box and its contents, without seeing the latter, except a poor water-carrier, who, having painted his cups the color of a cornelian, sold his water "for the love of the Imam Hassan, and the Imam Husain." He poured out sweet water to the thirsty, and sold to them "waters of the Nile." "This box," thought the water-carrier, "has some hidden meaning;" and, as he was a person doing well, and had credit, he went to a merchant and borrowed at interest the sum of forty thousand aktchas: this he paid over to the broker, and took the box, which he then had placed on the back of a porter and carried to his house.

On opening the box the water-carrier was greatly surprised to find that it contained a most beautiful Peree-faced, jasmin-breasted maiden; and extremely delighted he helped the fair creature out of the box, and humbly assured her that he was her most devoted servant. He next asked to be informed, "of what garden she was a rose—of what vineyard the cypress." The girl was as intelligent as she was beautiful, and thought it best not to divulge the secret of her parentage; she therefore only replied, "I was a feeble creature, and they sold me; it fell to your lot to purchase me. From being a jewel of great value, I have become a stranger in a strange house; and, as a helpless maiden, I now throw myself upon the protection of your skirts, where let me be as a servant." The water-carrier (Saka) was deeply touched at her tale; and as the person from whom he borrowed the amount paid for her was his townsman, then about to depart for his own country, he placed the maiden as a pledge for the money in his hands, and sent her to the care of his mother. When the merchant, his townsman, had arrived at his own country, he went directly to the mother of his friend the water-carrier, and consigned the maiden to her charge, saying that she was sent by her son.

Now the mother of the water-carrier was so extremely poor as to need even a morsel of bread; and yet, for her son's sake, she received the maiden with tokens of respect and regard, and told her that she should be her daughter quite as much as he was her son. The maiden on observing the poverty of the woman took a jewel out of her bosom, and bade her take it to the person who had brought her, and say that they needed a purse of money. The woman did as the girl had said, and returned with a purse of money, which she expended for provisions and other necessaries. The woman, who so lately had been in the extreme of poverty, now clothed herself in dresses of different kinds, and put on cloaks of rich silk. "Go," said the maiden to her again, "and tell the merchant to send me two more purses of money;" which she did, and they bought slaves and domestics. The woman now became like one in Paradise; and the maiden, famous for her beauty, intelligence, and spirituality, erected a palace-like building, in which they took up their abode.

Now about this time a gay young man fell in love with her, and, becoming greatly affected by his passion, asked for a meeting with her. To bring this about he tried numerous manœuvres, but all without ever succeeding in inducing the maiden to act improperly. Finally, losing all hopes of effecting a meeting with her, he went to the city where the water-carrier resided, and addressing him said, "My poor fellow, you remain in this strange place without any happiness, whilst your female slave amuses herself magnificently, by erecting palaces as large as caravanserays, and getting up all kinds of amusements and pastimes. You were formerly known as a pious and religious man, but now you have a bad name." The water-carrier was a man of an honest character, and he believed all the falsehoods which the fellow related to him; so disposing of his water-skin and cup, he purchased a sharp dagger and set out for his native town with the intention of killing the girl. On reaching the place he found, to his great surprise, that his house had become an immense palace, in front of which slaves and guards were in attendance. When the maiden saw the water-carrier from the balcony, she ordered her attendants to, conduct her master in; and he, on seeing this, had all his evil suspicions strengthened. On approaching the jarieh, she came forward to meet him; and just as she was about to kiss his hand, the water-carrier struck her with the sharp poignard which he had with him for that purpose and wounded her. As he was about repeating the blow, she fled away from him, and throwing herself from the roof of the house, was dashed to pieces by the fall.

Just at this moment a Jew was passing by; and beholding a most beautiful young woman in this condition, he told her that he could find remedies for her bruises, and carried her away with him to his own dwelling. As for the water-carrier, searching throughout the house for the maiden, he went down stairs, but found no signs of the object of his search. Filled with grief, he sought his mother, and informed her what had occurred. The latter was greatly afflicted, and weeping for the fate of the poor girl, asked what would be his condition in the other world. She assured her son of the maiden's virtue and fidelity; on which he repented of what he had done, and sought for her in every part of the place.

As for the Jew, on reaching his dwelling he applied healing salves to the wounds of the sufferer, and did all he could for her relief. The health of the young woman daily improved; and her beauty being again restored to her, the Jew became enamored of her, and asked to be permitted to visit her. The maiden thus seeing that a Jew, one of an evil religion, dared to approach her, which, should she permit, would give her a bad reputation both in this world and the other, she gently repulsed him, saying, "Pray go first to the bath; and after you have purified yourself, come back to me." The Jew, now believing in her sincerity, did as she bade him; and as soon as he was gone, thinking that death was better than such a life, she threw herself from the top of the house into the sea, which was close beside it, and was lost in its waves. Now near that place were three fishermen, all brothers; and these, on pulling up their seine, were greatly surprised to find a rose-formed, Peree-faced maiden in it, quite lifeless. On being hastily drawn to the shore, she for some time breathed with difficulty, but finally came to her senses. They dressed her in other clothes, and then quarrelled about possessing her, each claiming her for himself. Whilst thus engaged a horseman suddenly rode up before them, who inquired the cause of their quarrel, and one of the three related to him what had occurred. "You are all brothers," exclaimed the horseman; "why should you quarrel for such a matter? I will judge and decide on it for you." Then taking three arrows from his quiver, he shot them off, each in a different direction, saying, that whoever brought him one of the arrows first, should have the maiden. All having consented to this arrangement, they ran after the arrows; but as soon as the horseman thus found himself left alone with the girl, he caught her up behind him on his horse and fled away with her, leaving the brothers to gaze after him as he sped.

The horseman on reaching his own village felt as happy as if he had captured a whole treasury of booty; he observed attentively the beauty of the fair creature who had thus fallen into his hands, and immediately became deeply smitten with her. His passion overcoming him, he pressed his suit with warmth; and the girl, to put him off, exclaimed, "Why, O young man, are you so impatient? there is no hurry; let night come, and then all your wishes will be accomplished." Then, with amorous gestures, she added, "Come let me don your armor, set me on your horse, give me your flag, and see whether it will suit me." The horseman, unable to refuse her anything, arrayed her as she had desired, and put her on his horse. After riding twice around him, she galloped the horse a short distance in several directions; then suddenly giving him the reins, she started at full speed for the open country, where she disappeared from the horseman's sight. She rode on all that night and the night following; and on the next morning arrived before a fortress, the gate of which was fastened. At daybreak the gate was opened; and the keepers of the fortress, finding the girl there, took her in.

Now the prince of that place had recently died, directing as his last will, that, as he had left no heir to inherit his throne, his people should adopt and pay obedience to whomsoever they might find under the walls of his castle. The persons who had found the maiden informed her of this; so attiring her in a costume like that of a king, they led her to the vacant throne, where having seated her, they all promised obedience to her commands.

Whilst the girl was thus a sovereign, she had a fountain erected in the gateway of the fortress, on which she had her own portrait painted; and she placed persons to observe those who came to the fountain, with directions that whoever should look at the portrait and sigh, should be conducted before her. Some time after this, it happened that the poor water-carrier visited the fountain; and beholding the portrait painted on it, he manifested much agitation at the sight. So he was immediately taken by those placed there for that purpose, and conducted into the presence of the sovereign;

where, on being questioned as to the cause of his sighing, he related the history of the maiden-slave from the commencement to the end. He was then confined in a prison. Soon after came the fishermen, the three brothers, who on seeing the portrait sighed. These also were apprehended and conducted before the sovereign; and when they had told what they knew of the person whose portrait they had seen, they too were put in confinement. After them came the horseman and the Jew, who on beholding the portrait, also sighed. These likewise were led before the sovereign, who commanded the former to be imprisoned, and the latter to be hung. The water-carrier and the fishermen were then brought out, and each received an office. The former was clothed in the dress of a king; and the maiden, after collecting around her the nobles and chief men of the place, related all that had occurred to her from beginning to end. She then said, "I am not descended from one of high birth, but from one of the people; this person is my legal possessor, and I now, of my own will, confide the kingdom to him. Accept of him, and may he be a blessing to you all." So they accepted of the water-carrier, and chose him for their sovereign; they showed him every evidence of respect and regard, and he sat on the throne of the kingdom. As for the pure and virtuous daughter of the vizir, she lived a long while in happy union with the water-carrier.

Now this tale shows how goodness and uprightness are never lost; and how those who are sorrowful and afflicted will, by means of the blessings of patience, become sovereigns. Difficulty terminates with facility; and it is a matter of certainty that all troubles end through the pity and compassion of God.

A TALE ABOUT TWO INDIVIDUALS IN THE SERVICE OF HAROON ER RASHEED, THE DOCTORS HAKIM HINDEE, AND HAKIM JEBRAIL.

It is narrated that during the time of Haroon er Rasheed, the Hakims Jebrail and Hindee once met together. Both of them were unique for their learning and wisdom. It is said that a disease fell upon Ibraheem, the son of Haroon's paternal uncle Salih. He became very ill; and Haroon, sending for Jebrail, made inquiries about his state. The latter replied, "He is in a very bad condition, there is scarcely a breath remaining in his body; and if he dies at sunset, it will be well for him." The caliph was very much grieved on learning this, and became very sorrowful. When dinner was placed before him, he drew back his hand, and began to weep. The vizir Jaafer Beramikee, on seeing this, sent for the Hakim Hindee; who, when he arrived and saw the patient, replied that there was no cause to be afflicted. At sunset a great cry was heard, on which the caliph sent to see what had happened; and the reply was, that Ibraheem had improved. Haroon exclaimed, that this was an evidence of the greater talents of Hindee; but the latter replied, that he had merited nothing. The caliph and Hindee now went together to Ibraheem, when the caliph discovered that his breath was stopped, and called the attention of the Hakim to the circumstance. The latter arose, and, asking for a needle, stuck it into the great toe of the patient, which caused him to draw up his leg. The Hakim on this exclaimed, "O Mussulmans, can a dead man feel pain?" Then asking for a little incense, he mixed with it a perfume, and let the smoke ascend into the patient's face. Ibraheem now sneezed three times, and, rising up from the bed, sat upright. The caliph inquired of him what had been his sensations; when the latter replied, "I was in a most pleasant and agreeable state, when a black dog bit my foot, the pain of which awoke me."

Ibraheem lived thirty years after this, and the caliph conferred great honors and distinctions upon the Hakim Hindee.

CHAPTER THIRTY-FIVE.

On the Science of Enchantment and Sorcery.

The Sheik Abdallah Andalusee (of Andalusia) was one of the most distinguished men of his time. He was particularly well versed in the science of conformity, of talismans, of alchemy, and enchantment, and performed the most remarkable things by their aid. One of the strangest of them is the following:

Hafiz, one of the Fatimite sultans of Egypt, was a most eager student of the science of enchantment; and in his time many persons made their appearance as professors of the science, among whom was the sheik above mentioned. The sultan begged the sheik to exercise his art; whereupon he caused a large city to appear on the summit of Mount Karafa. Around it were vineyards and gardens, with all kinds of fruits; its inhabitants appeared engaged in trafficing in the bazars of the city; and the air was filled with birds, at the novelty of which the people gazed with admiration. The inhabitants of Egypt beheld these things, which formed a specimen of Paradise to believers. They were amazed at the edifices which the city contained; and they all exclaimed, "Blessed be He who is able to effect whatever He desires."

ANECDOTE.

It is narrated by one of the sheiks of Egypt, that Sheik Abdallah had a banker, a friend of his, of long standing. One day the sheik sent for the banker, and asked him for the loan of a thousand pieces of gold, of which he stood in great need;

but the unjust banker delayed the delivery of the money, and at length excused himself from granting the request. The sheik kept silence, and made no reply. On the following day, as the banker was seated in his shop he received from a friend the present of a large fish, which the banker placed in the hands of his servant, with orders to carry it to his house, and have it dressed for dinner. Just at this moment the sheik called on the banker, to whom he said, "I have come to-day to take you with me to an entertainment which I am going to give in the plain of Karafa." The banker made objections; but his excuses not being sufficient, he arose and set out with the sheik.

The relater states what followed in the words of the banker himself: When we reached Karafa, we went out through the Gate of the Plain, and passed over the ruins near that place. We walked on over the sands of the plain, when lo! an immense palace appeared before us, which greatly surprised me. Whilst thinking who could have erected it, a great number of people, servants and attendants, issued from the palace, and came forward to meet the sheik. We entered the garden, which was like that of the exalted Paradise. On one side, the most pure and delicious waters flowed into reservoirs, in delightful streams, purling and meandering through the pathways, along which grew divers kinds of flowers and fruit-trees. Around the sides of the reservoirs were spread sofas of the richest stuffs, on which sat youths of both sexes (gholams and hoorees), served by attendants, the like of whom I had never seen, except in the service of sovereigns. The sheik made a sign to those, and forthwith a collation of numerous meats was served for us, with goblets of delicious sherbets. We here sat ourselves down; and we ate, drank, and made merry. After that the sheik made inquiries about the treasury; when the attendants brought before us some forty or fifty purses of money on their shoulders, and placed them in the middle of the apartment. The sheik now turning to me said, "So you thought me destitute of money, and refused to loan me a hundred pieces of gold." At this I was greatly ashamed, but the sheik changed the conversation to a subject of amusement, much to my relief.

After this we remained one or two weeks in the palace, enjoying ourselves. The sheik remarked to me, that he did not bring me there merely to spend a few days. "I have," said he, "a most angelic daughter, to whom I have given all this wealth and these servants; so that she is in need of nothing. I now give her in marriage to you. I may then see your children and spend some days in enjoyment." Acquiescing in his request, I replied that I would be governed by his commands. So he sent for witnesses from the Mehkemeh (Islam legal religious magistracy), and the marriage ceremony was performed; after which he ordered his daughter to be brought in. On beholding her I imagined that I saw a moon-like angel rising from beyond the palace, as fair as the moon in her fourteenth night. Never in my life had I seen so extremely beautiful a creature. Putting her hand in mine, he bade me be happy and enjoy myself, after which he returned to his own residence. I led my bride into our apartments, and we lived for the space of one or two months in the most perfect enjoyment and happiness.

One night, whilst reposing as usual beside my wife, I awoke, and beheld her lying dead, and covered with her own blood. I cried out with feelings of surprise and distress, which awoke the sheik, and caused him to come to me. He seemed greatly incensed against me, and asked if that was the return I made for his generosity towards me, or the manner to treat one who in all his life had never in any way injured me. "Go," exclaimed he to the attendants, "bring here the governor of the city." They forthwith departed. I almost lost my senses, and wondered what would be the end of all these strange occurrences. Overcome by my feelings, I fell in a swoon upon the floor. At length, the sun beating in upon me, my eyes again opened; and lo! I found myself lying on the sands of Karafa, and neither palace nor people within my view.

I arose and returned to my own home, where my wife made no remark on seeing me. At length I related to her the occurrences of the two months; but she replied that I had gone crazy, —that the fish which I sent from the shop in the morning was still uncleaned, for it was not yet noon. My amazement, on hearing this, was increased, and I felt convinced that the past was the effect of the sheik's science. I went to see him; and on perceiving me he smiled, and exclaimed, "In the abundance of your mirth and happiness, you have quite forgotten us." I kissed his hand; when he added, "You have witnessed the great power of divine science —have you not?" and when I begged his forgiveness, he said, "There is no end to strange things like this." May Allah have mercy upon him!

TALE ABOUT JIFTAN KHAN, YAKOOB SEKAKEE, AND SOME OTHER INDIVIDUALS.

It is related that Yakoob, who was one of the most learned men of his age, and unique for his knowledge of rhetoric and the art of description, was once praising the former science to the vizir of the Ameedi Habesh, Jiftan Khan, and remarked that he was a perfect adept in the art of sorcery (*neiri nedjat*), and had performed numerous strange things by means of it. The Khan placed much confidence in him; he considered him capable of aiding him through every difficulty, and in all cases had recourse to his assistance, so much as that he never deviated from whatever he was pleased to advise. The Molla performed the most curious things in the service of the khan, of which the following is the most remarkable.

One day he was seated outside of his tent, when a flock of

cranes flew over him. On observing them, the khan asked the molla if he was able to bring down one or two of them. The molla replied by asking which of them he desired. The khan pointed out one in front, one in the centre, and another in the rear of the flock; all of which were immediately brought to the ground. This circumstance caused great faith to be placed in the powers of the molla; and the khan ever afterwards knelt in his presence.

Once the caliph's vizir, at Bagdad, injured himself; and for three days the fire would not come out, and all the endeavors made by the caliph proved ineffectual. Finally a crier proclaimed that the whole affair was caused by Sekakee, and that it was necessary for the vizir to kiss the hinder part of a dog, after which Sekakee would release him. The vizir, quite desperate, kissed the unclean animal, and the matter was loosed. The vizir was deeply offended at Sekakee, which the latter well knew. So going to the khan, he said, "By computations of the stars, it is evident that reverses of fortune are to happen to vizirs,—may no evil influence come upon the members of the government therefrom." The khan, having no other resource, dismissed the vizir from his office. A year after this he placed Sekakee in the service of the vizir; and the latter conciliated his good will, though at the same time he cherished anger against him in his own heart, until an opportunity should offer to gratify it.

By divine destiny about this time the Ilameh had bewitched a standard-bearer, and the soldier made his appearance out of the fire, with his arms in a blaze before the khan's attendants, who were all assembled at his pavilion. The khan was much disconcerted at this circumstance, and the vizir remarked it. He regarded this as a favorable opportunity for making an impression upon the mind of the khan; so he remarked to him, that he (the khan) was not ignorant of the fact that the molla was ambitious of possessing the kingdom, and that he was able to bewitch not only the soldier, but all the people on the face of the earth. The khan on hearing this was greatly alarmed; so that he bound the Ilameh and threw him into prison. Thus, by divine command, this man's talents were a source of injury to himself; for, after remaining in prison a year, he died there in great grief and suffering.

The author of the work entitled Jami ul Hikayat, says: One of my friends relates that, a number of Yaras once having assembled together for the purpose of going to war, we set out for the country of the enemy, and on the way fell in with a place shaded by a grove of oaks. Amongst the company was a youth, who remarked that he had a presentiment that a lion would seize him in that grove and be the cause of his death. "Should this indeed be my fate," added he, "I beg you to send my ass and clothes to my family." We were much troubled at what he said; and it happened that, on our way, a lion really did spring out of a thicket upon the young man, threw him off his ass, and, whilst the youth was still repeating the confession of faith, carried him into the deepest part of the grove. We were all very much grieved at what we beheld; and, on arriving at our city, so as to deliver his effects to his wife, we went to her dwelling. On knocking at the door, it opened; and the young man, to our very great astonishment, stood before us. To our questions as to how he had escaped, he replied, "As soon as the lion carried me off I heard a loud voice calling out; this frightened the lion so that it laid me down, and went away in the direction from which the voice seemed to come. Raising up my head, I saw the animal engaged in conflict with another more terrible than itself; and thinking this a good opportunity to effect my escape, I fled away. On my way I met with the body of a dead person, half devoured, with a money-belt girded around his waist. I found several pieces of gold in the purse; and taking them with me I fled on, until at length I fell in with several people, and felt safe.

The Cadi Abool Casim Moosa relates the following, in the book called Ferdjbaad esh Sheddeh: One day, whilst seated in Cufa, beside Aboo Alee Omar, one of the attendants rushing before us screamed out that a certain person had been seized by a lion and carried away into a thicket. All present were much affected by the news, and hastened to inform Aboo Alee of the same. "God have mercy on us," exclaimed Aboo Alee, "how strange this is! for the father of that person was also killed by a lion." Several days subsequent to this I went again to Aboo Alee; and whilst conversing with him, lo! the man who had been carried off by the lion suddenly appeared and saluted us. Greatly surprised, we asked him how he had escaped; and he answered, "When the lion first seized upon me I became insensible, but soon after recovering my senses I found myself alone with all my limbs sound, and so fled away. Whilst running, my foot struck against a purse, which I put under my arm, and continued on until I was safe. On examining the purse I found in it, sealed with the seal of my own father, a note in his hand-writing." Aboo Alee on seeing the note and its seal was greatly surprised.

CHAPTER THIRTY-SIXTH.

On remarkable coincidences.

STORY ABOUT THE SON OF THE BERAMIKIDE FAZEL BIN YAHIYA.

Mohammed Damashkee relates as follows: Fazel bin Yahiya, who was the vizir of the Caliph Mamoon, had a son born to him during the period of his power. All the poets of the time wrote and composed kasidehs and ghazals (poems) in compliment to the child, for which they received presents; but none of them pleased Fazel. I was then in great poverty; and Fazel kindly directed me also to compose some lines on the same subject. I replied that respect for his presence prevented my doing so; but he urged me to compose something, saying that I must write whatever came into my head. I composed several lines on the inspiration of the moment, and presented them to Fazel. Pleased with what I had written, he presented me with ten thousand pieces of gold. With these I put my affairs in order, and purchased houses and land, until I was quite comfortable.

Some time after this the sun of the Beramikides began to set; and when their fortunes had changed, I one day went to a bath, where a fair featured youth served as *tellak* (to kneel and rub him). The benefits which I had received from the Beramikides recurred to my recollection, and the verses which I wrote on the son of Fazel came upon my tongue. On my reciting them, the youth who attended upon me became quite beside himself, and fell down upon the floor of the bath. Supposing him affected with epilepsy, I left the bath, and scolding the keeper, accused him of having given me a silly fellow for my *tellak*. But he excused himself by swearing that the youth had been for some time past employed in the bath, and nothing like it had happened before. So I returned to the bath, when the youth coming up to me kissed my hand, and asked me if I knew who had composed the lines which I had recited. I informed him that I myself had composed them. "On what occasion did you write them?" he next inquired. I told him that Fazel having had a son born to him, I wrote them on his birth. "Where is that child now?" he continued. On my replying that I did not know, he exclaimed in a tone of affliction, "Behold that unfortunate youth before you!" On being thus reminded of times long past, I was quite overcome.

Mohammed Damashkee adds: On thus learning that the youth before me was indeed of such high rank, and that it was on the occasion of his birth that I, as above stated, became possessed of my wealth and comforts, I exclaimed, "Dear boy! I am now an old man, and all that I possess has been bestowed upon me by your generous father. I have no one to leave behind me. Come therefore with me before a cadi; and I will confer upon you all that I am legally worth, which will be making some return for the benefits your parent bestowed upon me." On hearing this the eyes of the youth filled with tears; and he exclaimed, "Never, never will I take back from you one *hubbeh* (cent) of what my father gave you." Nor indeed, adds Mohammed Damashkee, was I ever able to induce him to accept any thing from me.

One of the effects of divine power is related by Mohammed bin Casim Aniyar. The Emir Sivar was for a time the governor of the country of Rehba. Bin Casim says: One day after leaving the presence of the caliph I went direct to my own palace, when I entered into the harem of my family, Being hungry, some food was laid before me. But I did not like it, and bade the attendants to remove it; which was done. I was troubled in my mind, and did not feel disposed to associate with my family; so I lay down to take a little repose, but could not sleep. I therefore again arose, and ordering a horse to be saddled for me, I mounted him, and rode over the bridge of Bagdad, following unwittingly whatever route I chanced to meet. Whilst riding on one side of the city, one of my men came up to me and kissed my hand. I inquired of him whence he came; and he replied that he had been to dispose of the produce of a certain village, and had received for it a hundred thousand pieces of silver. "Come along after me," said I; and continued on. Soon afterwards I came to a part of the city where there was a chapel, and alighted from my horse for the purpose of performing the noon-day namaz in that place.

I performed one or two rikats, and seated myself, when I observed a blind man coming towards me, holding by the wall as he groped his way. Inquiring of this blind person what he wished, he replied, "I smelled an odor about you which caused me to know that you are a generous and benevolent man, to whom I can relate my circumstances, when perhaps you may fulfil my hopes." "Speak," said I; "let me hear what you have to say." The blind man added, "The houses which you see opposite this chapel once belonged to my father; he disposed of them, and we left here for Khorassan. But not long afterwards my father died, and I became blind. Being unable to work, I sank into poverty; so once more setting out, I returned with a caravan to this country. The request I have to make is, that you will be so good as to aid me in finding the owner of these houses, whom I will request to conduct me into the presence of the governor of Rehba, the Emir Sivar, who was once a sincere friend of my father." I asked the blind man what was his father's name; and he answered that he was known by the name of Jeleel Salar. It happened that this person had once been a warm friend of mine, for whom I had great regard; so I exclaimed, "Welcome, good sir, welcome! tell me what you need. Emir Sivar has plenty to eat and drink, blessed be God, who has conducted you to his feet; for I am the Emir Sivar whom you seek." Then calling in the servant who had the hundred thousand aktchas, I took that sum from him and presented it to the blind man. I also bade him come to me early in the morning, at a certain place; after which I mounted my horse and returned directly to my own house.

I next went to the Commander of the faithful, to whom I related the whole incident. The caliph was much pleased, and ordered me to give out of his own treasury two thousand pieces of gold to the blind man. He next asked me whether I had any debts; and I answered, "Yes, O Emir el Mumineen, I owe to such a person a hundred thousand aktchas." So he immediately commanded me to be paid that sum, with an additional one of the same amount;

which I took, and returned to my own palace. There I told the blind man that the Most High had sent him two thousand pieces of gold, and two hundred thousand aktchas; for which he must pray for the caliph. I next gave the blind man, from my own property, a thousand pieces of gold. He remained some days as our guest, and then returned with the cafileh to Khorassan, where his wife and children were. He frequently sent me letters and presents from that country; and I was then kept constantly acquainted with his circumstances.

AN ACCOUNT OF THE DIVINE FAVOR SHOWN TO THE IMAM MOOSA ER RAZEE IN A DREAM, AND WHICH WAS THE SOURCE OF IMMENSE WEALTH TO HIM.

To the well informed it is known that the Sultan of Khorassan, Alee bin Moosa er Razee, from being a man of great wealth, and pure in conduct and character, was, by the changes of time, reduced to the greatest want. In his extremity he waited upon a learned old man for advice, who counselled him to prostrate himself in prayer, and ask aid of the Most High, and then perform whatever commands might be given him.

PERSIAN VERSE.

"Whatever occurred under the shadow of His Majesty,
"Brought shame to no one."

The sultan having rubbed his forehead against that pure garden (the Prophet's house), spent the night in prayer. He performed two rikats, and made supplication to the Giver of all gifts and the Judge of all wants; and whilst in tears he fell asleep. During the repose of the sultan, he beheld the "Beautiful of the beau teous" (the Prophet), who addressing him said, "Your condition is known to me; but just at this time our hands are empty: we are therefore excusable. Take, however, the tablet which is hung up in our box, and expend it for your relief until you become the recipient of divine favor." The unhappy man took the tablet, broke it up, and, by disposing of it, soon became possessed of much wealth. The tablet, however, renewing its form, the sultan asked permission to restore it to the place where it had hung suspended. He saw the Glory of the universe (the Prophet) in his sleep, who said to him, "We are the heirs of the house of the Apostle of God; is it, therefore, proper or becoming in you not to deem right the favor which we have shown to our guest? We gave it to you gratis, to supply your innocent wants, and we have no need ourself of such things. We are also thankful for the services which you have rendered to us." May the Most High bless his secrets, and bestow upon us the blessings of his person!

AN ACCOUNT OF THE HERO RUSTEM APPEARING TO THE CELEBRATED FERDOOSEE IN A DREAM, AND THE BENEFITS WHICH THE LATTER RECEIVED FROM HIM.

That most celebrated poet, Ferdoosee, was in the service of the Sultan Mahmood; and whilst engaged in composing the Shah Nameh he received so much attention from the sultan as to become the object of the envy of his associates. He took precedence of all the other poets before the throne of the sultan; and their envy and jealousy being thus excited, they began to intrigue against him, until they succeeded in producing a great aversion in the mind of the Vizir Hassan Maimandee against Ferdoosee.

This ill will on the part of the vizir, which continued for some months and even years, occasioned much trouble to Ferdoosee;

and after finishing the work of the Shah Nameh, he found himself without recompense. The story about this matter being generally so well known, we refrain from reproducing it here. The result of the affair was, that the other poets prevailed upon the Sultan Mahmood to command Ferdoosee to compose a poem on the subject of the war between Kiavkeshany and Eskibos, and what occured to Rustem in the said war; which poem would show the degree of his talent and eloquence. This the sultan asked Ferdoosee to do; and the great poet so performed his work on the exploits of these two warriors, that his eloquence and talents left the other poets as much astonished as the magicians of Pharaoh were; and he himself appeared as fair and white as did the Prophet Moses when illumined by divine interposition. His work thus being sealed with the acceptance of the other poets, Ferdoosee's standing became higher than ever in the consideration of the sultan.

The pith of the poem is, that Kiavkeshany sent Eskibos, that celebrated prince, to the wars of Iran. The latter formed an agreement with the Imam, and the army stopped in front of the troops of Toolus, and invited them to fight. Toolus finally put his troops in battle array, the conflict commenced, and he and Eskibos joined in single combat. Eskibos, placing his back against a mountain, gave space for Toolus to march out and fight. The warrior Rustem, however, prevented him from so doing, saying "You are the commander of the army and must remain in its centre; but under your auspices I will soon teach him his bounds," adding:

PERSIAN VERSE.

"As heart of the army, you keep up the line,
"But I will soon teach them their heads to incline."

Rustem, so celebrated for his valor, was on foot, and at once marched on against Eskibos, who let fly an arrow at him. Rustem took his buckler, and shot an arrow in return, which knocked over the horse on which his enemy rode and killed it. Eskibos now sped another arrow at Rustem, which passed quite through his buckler and wounded him. Enraged at this, Rustem marched onwards against him and let fly another arrow, which, striking him in the breast, at once put an end to his life. This valiant act of Rustem was described in detail in the Shah Nameh; and on the sultan seeing a drawing of it, he exclaimed that if Ferdoosee were to receive for his work the revenues of Iran and Tooran, it would not be a sufficient recompense.

Now on that night Ferdoosee saw Rustem in a dream. He was in the market of the town called Yekta Abad, with a gold helmet on his head, and his cuirass adorned with jewels. Placing his lance on the ground, and standing on the place of conflict, he struck his hand forcibly against his breast, and saluted Ferdoosee, who was preparing to express his request to him with words of regard and respect. Ferdoosee returned his salutation, saying, "*Salam alaik,* O valiant prince, the champion of the world, and the joy of those who register the deeds of the brave." Pleased with these words, the hero of the age smiled like a rose; then weeping, he said to the Molla (Ferdoosee), "We are unable to express to you the degree of acknowledgment due to your learning: you are aware of our inefficiency, pray then excuse us. Once upon a time I fought with a celebrated warrior, and at such a place cut off his head; and not liking the golden collar which was around his neck, and which was a sign of heroism, I left it there." Then letting fly an arrow, Rustem pointed out the place where the collar was, a huge mound of earth; and he added, "Be it a gift from me." When Ferdoosee awoke he was greatly surprised, and thought to himself, "If I speak of this the people will not believe me, but regard it as an idle fancy." Consequently he kept the dream to himself.

Some time after this Sultan Mahmood went on a hunting excursion to Yakta Abad, and visited the tumulus which Rustem had pointed out as being the place of the golden collar. Ferdoosee was with him. The sultan's escort encamped without the city. Ferdoosee's dream came into his mind, and he paid a visit to the tumulus, which he perceived to be just where the arrow had fallen. He was on friendly terms with the chief Ayaz of the sultan, and to him he related what had occurred to him. The former told him to have no doubts of his dream; "for," said he, "it will, Inshallah, come true." The Ayaz now went to the sultan and remarked, that, as his majesty was in the habit of going frequently to that place to exercise himself in shooting, it seemed to him that a proper target ought to be prepared for him. "Let it be erected," replied, the sultan; and the Ayaz, preparing without loss of time for the labor, set seventy yoke of oxen to work, and soon had the tumulus removed. On digging up its foundation, the Ayaz related Ferdoosee's dream to the sultan; who replied that if it was not all a wild delusion, the contents of the tumulus would now soon testify to its correctness. Just then, and at the moment when the story was being related, the plough of one of the workmen caught in a link of the collar and could not be moved. The earth around it was removed, and the collar was brought forth and exhibited to the sultan, who exclaimed that it was justly due to the Molla Ferdoosee, and should be given up to him, which was immediately done. But Ferdoosee spoke to the Ayaz, saying, that it was the recompense of eloquence, and ought to be divided equally amongst all the poets there present. The Ayaz did as he was requested by the Molla, and the share of the collar that fell to him (Ferdoosee) was three hundred miskals of gold. Now, as in our days, the brave are recompensed for their deeds by receiving crowns and belts, so at that time they had a golden collar thrown around their necks. The Khodjah Abd ul Alee wrote the following lines:

"O Time, why in our days are great men without generosity? Did not Rustem say of Henor, that Behram held our stirrup and reins? One night he said to Ferdoosee, 'O dear one, our heart is ready to perform its duty to you. The silver is collected and hidden in a secret place; with the labors of our club, our poignard, and our blows, be prepared, so as to need no aid from our hand. Great as is the shame which our moving away causes us, know that there is no glory in life, since the debased are in more honor than the distinguished.'"

CHAPTER THIRTY-SEVENTH.

On miracles which have occurred to persons of distinction.

The author of the work entitled Keshf el Gameh, relates: I was often in the habit of narrating the strange story of what occurred, in recent times, to Ismaeel Herkeel; and one day whilst about to do so, one of the persons present rose and said, "I am the son of that Ismaeel mentioned by you, and my own name is Shems ed Deen." I was much pleased at this meeting, and inquired of him whether he had ever seen the complaint which existed in his father's thigh. The young man replied, "At that time I was very small, and could not judge of such matters; but I remember that after he recovered, hair grew out of that place."

The story is as follows: A sore made its appearance in the right thigh of Ismaeel Herkeel, which no medicines could cure. At length he represented the matter to the Kiazroonee Said Razee ed Deen Taoos, who assembled together all the surgeons of Aleppo, and asked of them a remedy for the complaint. They all agreed that there was no help for it but amputation; which was also extremely dangerous, on account of the sore being in the midst of the veins of his thigh, so that its excision might cause his death.

About that time Said made a journey to Bagdad, and Ismaeel accompanied him; on which occasion he showed his complaint to the best surgeons the place contained. These also replied that they were unable to offer any remedy; whereupon Ismaeel exclaimed, that since he had no hopes of any cure from the surgeons, he would turn his face towards the Lord of all doctors, and implore Him to vouchsafe a remedy for his affliction. Accordingly he visited all the *mabids* and *mesjeds* (places of worship and prayer), and the tombs of the martyrs (Hassan and Husain), where he offered up his supplications night and day.

"I passed my time," says he, "in imploring some relief from my sufferings; until one day, when employed on the banks of the Tigris in cleansing my clothes, I beheld, on turning round, four horsemen with their swords buckled to their sides; one of whom was covered with a cloak. The person on his right made a huge jump and stood near me; he saluted me, and remaining between me and his companion asked me, 'Do you wish to go to-morrow to your wife and children?' 'Yes, my lord,' I replied. 'Come near me then,' added he; 'what is your difficulty—let me see it.' So approaching him, I exhibited my sore to him. He stretched forth his hand and squeezed it violently, causing me very great pain. One of the three, who bore a spear, addressing me in Arabic, exclaimed, 'Health to you, O Ismaeel! you have attained your wishes, and are now free from fear.' I was surprised to find that he knew my name. Turning to me, he added, 'You have merited the good will of the Imam.' On hearing this last word, I rushed quickly to his side and embraced his blessed stirrup. I rubbed his foot against my face, and even followed them a short distance. At length he bade me return; but I replied, that I would never leave his service. Again he bade me return; 'for in that is your tranquility,' said he. Still I persisted in remaining; when the horsemen who bore the spear exclaimed, 'Are you not ashamed to disobey the words of the Imam?' I then, from necessity, stopped; and when they had proceeded a short distance from me, the face of that blessed person turned again towards me, and he cried out, 'When you return to Bagdad, Mustanser will ask for you and offer you something, which take good care not to accept.' On hearing this, my astonishment was increased; and whilst in this state, the horsemen all disappeared from my sight.

"After this occurrence I visited the tombs of the great martyrs, and made inquiries after the four horsemen whom I had seen.' No one knew anything about them; all that people could say was, that perhaps, from the description which I gave of them, I had met with some holy and pious persons. 'No,' said I; 'the person of whom I ask was the Imam himself.' 'Was he clothed in a cloak, or did he bear a spear?' 'He was dressed in a cloak,' I answered. 'Why did you not show him your sore?' they asked. 'I did so,' said I; and in my trepidation having looked down at my right thigh, I perceived that there was not the least sign of a sore. Turning next to my left thigh, I found it also perfectly sound; and those present becoming aware of what had occurred to me, they rushed upon me, and tore my clothes in pieces, each one seizing a fragment as a blessed memento of the miraculous cure performed upon me. Indeed I suddenly became so much the object of the people's regard, that I was almost killed with their attentions; and I was only relieved from them by the friend with whom I had visited the city, who placed me for security within the treasury, where I passed the night.

"On the following day I went to Bagdad. The citizens having already heard of what had occurred to me, they besieged me in the same manner; so that I was near being crushed to death by them. Said Razee ed Deen, on observing this, freed me from their hands, and conducted me to the vizir of Said Mustanser, where he related my cure. The Said assembled the physicians and inquired of them how long after cutting out my sore it would require to heal the wound. They all answered that the shortest space of time would certainly be two months; it would also remain white and no hair grow out of it. 'Uncover it,' said he, 'and let us see the place.' The physicians present added, 'It was only three days since we saw it and pronounced it incurable.' At the vizir's command, my thigh was exposed; and all the physicians present cried out and were amazed at the sight. The vizir now conducted me to the presence of Mustanser, to whom he related the story as it had occurred. Mustanser offered me a thousand filoorees (golden ducats), which I declined accepting."

The son of this person, Ismaeel Herkeel, adds, "By the command of the Shah (Mustanser), my father took up his residence in Bagdad; and in the hope of beholding the blessed person who had cured him, he passed by the same place some forty times in the course of a year."

It is related in the work of Ibin el Joozee called Muntazim, that in the four hundred and fourth year of the Flight of the blessed Prophet, a woman was attacked with leprosy. Portions of her nose, cheeks, toes, and fingers fell off, and her reins were affected. Her husband and children conceived an aversion for her, and left her outside of the city; whither her son daily carried two loaves of bread, and threw them to her. One day she said to him, "For the love of God, pray bring me a jar of water, that I may appease my thirst." Her son threw down the jar near his mother and fled away. Overcome by thirst, the poor woman made an attempt to reach a stream near her; but being unable from weakness, she fell prostrate on her face, and lay there covered with blood and dirt. This helpless being now became the object of that divine favor which is unending: her senses were restored to her, and all her members and her body were made whole. Kneeling down on the earth, she offered up prayers of gratitude and thanks. When the people of the neighborhood learnt the cure she had undergone, and heard her story, they asked to be informed of the manner in which it occurred; and the poor woman related simply what she knew of it. "When I asked for water," said she, "I fell down on the road, quite insensible. Two blessed persons in the shape of men appeared before the eyes of my heart, and two females, who resembled angels; they gave me a loaf of bread, a portion of vegetables, and a cup of water. I ate the bread, and drank the water; and never before had I eaten or drunk of such bread and water, nor indeed ever heard of the like, so delicious were they. I prostrated my face in the dust before those persons, and inquired who they were. I then learned that these two excellent people were the Imams Hassan and Husain; and the angel-like females were Fatimah the lovely and Hadijah the great, on whom be peace, and may their intercession be made for us!*

PERSIAN VERSE.

'There is one great rite in that congregation,
O'er which they have passed to the highest point.
To love them is an evidence of fidelity and happiness;
To hate them is a sign of blasphemy and wickedness.
To be near them is an elevated distinction;
To despise them is a token of evil and wickedness.'

The blessed Imam Hassan rubbed his hand over my face and my ears; and the blessed Husain leant his foot against my back, until I arose. My nose, lips, toes, and fingers were again restored to me; and I felt my strength return."

Ibin el Joozee adds that the inhabitants around the country where this miraculous cure occurred flocked in crowds to see the woman, and ask her good prayers in their behalf. May Allah have mercy on them all!

* These were the two favorite wives of the Prophet, whose intercession is thus shown to be desired by Mussulmans.—A. T.

STORY ABOUT JESUS, ON WHOM BE PEACE, AND THE PURE WOMAN.

Hazreti Isa (the Lord Jesus), on whom be peace, was once informed, through divine inspiration from Him who knows all things, as follows: "There is a pure and pious woman amongst our worshippers, who on the day after the judgment must be a companion of thine, O Jesus, in Paradise. She desires ardently to see you, and resides in such a ruin. Go, therefore, and see her."

Jesus went to the place indicated, and there found a blind female without hands or feet, engaged in offering up prayers and thanks to the Almighty. Jesus saluted her by exclaiming "*Es salam aleik;*" and she responded, "*Ve aleik es salam,* O thou of high regard." Jesus said to her, "O woman of God, how are you able to reside in these ruins?" and the female answered, "Thanks be to Allah, I here enjoy all the benefits bestowed upon sovereigns and kings." "How can you thus enjoy yourself, hidden from all the world and from mankind, and without hands or feet; what kind of pleasures can you find here?" The pious woman replied, "O Abd Allah (servant of God), if I had hands and feet, they might have been engaged in perdition and sin; my eyes might have been looking on what is forbidden to them; and what would my condition have been in the day of resurrection?" Jesus was much surprised at what he heard, and exclaimed, "O woman of God, if you have any thing to ask of me, ask it, and I will serve you." The pious female replied, "My only request is for the pardon of my sins." Jesus told her, "Pardon is of God, and appertains to Him alone. If you have any other request, pray make it." The woman said, "Then give me your assistance to renew my ablutions, and to turn towards the *Kibla*" (of Mecca). So Jesus brought her water and aided her to turn towards the Kibla; and when she had performed her prayers to God, he commenced offering up supplications to that place where none ever apply in vain. At their termination, a great outcry was heard, of which Jesus inquired the cause from the persons near that place. They replied, "That poor woman had a son, whom she gave into our care; we were neglectful of him, and he has been torn in pieces by a wolf; this caused the noise which you just now heard." Jesus approached the woman, and informed her of what had happened to her son; whereupon she returned thanks, saying (in Arabic), "Thanks be to Allah, who has placed him above want, and relieved him from the difficulties of ablution and interment." "Joy to thee, O woman," said Jesus, "whom the Most High has caused to be in perfect submission and resignation to Him; and who has blessed and pardoned thee, and vouchsafed to thee the happiness of being my companion in Paradise." The pious woman answered, "You must be Jesus?" To which he replied, "Yes, I am Jesus." "Blessed be God," the pious woman exclaimed, "for the promises you have made to me;" and immediately she expired. Jesus washed and interred her, and exclaimed, "Happy art thou, O woman, who goest before me into Paradise!"

THE STORY OF THE JUSTICE WHICH, AT THE REQUEST OF MOSES, GOD ALLOWED TO BE BROUGHT ABOUT BY HIS POWER.

It is related in some works of repute that once, when the Prophet Moses, on whom be peace, was offering up his adorations to the Almighty, he said, "O God, I beg of thy great mercy to be allowed to witness an act of justice brought about by thy power." God's command came to Moses, saying, "Go to such a fountain in the desert; remain there, and witness the effect of divine wisdom."

Moses consequently went, and remained hidden in the place indicated to him. Soon afterwards he descried a young man approaching the fountain on a steed swift as the autumn wind. He dismounted from his horse, undressed himself, took from his pocket a purse of gold, and placed it near the fountain. He next made his ablutions, performed one or two rikiats of prayer, and again mounting his horse departed, forgetting the purse of gold. After him came a fair youth over the plain, who drank of the water; and perceiving a purse, of which there was no owner present, he took it up, tied it around him, and departed. A little while later, a blind man came to the fountain, leaning on his staff, who performed his ablutions and prayers. Scarcely had he ended, when the young man who had forgotten his purse returned in search of it, bending to his horse's neck as the latter flew over the ground. On reaching the edge of the fountain, and not finding the purse where he had left it, he demanded it of the blind man, who replied that he had not seen it. The oaths of the latter were however insufficient. The young man, becoming enraged, drew his sword and struck the blind man's head from his shoulders; then searching the body for his purse, he was unable to find it, and at length departed in disappointment.

The Prophet Moses, grieved at what he had witnessed, prostrated himself to the earth, and implored the Most High to acquaint him with the wisdom of this occurrence. Suddenly the angel Jebrail (Gabriel), that faithful bearer of God's commands, descended near him, and exclaimed, "O Moses, the wisdom of the occurrence which you have just witnessed is this: The father of the young man who took the purse filled with gold, after serving the other young man who owned the purse for several years, under a promise of so much recompense, was finally refused what was his due. Injustice was done, and the obligation of the Mussulman remained upon his debtor. The man died, and the sum due him became the inheritance of his son. The exact amount of gold in the purse was precisely the wages due to the father of the orphan, who has thus obtained his rights. As to the blind man whom you saw, previous to becoming blind he had murdered the father of the youth who owned the purse. The youth was then quite young, and he is now possessed of much wealth; the blood of the father has thus been expiated by the performance of the law of talion.

PERSIAN VERSE.

"He that does evil to another
Will one day have evil done to him.
Do good then, that good may be done to thee;
For surely every thing has its recompense.
I once saw with mine own eyes, in a certain place,
A bird pounce down upon an ant;
And whilst the victim was yet in his bill
Another bird bore the first away in its claws."

The author of the work called, "The Mirror of the Times," Sebet ibin el Joozee, narrates the following, as told by Cadi Husain, one of the Mosahibs, or companions of pleasure, of the Abbaside caliph Mutasid Billah.

Once, after amusing ourselves for some time with the caliph, he at midnight dismissed us, and we all withdrew for the night. I arose and returned to my own dwelling, where, as it was late, I entered the harem, undressed myself, and went to bed. I scarcely had got to sleep when some one knocked at my door, and I was awoke and told that the caliph wished me to come to him. Much surprised, and feeling assured that something of moment had occurred to induce him to send for me, I arose and went in haste to the palace of the caliph. His Harem Agasee told me that his master was in his private apartments, and that I was to follow him there. Accordingly I went after him, in great mental agitation, to the caliph's bedside. I found him sitting up in bed; and when I saluted him he asked for the chief police officer of the city. Immediately some one went for him, and conducted him to the room in which we were. The caliph, on seeing this officer, asked him if there was not an individual in prison named Jemal ed Deen; and ordered him to be brought immediately, which the officer forthwith set out to do. We all in the meanwhile remained perfectly silent, and I was greatly alarmed, being aware that the caliph was a man of violent passions.

Soon after the officer returned, bringing with him Jemal ed Deen; of whom the caliph inquired the cause of his imprisonment. The man replied, "I had four camels in the charge of such a one of the caliph's servants, who used them to carry grain from his village to the city, and this helped to maintain me. The servant having once loaded them and set out for the city, robbers, during a dark night, stole one of them with its load; and accusing me of being the thief, he cast me into prison, where I have now remained for three years, having no one to interest himself in my behalf and see justice done me." The caliph on hearing this, sent for his treasurer, and commanded him to present Jemal ed Deen with five hundred pieces of gold; he then ordered the chief officer of the city immediately to take measures to find the four camels, and, requiring four years' hire of the same from the man who had them in charge, to deliver them and the amount collected to their owner. The officer took Jemal ed Deen and departed, leaving us again standing in silence by the caliph's bedside, until he returned and announced that the orders of the caliph had been executed.

The caliph next told him that he also had a blacksmith of Damascus confined in prison, and ordered that the latter should likewise be brought before him. The officer departed, and soon returned, bringing the individual. The caliph inquired of the smith why he had been imprisoned; and he answered, "I came here from Damascus; and being a stranger, I apprenticed myself to a smith in order to procure a livelihood, and served him for a stipulated amount of wages. As usual, we commenced our labors one morning very early: and besides myself there was another apprentice, a young lad. I worked at the bellows whilst the boy and the master smith worked with the hammers. Whilst beating the iron, the hammer slipped from the boy's hand, which caused the horse-shoe to fly from the anvil and strike the youth in a tender part of his body, killing him on the spot. On seeing this, the smith sprang out of the shop and fled, leaving me alone there with the dead boy. Just at that time, it so happened that the chief of the police passed by; and seeing me and the deceased in the shop, he apprehended me, and threw me into prison. Being a stranger in the country, and not knowing how to write, I have remained there up to the present time." The caliph gave this person also five hundred pieces of gold, and directed that, after being taken to a bath and dressed in clean garments, he should be released. After this, covering himself with a quilt, he lay down again to sleep.

As for me, I followed the Harem Agasee (chief eunuch), and returned to my own dwelling, where I retired to rest. Early the next morning I arose, and according to my habit went to the divan of the caliph, whom I found in good humor conversing with his companions. I heard nothing of what had occurred during the previous night, and I circumspectly asked some of the persons present whether the caliph had spoken to them of the great acts of benevolence he had performed. All however remained silent, and the caliph himself asked what sort of benevolent acts I alluded to; "for," said he, "I know of none." Supposing he was joking, I exclaimed, "O Emir el Mumineen, last night you commanded the chief of the police to bring out of prison into your presence Jemal ed Deen and the smith of Damascus; and after having their suits decided upon with all justice, you dismissed them with a present. This took place in the presence of that officer, and of all your attendants of the harem; and I also remained for two whole hours in your presence listening to your sentences. "Praise be to Allah," exclaimed the caliph, "who directed us in the right way! I am thankful for what he does;" adding, "I swear by the glory of the Lord, and the love which I bear for the pure soul of the Prophet, I know nothing of what you have just related. Nevertheless my respect for yourself and my confidence in the testimony of the several persons whom you cite, cause me to believe it." "Praise to God," I exclaimed, "that the blessed Prophet has bestowed upon you the disposition to benefit the oppressed servants of God in this manner. It is no doubt a divine gift." All the individuals present were greatly surprised, and offered up thanks to the Almighty. May he have mercy upon them all!

Mutasid Billah, one of the Abbaside caliphs, was a prince of a most benevolent character, and was celebrated for his justice and the protection which he accorded to his subjects. One night being unable to sleep, he commanded the head of the police to be sent to him early the following morning. This being done, the caliph ordered him to proceed immediately to the sea-shore, where a vessel was then arriving. "As soon as she is come to anchor," said he, "and has lowered her sails, go on board, where you will find a young person dressed in a blue shirt. Take that person and immediately conduct him to me." The officer did as he was directed; he proceeded to the sea-shore, and beheld a vessel arrive there. The person whom he was in search of came on shore from the vessel; and apprehending the man, he conducted him before the caliph, who, on seeing him, exclaimed to the sailor, "Where, fellow, are the woman's clothes; what have you done with them?" He asked this in anger; and the sailor, surprised at what he heard, was unable to deny the matter; but at once acknowledged that he had killed the woman. "Where then are her clothes?" asked the caliph again; and the sailor pulled out from his breast, an embroidered pocket handkerchief, a gold bracelet, and armlets worked with pearls. "When did you kill her?" next demanded the caliph. The sailor replied that, tempted by the devil (Shaïtan), he had, at a certain place, thrown her into the sea.

The caliph next ordered the public criers of the city to proclaim that whoever had lost a relative should come and see the murderer. Now the deceased was the daughter of a poor woman, who, coming to the caliph, represented that she had legally married her to the sailor, and that he had taken her away with him. The caliph delivered the handkerchief and jewels to the woman, and informed her that the man before her was the murderer of her daughter, adding, that he should be dealt with as she might demand. The woman having demanded the execution of the law of talion (viz. death for death), the caliph commanded the sailor to be hung on the yard-arm of his own vessel. The law was therefore executed, and the act served as an example to other evil-minded persons.

Cadi Husain relates: I exclaimed to the caliph, "O Emir el Mumineen, here is another miracle. But he replied, 'No, it is no miracle; for whilst I was asleep I beheld the sultan of all beings (the Prophet), on whom be peace, who commanded me to send quickly to a vessel which he pointed out to me, and I then beheld a person precisely agreeing with the appearance of this fellow. 'Execute justice upon him,' commanded the Prophet, 'for he has murdered an innocent woman;' and it was my duty to perform the injuctions of the Holy Law. I awoke, and forthwith called for the head of the police, who, thanks be to Allah, has performed his duty."

One day when the Caliph Haroon er Rasheed was seated in the place of state, he exclaimed hastily, "See which of the pages are in attendance at the door." Fazel bin Rebia was there, with one of the servants of the Benee Ommieh, named Hashim bin

Suliman. At the caliph's desire the latter only came in. The caliph spoke kindly to him; and, after some conversation together, he took off his costly girdle and presented it to Hashim, who kissed it respectfully, put it over his head, and began to weep, his tears falling down upon his beard. The caliph, in surprise, asked him the cause of his grief; and Hashim replied that if the caliph would give him permission, he would tell him the occurrence which had made his tears to flow. As the caliph granted the desired permission, Hashim related as follows:

"One day I went to see Valeed bin Abd el Melik of the Ommiades. I found him with two very fair female slaves (*jariehs*) seated at his side, both as beautiful as angels. They had never seen me before, and they asked the Melik to allow them to make sport of the Arab (lit. laugh at his beard). Valeed also did not know me; he called me to him, and I approached and sat down by his side. He handed musical instruments to the two female slaves, and they commenced playing on them. In performing they made two or three mistakes, on which I made a remark. 'See,' exclaimed the girls, 'the Arab points out our errors!' Valeed looked at me in great disdain; and I asked his permission to show to the performers the parts in which they had made the mistakes. 'Good,' said he, 'let us see.' So taking an instrument in my hand, I tuned it, and bade them try it again. Much pleased, they both exclaimed, '*Barik Allah!* Hashim has become our master.' Valeed now asked me if I was not Hashim bin Suliman; and when I replied in the affirmative, he was much pleased, and presented me with thirty thousand aktchas. One of the female slaves also asked Valeed's permission to offer something to the master Hashim; and it being accorded her, she took off her necklace and gave it to me. They spent that day in great joy and merriment, and afterwards asked for a vessel in which to cross over to the other side.* They entered it and were going out, when the

* This probably occurred at Bagdad.—A. T.

female slave's foot slipping, she fell into the water, and was drowned. Valeed was greatly grieved at this occurrence, and addressing me, exclaimed, 'O Hashim, pray dispose of that necklace to me, and let it be a memento of the fair creature whom I have just lost, to remind me of her.' He gave me in place of it thirty thousand dirhems; and I just now, being reminded of the sad occurrence, could not refrain from tears."

The caliph, at the conclusion of this tale, exclaimed, "*El hamdu Lillah,* praise be to God, for permitting me to inherit both the caliphat and his kingdom!"

It is narrated by Alee bin El Jehem, that when the Caliph Mutavakkel ala Allah succeeded to the caliphat, there was sent to him, among other choice presents, a beautiful female slave, named Mahboobeh (the beloved) from Abd Allah bin Tahir, then governor of Khorassan. This slave, besides being a good singer, could also compose verses of much merit. The caliph was greatly pleased, and became warmly attached to his slave; but some time afterwards becoming angry with her, he for several days did not go near her. One evening the caliph had some friends with him, and I also was present. After making merry for some time, we all retired to rest. In the course of the night, the caliph awoke, and calling out to me said, "O Alee, I have just had a dream, in which I thought I made friends with Mahboobeh." I replied, "Whatever favor you show to your beloved and to your own slave, is done justly." Whilst we were talking about this, one of the female slaves in waiting remarked that a voice had just been heard proceeding from Mahboobeh's apartment. So we both arose and began listening; whereupon we distinguished her voice, accompanied by an instrument, singing the following verses:

ARABIC VERSES.

"I wander about the palace, and know none to whom
I can complain of my grief. He will not address me;
As if I had committed some crime.
Is there none to tell me my fault, so that I may be forgiven;
Is there no one to intercede with the prince?
It seems to me that he has pardoned my fault.
Oh when will morning come;
So that his heart may return to me, and I evermore be his!"

The caliph listened attentively until she had ceased, and then immediately cried out, "Why have you stopped so soon?" Mahboobeh on this, perceiving that the caliph had heard her sing, rushed from her apartment, and throwing herself at his feet, "O Commander of the faithful," cried she, "I dreamt that I had been restored to your affection, that you were again pleased with me. The joy which it gave me, awoke me; I arose, and after composing the lines which you have just heard, was reciting them." The caliph was astonished at the coincidence, "*Billahi el Azim!*" exclaimed he, "I have had precisely the same dream, and, in amazement at the circumstance, was relating it to Alee." He conferred large presents on his slave, and she again became the object of his affection.

DARIUS AND ALEXANDER.

Darius, complaining to Alexander of the reverses of fortune in this world, asked, "When the celestial sphere (*felek*) turns too late, and fortune is unpropitious, what can be done to remedy it?" Alexander replied, "There is but one remedy for such an evil. Pray order me four nails, each of sixty thousand kantars of iron."

"What do you wish to do with them?" asked Darius. Alexander added, "I will put one of these nails in each of the four corners of the world, so as to prevent the sphere from ever retrograding; for I know of no other remedy."

It is related that there was once in Bagdad, that abode of Paradise, a very wealthy merchant who was extremely penurious: never in his life had he given an aktcha in alms. In the same city there was likewise a very poor and pious porter, who, one day, when pressed by want, left his humble home and wandered about the city in search of food for his family. God's providence led him before the door of the rich merchant, where bread was just then being baked; and the odor of it reaching the porter's nostrils, he involuntarily knocked at the door, and begged "a piece of bread for the sake of Allah." The wife of the merchant, on hearing the voice, felt pity for the poor man who was thus compelled to beg. She had a grown up daughter, to whom she gave a loaf of bread, directing her to go and give it, in God's name, to the beggar. The latter received it with gratitude, and, after expressing his thanks, departed. On his way, by God's providence, he met the merchant who owned the house where he had received the bread. The merchant inquired where he had got it; "for," added he, "there is no house in this city, besides my own, in which bread like that is made." The porter, preceding him, conducted him to his own door, saying, on reaching it, "There is the house in which I received the bread."

The merchant was very much displeased, and said to the porter, "Never let me see you here again;" adding severe censures on his conduct. Then turning round, he entered his house, where he demanded of his wife whether she had given the bread to the beggar. The woman answered in the affirmative; but added that she had sent it by the hand of her daughter. The merchant now blamed his wife severely, and cut off his daughter's right hand as a punishment for what she had done, thus maiming her for life. Submissive to the will of God, she remained in this pitiful state.

Not long after this, this same wealthy merchant became so poor as to want even a supper. All he could gain in a day was scarcely sufficient for the support of one person, and he was unable to provide food for his daughter. So he at length had to say to her, "I am unable to-day to give you any thing; go therefore and procure food for yourself as best you can." The poor girl had never before been out any where; and deeply afflicted with her destitute condition, she set forth on her way.

The place she went to was a market; and she saw that several persons were assembled for traffic in front of the door of a merchant's shop. Unable to tell her wants, she stood aloof; but the merchant, happening to observe her, was convinced that she was a female of good character. So addressing her, he inquired if she was of age. The girl replied in the affirmative. "Then you need neither *vassee* (executor) nor *vekeel* (proxy); come, and I will, by God's command, take you as my lawful wife." The other merchants who stood by approved of what he did; and he forthwith conducted the girl to his own dwelling, where the marriage ceremony was performed. At night food was placed before them; and after the merchant had eaten a little, he bade the girl also to partake of the food. But she hesitated, and thought to herself, "I have but one hand. If I stretch it forth to partake of the meal, he will perceive the defect; and as he supposed that I was perfect in all my limbs, he will immediately divorce me on account of my being thus maimed. I know not how to find my father's house; and at this hour whither shall I go?" Whilst thus engaged, she heard a voice, telling her not to be grieved, for He who created her from nothing was able to restore her hand to her. The girl, on this, said a Bismillah; and then stretching forth her maimed hand, by the power of the Most High it was restored precisely as the other.

The merchant, ignorant of this, asked her why it was, that not till after being pressed three times, she had stretched out her hand to partake of the food. The girl was now embarrassed; and to relieve herself, she related the whole of what had happened to her.

The merchant was greatly surprised at what he heard; and turning to the girl, he asked her if she did not recognise him. On her replying that she did not, he added, "Behold in me the poor porter who went to your door to beg for bread. The shop at which you found me was once your father's; he sold it to me, and it is now mine. It was for me that your hand was cut off; the Most High blessed the loaf of bread which you bestowed upon me, and, in remembrance of it, has restored your hand. He has also reduced your father to poverty, and made me rich; and thus destiny has rendered me prosperous."

Now the moral of this tale is, that you forget not the poor, but give bread to the hungry; for the advantage which results from the bestowal of alms is as evident as the sun.

This book, called "Nevadir es Sohailee," (Sketches of Remarkable Occurrences by Sohailee,) filled with strange tales, agreeable anecdotes, and sprightly sallies, has, by His assistance, been printed at the Royal Press, under the superintendance of Mustapha es Samee,—may Allah abundantly endow him with his gracious favors,—in the middle of the month of Ramazan the blessed, and in the year (of the Hedjreh) one thousand two hundred and fifty-six.

END.

9 Bow Lane, London. 155 Broadway, New-York,

Dec., 1849.

G. P. PUTNAM'S

LIST OF

NEW PUBLICATIONS

AND

WORKS IN PREPARATION.

IMPORTATION OF FOREIGN BOOKS.

MR. PUTNAM'S Branch of the American Literary Agency (established in 1838) is ill continued by him in London, under the charge of MR. THOMAS DELF, an experienced ıd competent bibliographer. Mr. Putnam has also special agents in Paris, Brussels, Leipsic, ıd Leghorn, and can thus afford every facility to private persons, as well as to Booksellers ıd Public Institutions, for procuring *Books, Stationery, Maps, &c., &c.*, from all the princi- al cities in Europe, in the most expeditious and economical manner.

Particular attention is given also to the procuring of old and scarce books, by means of ıvertising, &c., &c. Mr. Putnam believes that his twelve years' experience in the execution of rders of all kinds, gives him advantages that are inferior to none, and which cannot fail to be ppreciated by those who favor him with their business.

An order for a single volume will at all times receive the same careful attention as larger or- ers. Any party preferring to correspond directly with the London house, will find his orders romptly attended to, provided they are addressed "T. Delf, *Putnam's American Agency, ondon*," and accompanied with a remittance or satisfactory references.

BOOKS, &c., DUTY FREE.

*** *By a recent Act of Congress*, all Colleges, Academies, Seminaries of Learning, r other Societies established for Philosophical or Literary purposes, or for the ncouragement of the Fine Arts, may Import Books, Maps, Coins, Statuary, Phi- osophical Apparatus, &c., Free of Duty. Public Institutions of this description, wishing secure this advantage, will have their orders executed in a most satisfactory manner by for- 'arding them to G. P. Putnam direct.

N. B.—CATALOGUES of New Books published in London, with CHEAP LISTS, &c., are ut up *monthly* in small packages, and forwarded gratis to all who may desire them.

ORDERS FORWARDED BY EVERY STEAMER;

ınd, if desired, and the books can be readily procured, they will be received by return steamer.

Subscriptions received for Periodicals, Newspapers, &c., published abroad. Lists supplied on application.

A General Catalogue

OF A VERY EXTENSIVE COLLECTION OF

STANDARD WORKS IN EVERY DEPARTMENT OF LITERATURE, SCIENCE & ART,

INCLUDING FOREIGN AND AMERICAN PUBLICATIONS,

Nearly Ready.

It will be sent gratis on application.

Latest Publications of 1849-50.

The East; or, a Visit to Egypt and the Holy Land.

BY REV. J. A. SPENCER, M. A.,

Editor of the New Testament in Greek, with English notes. Member of the New-York Historical Society, &c., &c.

Splendidly Illustrated with Original Drawings. 8vo, pp. 500. Uniform with "Layard's Nineveh," &c.; "Hawks's Monuments of Egypt," &c.

The Neighbors;

A Tale of Every-day Life.

BY FREDRIKA BREMER.

A New and Revised Edition, with an Introduction written expressly for this Edition by Miss Bremer. 12mo. cloth. Uniform with Irving's, Cooper's, and Sedgewick's Works; and Illustrated with Portrait, and View of the Author's Residence. $1.00. *To be followed by* "HOME," *&c.*

"To all our readers who are not familiar with these admirable characters, we beg leave to tender a cordial introduction, with the confident assurance that they will find them exceedingly 'pleasant acquaintances.'"—*New-York Mirror.*

"The present edition is very beautifully printed, and must be universally welcomed."
N. Y. Evening Post.

The Works of Oliver Goldsmith.

Complete in Four elegant volumes, thick 12mo. With Vignettes engraved on steel. Vols. I. and II. now ready. $1.25, each.

EDITED BY JAMES PRIOR.

"The book will embrace quite a library in itself; and the polished style of the accomplished author should become a model to the careless scribblers of the present day. The typography of the work is beautiful."—*New-York Mirror.*

The Iliad of Homer; with Flaxman's Designs.

Homer's Iliad.

TRANSLATED BY WILLIAM COWPER.

With Notes, by M. A. Dwight. A splendid edition, on large paper. Royal 8vo, cloth. Illustrated with Twelve engravings in outline from designs by Flaxman. Also a cheaper Edition for Schools. $1.25.

The Shakspeare Calendar;

Or, Wit and Wisdom for Every Day in the Year.

EDITED BY W. C. RICHARDS.

In a very neat volume. 32mo, cloth.

American Historical and Literary Curiosities.

Containing fac-similes of many memorials of the Revolutionary Period—of Letters, Autographs, Portraits: also of Drawings and Letters by persons active at that time; with the Lives of several eminent Statesmen, Legislators, Divines, and Philosophers concerned therein; with divers other marvellous and curious things, worthy of being treasured up. In one vol. 4to, half morocco. Price, $6.00.

B

INDEX TO G. P. PUTNAM'S PUBLICATIONS.

On those marked thus (*), a special discount to the Trade.

www.ingramcontent.com/pod-product-compliance
Lightning Source LLC
LaVergne TN
LVHW020121110826
845151LV00001B/239